——— The ———
Nominated Member of Parliament Scheme

Are Unelected Voices Still Necessary in Parliament?

A Collection of Perspectives and Personal Reflections by NMPs

The Nominated Member of Parliament Scheme

Are Unelected Voices Still Necessary in Parliament?

A Collection of Perspectives and Personal Reflections by NMPs

Edited by

Anthea Ong

Hush TeaBar/Anagami
A Good Space Co-operative
WorkWell Leaders
SG Mental Health Matters
Singapore

NEW JERSEY · LONDON · SINGAPORE · BEIJING · SHANGHAI · HONG KONG · TAIPEI · CHENNAI · TOKYO

Published by

World Scientific Publishing Co. Pte. Ltd.
5 Toh Tuck Link, Singapore 596224
USA office: 27 Warren Street, Suite 401-402, Hackensack, NJ 07601
UK office: 57 Shelton Street, Covent Garden, London WC2H 9HE

National Library Board, Singapore Cataloguing in Publication Data
Name(s): Ong, Anthea, editor.
Title: The Nominated Member of Parliament scheme : are unelected voices still necessary in Parliament? : a collection of perspectives and personal reflections by NMPs / edited by Anthea Ong.
Description: Singapore : World Scientific Publishing Co Pte Ltd, [2023]
Identifier(s): ISBN 978-981-12-5842-8 (hardback) | ISBN 978-981-12-5894-7 (paperback) | ISBN 978-981-12-5846-6 (ebook for institutions) | ISBN 978-981-12-5847-3 (ebook for individuals)
Subject(s): LCSH: Legislators--Singapore. | Legislators--Selection and appointment--Singapore. | Nominations for office--Singapore. | Singapore--Politics and government--20th century. | Singapore--Politics and government--21st century.
Classification: DDC 320.95957--dc23

British Library Cataloguing-in-Publication Data
A catalogue record for this book is available from the British Library.

Notes on the cover design: The NMP scheme was first introduced to address the shifting sands of Singaporean politics, as a different path to a Parliament that seemed set in its partisan ways. This book now seeks to explore how, over three decades later, this electoral innovation can move with the times to better serve Singaporeans into the future. The mindfulness practice of making sand art with stones and the minimalist feel of neutral, earthy tones also illustrate the Editor's wish for a mindful Parliament that is grounded in integrity, humility and empathy for the people.

Copyright © 2023 by World Scientific Publishing Co. Pte. Ltd.

All rights reserved. This book, or parts thereof, may not be reproduced in any form or by any means, electronic or mechanical, including photocopying, recording or any information storage and retrieval system now known or to be invented, without written permission from the publisher.

For photocopying of material in this volume, please pay a copying fee through the Copyright Clearance Center, Inc., 222 Rosewood Drive, Danvers, MA 01923, USA. In this case permission to photocopy is not required from the publisher.

For any available supplementary material, please visit
https://www.worldscientific.com/worldscibooks/10.1142/12895#t=suppl

Desk Editor: Jiang Yulin

Typeset by Stallion Press
Email: enquiries@stallionpress.com

Printed in Singapore

To those who say "Huh, NMP?",
you inspired this book.

And to our Singapore,
with much love.

Contents

Foreword by Prime Minister Lee Hsien Loong   ix

Prologue   xi
Anthea Ong

Section 1 — (N)OVEL   **1**

    Preface   3

    One Way   10
    Maurice Choo

    Origins of the NMP Scheme: Contributing an
    Independent Perspective   22
    Walter Woon

    Democracy, Legitimacy and Civil Society   36
    Simon Tay

    NMPs as "Loving Critics" of Singapore   49
    Chandra Mohan Nair

    Then and Now, for the Future   62
    Braema Mathiaparanam

Section 2 — (M)ERITS   **79**

    Preface   81

    Lessons from My Extended Classroom: Tempering
    Technological Utopianism with Circumspection   88
    Lim Sun Sun

    Sport and Institutionalising a Sports NMP   103
    Nicholas Fang

Speaking for the Trees in Parliament *Faizah Jamal*	117
POFMA: Duty, Conscience or Both? *Walter Theseira*	132
Dilemmas and Challenges for the Labour NMP *Thomas Thomas*	148
A Baptism of Fire *Viswa Sadasivan*	160
NMP as Advocate, or Advocate as NMP? *K. Thanaletchimi*	174
Speaking Personally, Clearly and Kindly *Kuik Shiao-Yin*	186

Section 3 — (P)OSSIBILITIES — 203

Preface	205
Make the NMP Scheme Irrelevant *Laurence Lien*	213
Not Just a Youth NMP *Shahira Abdullah*	227
Choosing an NMP for the Arts: A Unique Process *Audrey Wong & Janice Koh*	237
The Education Motion: Animus, Process, Potential *Mahdev Mohan*	254
Constitutionally Engineering Non-Partisanship *Eugene K B Tan*	271

Are Elected MPs Enough? 288
Anthea Ong

Appendices
    A: Constitutional Provisions 307
    B: Timeline of Key Developments 310
    C: Comparison of NMPs and NCMPs 314
    D: Fun Facts and Figures 318
    E: Examples of Other Appointed Member Systems 338
    F: Further Readings 341

Author Bios 343

Editor's Profile 355

Acknowledgements 357

Index 359

Foreword

Singapore's system of government is modelled on the British Westminster parliamentary model, but we have evolved it over time to suit our own circumstances and needs. The Nominated Member of Parliament (NMP) scheme is one such innovation.

We introduced NMPs in 1990 to make our political system more inclusive and widen the range of views aired and considered in Parliament. The NMPs are individuals who have made their mark in diverse fields, such as business and industry, the labour movement, social services, arts and sports. They bring to bear their professional knowledge and practical experience in their respective domains. Being politically non-partisan, they can offer perspectives independent of both Government and Opposition MPs. NMPs can be dissenting but constructive, or supportive but not uncritical. Thus they can help to sharpen parliamentary debates and improve policy making and legislation.

The arrangement to have some MPs who are nominated rather than elected is not unique to Singapore. Other parliamentary democracies have also recognised the valuable role such MPs play in enriching the national discourse and have instituted alternative routes for MPs to enter Parliament, to participate in debates and to vote on legislation. We have similarly done so.

Looking back after three decades, the NMP scheme has fulfilled its original purpose. Many NMPs have enriched the diversity of views expressed in Parliament and raised the quality of debate. NMPs have pushed for new legislation on issues important to them, and some have moved Private Member's Bills.

Looking ahead, Singapore's political landscape is likely to become more contested. Is there a role for NMPs in such an environment? I believe the answer is yes.

A more intense political contest makes it all the more important that the national debate does not deepen divisions between ourselves, but brings Singaporeans closer together. We all need to listen to different perspectives and voices, respect views different from our own and understand problems from multiple angles, in order to reach a wise national consensus on the way forward. The NMPs can play a useful role in this, as long as they remain non-partisan.

It is thus timely that former and current NMPs have put together these recollections and reflections on their personal experiences. They have expressed a wide range of views. Not all are aligned with one another, nor should we expect them to be. This is precisely the diversity of perspectives that the scheme seeks to foster, to better enable Parliament to fulfil its function at the apex of Singapore's system of government.

Lee Hsien Loong
Prime Minister of Singapore

Prologue

It was almost exactly a year after I completed my term as a Nominated Member of Parliament (NMP) on 23 June 2020, when the deafening idea of this book came to me after my morning practice of silence. The immensity of the NMP experience also hit me then as a much-delayed reflection, despite the mindless rambling to Mothership in an exclusive interview[1] in July 2020.

I was, and continue to be, inspired by this deep privilege of giving voice in the highest hall of the land to the underclass who cannot vote, and bringing to light the gaps and shadows of an efficient meritocracy that is increasingly less equal and getting in the way of every citizen and resident becoming the best and happiest human they can be — without the distraction of political agendas. I also became increasingly impatient with the constantly binary discourse about the NMP scheme that changes nothing for Singapore. On one end, there is the view that NMPs have been effective in adding value and diversity to the debates in Parliament, yet no sincere nor commensurate effort has been made to strengthen the institution. On the other, the same old cry that it is not democratic, yet the ground has been slow in organising itself or showing the need for this "democracy" and diversity of parliamentary voices at the ballot box as an electorate until the 2020 General Election (GE).

Two different strangers wrote to me kindly offering to volunteer for my "campaign" with the ruling party for GE 2020 before Nomination Day; later a well-spoken neighbour in my block urged me to join the

♦ The Nominated Member of Parliament Scheme

Workers' Party. Remembering these isolated episodes confirmed for me that the NMP scheme is no closer to being understood by all Singaporeans, three decades later. It also prompted the curious cat in me to do a quick search, revealing that there has not been a "popular" book on the NMP scheme, only academic papers and commentaries.

The book began to form in my head: it must be accessible to and enjoyable for the mainstream reader, rather than an academic text or one which speaks only to the very politically informed. And the NMP story must be told by this special group of Singaporeans who have served as nominated members in the hallowed chamber across 32 years from their personal lenses, as *their* stories. Singaporeans must hear directly from them, not through the filters of the media nor the distanced analyses of political scientists and commentators.

We were a young Parliament at 25 years when the NMP scheme was introduced by then-First Deputy Prime Minister Goh Chok Tong on 29 November 1989 to "... encourage participation, to build consensus, to accommodate alternative viewpoints and dissent".[2] At that time, there were only two Opposition Members of Parliament (MPs) in Parliament.[3] The Bill provoked a two-day debate that was robust and often testy (a riveting read on Hansard that I humbly think should be mandatory reading for all incoming NMPs!).[4]

Some government MPs seemed to take offence to the introduction of such a scheme as "an indictment of the existing system and the elected MPs we now have, especially of the Backbenchers" (Abdullah Tarmugi). Others argued that the NMP scheme would be seen as "government overload", given the selection process instead of "proxy for opposition" to the citizens (Chandra Das). Many were more than unhappy about the "back door" entry into Parliament for NMPs, and whether they therefore lacked mandate and accountability — even calling them "armchair politicians if they do not do grassroots work" (Aline Wong).

The Opposition argued against the scheme on grounds of democracy and representation, in addition to alleging that NMPs "...naturally represent the interest of the political party that appoints them", describing it as a form of "colonialism", and suggesting that Singapore was headed towards "a dictatorship of one-party rule" (Chiam See Tong).

The most illuminating arguments for me against the scheme were by the People's Action Party (PAP) MPs: first, on the need for "a change in the attitude of the Frontbench towards the Backbench so that there can be much more dialogue" (Arthur Beng); second, that there was already a multitude of views offered by elected MPs but "...the Government is not taking the views of the PAP MPs seriously" (Philip Tan), which may explain why the electorate was wanting alternative views.

A difficult birth to say the least, but there was also no lack of supporters pushing it through. The Bill for the NMP scheme passed without the Whip lifted.[5]

Here we are, 32 years later in 2022, with 97 NMPs past and present, 2,000 speeches made and 3,000 questions asked.[6] Was the birth justified? Have NMPs achieved the intent of raising alternative and dissenting views that elected MPs — on both sides of the House — could not/did not? Has the presence of these nominated members kept voters away from the Opposition, notwithstanding the largest ever number of opposition seats won in GE 2020? Are we letting this electoral innovation that is uniquely Singapore simply just plod along every 2.5 years or less when the world and our society look very different to what they were three decades ago? Aren't we being complacent with the status quo of a parliamentary system based on a 200-year-old system that may no longer be relevant?

These questions guided me at some level on which NMPs to invite as contributors, aside from the intention of diversity on gender/age/race/sector, issues, views and their contributions in Parliament. In this book, we have at least one NMP from each of the seven Parliaments. Needless to say, the final 20 contributors are neither exhaustive nor definitive of the contributions of NMPs over the years; I merely started with the ones I know, sleuthed out a few, got turned down by some, let go of two and am still crestfallen that the last one could not work out.

Asking these important questions also helped us organise the book in three main sections, playing on the letters N, M and P to capture the significance of the NMP story as a parliamentary evolution.

Section 1 (**N**ovel): Five NMPs from the early days of the scheme share what they saw, championed and experienced in and outside Parliament, as part of a new parliamentary innovation that was not totally welcomed by members from both sides of the bench.

Section 2 (**M**erits): Eight contributors highlight key issues/sectors they represented or championed, and/or notable contributions they made in Parliament. Professor Walter Woon remains the only NMP to have tabled a Private Member's Bill that was passed by Parliament,[7] though more than a few have raised important issues with parliamentary mechanisms such as petitions and motions (on repealing Section 377A and Education for Our Future respectively) as well as adjournment (Digital Divide) and amendment (Protection from Online Falsehoods and Manipulation Act) motions. Even more have given voice to significant issues in their speeches and stood their ground when it was time to vote.

Section 3 (**P**ossibilities): Seven NMPs draw from their own experiences and ruminate about the future from their own experiences, giving much food for thought about the possibilities not just for the NMP institution, but Parliament as a whole, that will serve us well into a future that is increasingly volatile, uncertain, complex and ambiguous. No future can be imagined without including the voice of the present and youths, so I invited the current Youth NMP too.

The reader will, however, find aspects of merits and possibilities in all the essays to some extent, no matter which section, as the authors answer the question: *Are Unelected Voices Still Necessary in Parliament?*

At the start of each essay, the "Editor's Note" is intended for the reader to feel like they are having an ongoing chat with me throughout their journey with the book before they "hear" from each NMP. We also hope that the reader gets to know the person behind the name through the "Editor's Cut" (Q&A) following each essay. For the instructive objective of this book, we compiled some fun facts about NMPs in the Appendices section, including the total number of speeches, motions and Parliamentary Questions asked by NMPs since 1990.

Many have warned me that doing a book as an editor is way more challenging than writing my own;[8] now I know it to be somewhat true. It was indeed a monumental task chasing and coordinating between 19 top leaders and accomplished academics with no white space on their calendars, and then editing each essay with care because I feel the heart behind each word written as I have been there too.

That this book project must be co-owned by all NMPs involved was crystal clear for me, so we met on Zoom, discussed ideas as a group and agreed on the book strategy before we went away to write our own essays. It took eight months for all manuscripts to be submitted, edited and ready: some took longer than others, a few struggled revisiting

◆ The Nominated Member of Parliament Scheme

unpleasant memories, but most were wholeheartedly invested and collegial. It has been a unique honour for me to work with them, each one an outstanding Singaporean who loves their country and truly wants to make a difference to the people who call Singapore home.

Sometimes, we have to create what we want to be part of. This book is a collective expression of this love and faith from us NMPs that I hope will invite a wider discourse amongst all Singaporeans on how NMPs can, and must represent them, aside from their elected MPs. And in so doing, ask what is the Parliament we deserve as an evolving society.

Endnotes

1. Mothership (2020, July 20) "'What a privilege to be able to serve this way': Anthea Ong shares her reflections on being an NMP".
2. Hansard, 29 November 1989, vol. 54 col. 695. Second Reading Speech by Goh Chok Tong, Constitutional (Amendment) Bill (No. 2).
3. In 1968, the Barisan Sosialis party boycotted the general election as part of their "extra parliamentary struggle", allowing the PAP to win all 58 seats that have entrenched a supermajority Parliament ever since. This means that all government bills introduced, including constitutional amendments, are essentially guaranteed a safe passage in the House.
4. Hansard, 29 November 1989 and 30 November 1989, vol. 54. Constitutional (Amendment) Bill (No. 2).
5. The Whip was not lifted for this Bill despite several requests from PAP MPs. Dr Tan Cheng Bock voted against the Bill and was given a warning by the party. (Wikipedia, Tan Cheng Bock).
6. Please refer to Appendix D.
7. NMP Dr Kanwaljit Soin also tabled a Family Violence Bill during her term which was rejected by Parliament.
8. I had written my own book, *50 Shades of Love*, in 2018 which was published just after I was appointed to Parliament as NMP.

Section 1

∞

(N)ovel

PREFACE

<u>N</u>OVEL: A Parliamentary Experiment

O ver a two-day session spanning 29 and 30 November 1989, Members of Parliament (MPs) gathered for the Second Reading of the Constitution of the Republic of Singapore (Amendment No. 2) Bill. The question before the House was: Should Parliament be expanded to include non-elected, nominated members?

At the opening of the debate, then-First Deputy Prime Minister Goh Chok Tong explained that the scheme was intended to encourage Singapore's political development. It would, he argued, offer Singaporeans "...more opportunities for political participation and to evolve a more consensual style of government where alternative views are heard and constructive dissent accommodated."[1] To that end, he acknowledged that appointed representatives were not in themselves a novel concept.[2] Rather, what was being presented was a new vision for Parliament itself.

"For many years, from 1966 to 1981, the people were happy with the total dominance of the PAP in Parliament," he said, continuing:

> *"But they have shown in recent years that they want alternatives to the Government views to be aired, whilst wanting the PAP to continue as the Government. We must take cognizance of this... [The Nominated MP scheme] broadens our political system and makes for a better Parliament. We have to evolve a system which meets the special needs of Singapore."*[3]

The Lead-Up to the Debate

By that time, the system was already in the midst of evolving. The NMP scheme was only the latest in a series of significant and controversial changes to Singapore's electoral system in the late 1980s. The Non-Constituency MP (NCMP) scheme, allowing the best-performing of the losing Opposition candidates to take up seats in Parliament, had been introduced in 1984.[4] In 1988, Mr Goh had presented a White Paper to Parliament on the creation of the Elected Presidency. That same year, the Group Representation Constituency (GRC) scheme came into effect, reassigning 39 of Parliament's 81 seats to wards which would elect teams of candidates rather than individual MPs.

However, Singapore in the 1980s was not known for embracing dissent and alternative views. Civil society at the time has been described as "stifled",[5] with the mass arrests and detentions under Operation Spectrum in 1987 still fresh in the public memory and marking "the beginning of a new era where Singaporeans became conscious of the operation of what would later be known as out-of-bounds (OB) markers in politics".[6] At the time, Parliament had only one elected Opposition MP, Chiam See Tong, along with NCMP Lee Siew Choh.[7]

Although the People Action's Party (PAP) considered it a "misconception"[8] that non-government voices did not get enough airtime, it nonetheless recognised that this view was in its interests to correct. Mr Goh's succession of Lee Kuan Yew as the leader of the PAP — and by extension, the government — was meant to herald a shift away from the paternalistic, hard-knuckled style of politics which had dominated post-independence, and towards a more consultative, softer version.

Even so, by Mr Goh's own admission, the Whip system and convention of collective responsibility prevented PAP MPs from voting against the party line, however vehemently they might have argued their personal views. NMPs, according to his vision, would be a helpful counterbalance: politically non-partisan members who could speak for those who disagreed with the government but did not identify with the Opposition. In not having to "play to the gallery", they could be "constructive while dissenting, thus contributing to good government."[9]

Responses to the NMP Scheme

Parliamentary debates do not always make for scintillating reading, but the Hansard transcripts of the Bill's Second Reading are a notable exception. In reading them, we were struck by the unfiltered intensity with which MPs expressed their views, both for and against the scheme — a candour which, perhaps, was due at least in part to the element of self-interest. (As Mr Goh wryly observed at the close of the debate, parliamentarians seemed far more troubled by the Bill than the general public.) In scrutinising the NMP proposal, MPs understood they were considering not only the composition of Parliament, but the conduct of democratic governance and their own role and standing as representatives in Singapore's evolving political landscape.

MPs who supported the scheme believed that Parliament, and Singapore as a whole, stood to benefit from the contributions of non-partisan colleagues. Although many expressed lengthy reservations,

◆ The Nominated Member of Parliament Scheme

they nonetheless accepted that making space for a "more complete body of views" in the legislative process was not only desirable in a maturing democracy, but could "contribute significantly to our longer term political stability."[10]

Those against it questioned NMPs' legitimacy and lack of mandate, the opacity of the selection process and the necessity and efficacy of such an intervention.[11] NMPship, they countered, was for "passionless men and women too squeamish for real politics";[12] free-riders who wanted the privileges of being in Parliament without the burdens of constituency work.

Could NMPs be truly trusted to subordinate their personal interests? Might they end up being convenient puppets for lobby groups? Was it an indirect indictment of backbenchers' performance that could end up creating a "class system" of MPs? Even the non-partisan label was interrogated; the scheme was simultaneously decried as a possible back-door route for the "Oppositionistic" to enter Parliament as well as a smokescreen for entrenching PAP dominance. In the words of one MP, "What the people want is not more NMPs. What they want is a government that is listening, what they want is a government that is receptive and is willing to accept alternative views."[13]

However vocal some MPs were in their objections, the Whip was not lifted for the final vote, and the Bill passed its Second Reading 74-1. Public opinion on the scheme was nonetheless similarly divided. Newspapers published a slew of commentaries and forum letters both for and against the scheme leading up to the debate, and even after the Bill was handed over to a Select Committee for review. Interestingly, the only survey of public opinion presented to the Select Committee came from a National University of Singapore (NUS) student society, which had conducted a poll amongst their peers: just over 50% of the 577 students surveyed disagreed with the need for NMPs, while 82% did not think the Bill should pass unamended.[14]

The First NMPs

For all the furore surrounding their appointment, there was ultimately very little clarity on how NMPs were expected to go about their roles in practice when the Constitution of the Republic of Singapore (Amendment) Act 1990 finally took effect on 10 September 1990. For all intents and purposes, the scheme remained an experiment when the first two NMPs, Professor Maurice Choo and Leong Chee Whye, were sworn in on 22 November 1990 from a slate of 16 names.[15]

The essays in this first section capture much of this initial uncertainty. From reading them, it is clear that the NMPs of the scheme's early years were themselves figuring things out as they went along. In between wrapping their heads around parliamentary procedure and preparing their speeches, they were also grappling with what sort of issues they would raise and what they hoped to accomplish — all without the benefit of party resources or official assistance. How well they would work with their colleagues (elected and non-elected alike) also remained to be seen; as more than one contributor observes, the guardedness, and in some cases hostility, to the NMP scheme meant their presence was not always welcomed.

Maurice Choo (NMP 1990–1991) opens the section by discussing his eight brief but significant months in office, an appointment he felt was "one way" of diversifying views in a one-party dominant Parliament, and how he sought to contribute by sharing his views on local and regional affairs. **Walter Woon (NMP 1992–1996)** expounds on the genesis of the scheme and the political climate at the time, including the development of checks and balances on the government. He also discusses the ability of NMPs to shape national policy, drawing on his experience as the only NMP to have passed a Private Member's Bill into law to date.

The tense reception of the NMP scheme is, in its own way, indicative of Singapore's traditional suspicion of dissent. In his essay, **Simon Tay (NMP 1997–2001)** reflects on taking office during Mr Goh's premiership, and argues that NMPs could bridge consultation between government and citizens, and indeed help to mediate the uneasy relationship between the state and civil society.

Similarly, **Chandra Mohan Nair (NMP 2001–2004)** writes about being a "loving critic" of Singapore both during his term and afterwards, even as he questions the effects of decades of one-party dominance and laments that the powers of the office rarely moved beyond debate to action. Finally, his colleague **Braema Mathiaparanam (NMP 2001–2004)** expounds on how her participation in civil society groups like Association of Women for Action and Research (AWARE) and Transient Workers Count Too (TWC2) equipped her for the role, and sets up a question to be revisited: whether the NMP scheme, 32 years on, has finally outlived not only its novelty, but its purpose.

Endnotes

[1] Goh Chok Tong, speech during the Second Reading of the Constitution of the Republic of Singapore (Amendment No. 2) Bill, Singapore Parliamentary Debates, Official Report (29 November 1989), vol. 54, sitting 8, col. 695.

[2] See Appendix E for a list of other legislatures with appointed members. A similar list was shared by Mr Goh in Parliament during the Second Reading.

[3] Goh Chok Tong, speech during the Second Reading of the Constitution of the Republic of Singapore (Amendment No. 2) Bill, Singapore Parliamentary Debates, Official Report (29 November 1989), vol. 54, sitting 8, col. 704.

[4] Amongst other points, proponents of the schemes argued that they would support democracy, while critics held that they would undermine it. Similar arguments would later be applied towards the NMP scheme itself.

[5] See, for example, Chong, T. (2005). Civil Society in Singapore: Popular Discourses and Concepts. *Sojourn: Journal of Social Issues in Southeast Asia*, 20(2), 273–301.

6   Barr, M. D. (2008). Singapore's Catholic Social Activists: Alleged Marxist Conspirators. In Barr, M. D., & Trocki, C. (eds.), *Paths not taken: Political pluralism in post-war Singapore* (pp. 228–247). NUS Press.
7   As an NCMP, Mr Lee was precluded from voting on amendments to the Constitution and was thus unable to vote on the Bill. The only other elected Opposition MP since independence, J. B. Jeyaretnam, had to vacate his seat in 1986 due to a criminal conviction.
8   Goh Chok Tong, speech during the Second Reading of the Constitution of the Republic of Singapore (Amendment No. 2) Bill, Singapore Parliamentary Debates, Official Report (29 November 1989), vol. 54, sitting 8, col. 699.
9   Ibid, at col. 700.
10 Speech by Chay Wai Chuen (PAP, Brickworks), Singapore Parliamentary Debates, Official Report (30 November 1989), vol. 54, sitting 9, col. 789.
11 These criticisms, of course, persist today.
12 Speech by Dr Tan Cheng Bock (PAP, Ayer Rajah), Singapore Parliamentary Debates, Official Report (29 November 1989), vol. 54, sitting 8, col. 725.
13 Speech by Dr Arthur Beng (PAP, Fengshan), Singapore Parliamentary Debates, Official Report (30 November 1989), vol. 54, sitting 9, col. 764.
14 Report of the Select Committee on the Constitution of the Republic of Singapore (Amendment No. 2) Bill (no 41/89) (Presented to Parliament on 15 March 1990).
15 Although up to six NMPs could be appointed, the Select Committee demurred to fill all the slots, noting that the scheme was new.

One Way

Maurice Choo
Nominated Member of Parliament (1990–1991)

> *Editor's Note: This book would be far less meaningful if we did not have Professor Maurice Choo raise the curtain with this first chapter as one of the first two NMPs to be appointed in the Parliament of Singapore more than three decades ago. I am grateful for his contribution, especially considering that he was leading the Covid-19 taskforce for his hospital at a time when Singapore was seeing an alarming spike in cases and deaths for weeks. The title "One Way" is a reflection of Maurice's love for haiku and brevity, and his humble reference to his short yet significant interlude of eight months as an NMP as one way, albeit a novel one at that time, for a "one-party dominant" Parliament to listen to diverse views.*

More than thirty years ago, the late Leong Chee Whye and I were appointed the first nominated members in the Parliament of Singapore on 22 November 1990. Six days later, a far more significant event took place: Lee Kuan Yew, who had led Singapore since 1959, stepped down as Prime Minister.

A few months earlier, on 29 March 1990, Singapore's 7th Parliament had enacted the Nominated Member of Parliament (NMP) scheme after much divisive debate, even within the ruling People's Action Party which held 80 of 81 elected seats. Not long after that, a government minister called and asked if I could meet him at his office.

Having been engrossed in academic and clinical activities, I did not connect the two events then. Some years earlier, the same minister had been attended to by me professionally; the outcome was a happy one. What could be the matter, I thought? To my surprise, when we met, it was not about health matters. Rather, the minister's question to me was whether I would consider serving as an NMP.

Not knowing much about what was involved, I asked for time to study the scheme. Many arguments, for and against the scheme, had been raised during the parliamentary debate. Goh Chok Tong, who was soon to become Prime Minister, was a strong proponent. Among the arguments, the one I felt was the most important was about modifying the perception that Singapore was a "one-party parliament" with an excessively autocratic government.

Saying Yes to Singapore

At that stage in my professional life, I had little interest in electoral politics. I was fully aware that an unelected NMP represented no geographical constituency. In its original form then, a nominated member did not even represent any sectorial constituency, such as the arts, sports or the disabled.

Our family had done well in post-independence Singapore. My mother had fled her village in Fujian with her widowed mother during the chaos of the civil war in China. They arrived in Singapore illiterate and impoverished. My father's family, from a neighbouring village, had arrived in Singapore a little earlier. Any modest progress made in their circumstances was later destroyed during the Japanese occupation.

In the early 1950s, my four siblings and I grew up in an attap hut in Siglap, next to our pigs, chickens and ducks. Water was drawn from a well. We had no electricity. In 1959, Singapore achieved self-government. From then on, our family's circumstances improved rapidly. In one generation, all five children of poorly educated parents completed tertiary education; two became doctors, two became corporate leaders and one was a lifelong teacher in the Ministry of Education.

The social uplifting of my family is neither unique nor uncommon in post-independence Singapore. It was the main reason I agreed to contribute to society in Parliament.

My Way to Parliament

During the selection interview, Chiam See Tong, then the sole elected Opposition MP, sought assurance from me that I was not affiliated to any political party. I replied truthfully that I had never been a member of a political party (not then, not since).

Unattached to any political philosophy or platform and unbound by electoral promises and assertions, a nominated member could range more freely. On the other hand, there were no party colleagues to consult with, nor party resources to depend on.

Chee Whye and I were sworn in as the first NMPs on 20 December 1990.

It took a few weeks of observation and introspection before I determined that my service in Parliament as a nominated member should help illustrate a sensitive and effective citizen's contribution to his country and community. To do this well, he had first to be knowledgeable and acutely perceptive with regard to contemporary local, regional and international affairs.

The years 1989–1990 were hugely significant in world history. In January 1989, following the death of Emperor Hirohito, the Japanese bubble economy started its relentless decline into recession which continues to this day. On 15 February 1989, an occupying Soviet army withdrew from Afghanistan, utterly exhausted.

From April through June 1989, massive student protests were held in Tiananmen Square before being violently put down on 4 June. Interestingly, the three decades since then have seen the most spectacular growth in the Chinese economy and its power. Trending in the opposite direction, the Berlin Wall fell on 9 November 1989, portending the fall of communist governments and the fragmentation of Eastern Europe and the Soviet Union.

In biology, 1990 marked the fulcrum when worldwide reproductive rates began to shrink, with potentially catastrophic consequences for human society. On the positive side, the first successful human gene therapy was announced on 14 September 1990, and the Human Genome Project was launched on 1 October 1990.

On 2 August 1990, Iraq invaded and annexed Kuwait, its small rich neighbour. Tim Berners-Lee introduced the precursor of the Internet on 20 December 1990, and today the Internet has invaded and occupied most of our living spaces, including our minds.

These pivotal events of 1989 and 1990, like a series of mega eruptions, reshaped our global landscape. What we did not know in late 1990 was how prolonged their effects would be.

Being a Voice of the Common Citizen

During that unsettled time, I began my brief interlude in Parliament, which lasted barely eight months.

It would be almost three months before I made my maiden speech. I resolved that I would not be typecast as a doctor, but would be a sentient common citizen, commenting wherever I believed there was something useful to say about the present and possible futures. Unattached and unbound, I could be simply Singaporean and voice some of our hopes and anxieties.

◆ The Nominated Member of Parliament Scheme

To accurately recollect what had been said so long ago for the purpose of writing this chapter, I reviewed all my speeches and questions as recorded word for word in the parliamentary Hansard. This memory lane that I walked down on reminded me of some of the pressing issues of that period, but it is not lost on me how they are still pertinent more than 30 years later.

My maiden speech on 24 February 1991 was completely overshadowed by breaking news that Saddam Hussein had been defeated on the same day, and Iraq's occupying army had been routed and driven out of Kuwait. I therefore chose to speak on the security of small states.

> *"Sir, almost exactly 40 nights after the expiry of the Security Council's deadline for Iraq to withdraw unconditionally from occupied Kuwait, and following intense air bombardment, a massive Allied land campaign was launched early this week. Within three days, the Iraqi occupation army crumbled.*
>
> *Each day of this conflict has cost more than a billion US dollars, and hundreds and thousands of lives. This enormous cost was borne not merely to liberate Kuwait, but to help free all sovereign nations from the threat and temptation of wars of aggression. I salute our small team of medical support personnel who exposed themselves to great danger in defence of an important principle."*

In the wake of the Soviet defeat in Afghanistan, another larger country had invaded a smaller one. Both had failed abjectly. It was important then, and now, for small countries such as ours to celebrate these failures, highlight the crucial principle that wars of invasion must never be tolerated, and that we as a country would do our part in defence of the principle.

On 12 March 1991, I participated in the annual Budget Debate and spoke about ageing and technology explosions.

"Looking ahead, it has been suggested that many health economies will be most devastated by two explosions — the explosion in the ageing population, and the explosion in medical technology. What is more, technology may increase longevity, and longevity will increase the use of technology.

Technology out of control in medical care is no longer hyperbole; it is real and it is frightening. Technology is multiplying and growing so fast that it may be impossible to know for certain what is useful, what is superfluous, what is redundant, what is extravagant, and, worse, what is harmful. Growth in technology appears to be limitless."

In 1990, global reproductivity rates began their precipitous fall. Today, national crude reproductivity rates in some countries have dropped to 1.0 which translates into a halving of the resident population in each succeeding generation. Simultaneously, in many countries, longevity is increasing, and the period of dependency at the end of life has lengthened. In time, the number of frail aged citizens supported by one economically active citizen will be intolerably high. As highly expensive medical technologies such as gene-based vaccine therapy proliferate, healthcare costs will likely be unsustainable, and societies must confront difficult choices between life and death, young and old.

On 21 March 1991, with the ongoing Budget Debate, I also discussed information discordance, giving the example of how two Ministers and an MP were interpreting the same information differently.

> "In this House a few days ago, on the issue of local wages, Mr Goh Chee Wee took the median point. Rebutting, the Finance Minister gave the mean. Later, Mr Goh argued that the raw data was skewed. The Labour Minister analysed subsets. Three clear-minded people saw the same basic information in quite different ways.
>
> In an information age, problems of perception become more acute and I shall highlight three factors: (1) sources of information become numerous and diverse; (2) information flow volume and velocity greatly increased; and (3) technology to capture information is decentralised.
>
> The effects of these can be deduced. For example, as Encik Yatiman alluded to earlier, innocuous words from a different social context may raise a storm elsewhere. Instant images evoke volatile emotions because the intellect has less time to operate."

This was more than 30 years back. In early 1991, few people had heard of, let alone experienced, the embryonic Internet. Yet even then, there were inklings of information overload and later widespread weaponisation of information (or disinformation). Since then, as we now know, the viral spread of the Internet in the virtual world as well as "of things" has created a metaverse where trust has shrivelled and scepticism is an indispensable survival skill.

On 7 May 1991, I spoke up for the students of National University of Singapore (NUS) on the issue of higher education subsidies.

> "The students in the National University of Singapore have communicated with me and I feel that I can air some of their more useful points. At issue is the level of subsidy. It may be

> argued, as the Minister has just done, that education which confers higher earning power should be subsidised less. Equally, it may be argued that education which confers higher earning power may benefit the State more in commercial as well as non-commercial terms and, therefore, deserves greater support.
>
> For university education, we must have a firm idea of what the desirable level of subsidy should be in the medium term. This can be fine-tuned, of course, to differentiate between different fields of study."

For countries poor in natural resources, human development, especially of the young and talented, is key. However, as societies age, there will be increased tension between resources allocated for development and resources allocated for welfare, between the future and the past.

The case for subsidising education is a compelling one, especially for primary and secondary education. For tertiary education, subsidies have historically been less but in a highly competitive world — of genomic therapy, of artificial intelligence, of robotics, of space exploration — we should, as I had spoken about then and still believe now, reconsider our education and research funding strategy.

Are There Better Ways?

There are many ways (even more nowadays) for people in society to express themselves and be taken into consideration by policy makers. The NMP scheme was one (early) way. As the number of ways increases (social media, professional platforms, etc.), the importance of the NMP scheme may decrease.

> "Sir, proportional representation implies disproportional representation is its antithesis. The first-past-the-post system undoubtedly leads to disproportional representation. However, its great merit is that it amplifies the rule of the majority and facilitates strong effective government during its tenure. The great merit of proportional representation is that wider views and interests can be promoted. Its recognised failings are that Government may be fragmented, a pivotal minority may exert disproportionate influence, and sectorial behaviour may become overly accentuated.
>
> Clearly, proportional representation can be, and has been, applied when circumstances are favourable. It need not be rejected out of hand, or accepted blindly, based on extreme arguments, but can be retained as a future option by this or another government."

The concluding statement in my maiden speech hinted at my own personal discomfort with some aspects of the NMP scheme. It was certainly one way then in a one-party dominant Parliament.

Was there another way? A better way? In accepting the appointment, I had concluded that the scheme was a quick fix and a useful one for our nation's needs then. In the 30 years since, the scheme has proven durable, but it continues to have many detractors.

On 4 August 1991, then-Prime Minister Goh Chok Tong dissolved the 7th Parliament to seek a fresh mandate.

In slightly more than half a year, I had learnt much and contributed a little to our country's political life. I gratefully returned to academia.

Editor's Cut: A Q&A with Maurice Choo
(This interview has been edited and condensed for length and clarity.)

What is your most memorable moment from your time in Parliament?
It was a very brief period and I don't recall anything exceptional in the House, but I think people may not really have known how to interact with NMPs in those days. Some were very cold and some were warm, depending on how they felt about the scheme, but in general it was quite pleasant. I had good friendships in the tea room, especially with Lee Siew Choh.[1] He was very good. Some PAP MPs didn't want to talk to me because they were against the scheme, but Ong Teng Cheong was very warm and gentlemanly, and Sidek Saniff from Geylang Serai was also very nice.

I realised then that people can be very different from their political personas. Some people who look very good in the papers may not be as attractive in person. And the people who are nice to be around are not necessarily the ones whom the press writes nicely about.

How did being an NMP change you as a person and/or the work you do?
Even though I was spared from Parliament early, I certainly wasn't spared from work. [Besides academia and medicine], I was on several committees and groups. There was an Advisory Council for how to make Singapore more disabled-friendly, which I served on with Dr Tony Tan. Some of the things we asked for didn't happen, like making the MRT accessible to the disabled...but politics always reflect the times, and I think we did make some good recommendations. Another significant one was a National Review Committee — coming up with a 10-year plan for national health policy which I think we did a good job with.

[In hindsight], I think some of these might have been more useful than making speeches in Parliament. In making speeches, you share your thoughts and principles, your views on where Singapore could be going and what the challenges are. But practical things, like making Singapore more wheelchair-accessible…you need to talk, yes, but you need to do as well.

Based on your time in Parliament, what words of advice would you give future NMPs?
I'm not sure I have any. NMPs nowadays go in for different reasons, like sector representation, and that wasn't the case in my time. Like I wrote in my piece, it was quite clear to my mind that we needed a so-called third voice to show the world that we have an avenue for views which are not the government or the opposition.

On the one hand, like I just said, if you just express views without doing anything practical, the layperson on the street will say these people are all just talking and doing nothing. If you're representing, say, the disabled or the culture sector [as an NMP], maybe you can help do something practical for these people.

But then again, the act of making speeches in Parliament — having a national platform — is a unique part of the appointment. Things like making networks, working for communities, all those can be done without being in Parliament. So if you're talking about why the scheme should exist at all, then the speech-making and giving voice to some segment of public opinion has to be an important part. And I think there's benefit to having a thoughtful person providing another view; not necessarily antagonistic, just another view.

Of course, you could always ask: Why can't existing MPs do this? And is it better to do it as an MP or an NMP? It can be hard for an NMP, because without a constituency or constituents you don't have *locus standi*, so to speak. And does that person have authority, or are they like those scholars in old China just philosophising from the mountains?

How would you sum up your time as an NMP in one sentence?
It was like an omakase.

You know, when you go to a Japanese restaurant and you just sit down and keep quiet and see what the chef serves you. You don't know what you're in for. And you just hope that in the end, you'll be able to go "oh, that was quite pleasant" — which it was.

Endnotes

[1] The former Secretary-General of the Barisan Sosialis and the first Non-Constituency MP (NCMP).

Origins of the NMP Scheme: Contributing an Independent Perspective

Walter Woon
Nominated Member of Parliament (1992–1996)

> Editor's Note: Walter was the first former NMP I invited for the two "firsts" that he held in Parliament; this book would be sub-optimal without his contribution. He was the first Member of Parliament since 1965 to have a Private Member's Bill become a public law in Singapore — the Maintenance of Parents Act, which was passed in 1995, and also the only NMP to do so in the 32 years of the scheme. Intrigued and even more inspired by this feat, I sought him out in my early days as an NMP. He was generous in his sharing with me but also brought me down to earth about my hope to reform our Mental Health (Care and Treatment) Act to include prevention. Walter is known to be incisive and no holds-barred with his views: this essay does not disappoint.

It wasn't very long ago that Singaporeans had no real choice as to who would lead them. For many years after independence, the prevailing philosophy of the ruling party and those who controlled it was that anyone who was not a supporter was an opponent. The election of J. B. Jeyaretnam in the 1981 Anson by-election was not greeted with graciousness by the powers-that-were at the time.

Giving credit where it is due, we in Singapore have been fortunate against the odds to have had a generally competent and honest government. I emphasise "against the odds". The experience of other former colonies that have emerged from the thrall of European imperialism since the Second World War demonstrates how uncommon this is.

However, countries cannot count on historical luck indefinitely. Over the years, some checks on one-party power have been introduced, notably the Elected Presidency and the Nominated Member of Parliament (NMP) scheme.

Checks on One-Party Rule

In 1984, Prime Minister Lee Kuan Yew suggested that the President could safeguard the national reserves.[1] No doubt he was concerned with the possibility that the ruling People's Action Party (PAP) could at some point lose power, having seen the election of his *bête noire* J. B. Jeyaretnam to Parliament in 1981. Four years later in July 1988, First Deputy Prime Minister Goh Chok Tong presented a White Paper in Parliament proposing the creation of an Elected President to safeguard national reserves and the integrity of the public service. The White Paper was followed in 1990 by a bill to amend the Constitution to provide for the election of the President.[2]

This Bill was committed to the Select Committee on 5 October 1990. Representations from the public were invited.

I was one of those who made representations[3] and was invited to appear before the Select Committee on 15 November 1990.[4] We had a spirited exchange on whether candidates for the Presidency should have to renounce their political allegiance before standing for election. My concern was to ensure that the President would be politically neutral, or at least would be seen to have cut his or her links to the ruling party. Despite the grilling I got from PAP members on the Select Committee, this principle was accepted and found its way into the amended Bill.[5]

♦ The Nominated Member of Parliament Scheme

Between the introduction of the White Paper on the Elected Presidency in July 1988 and the Select Committee in October 1990, First Deputy Prime Minister Goh Chok Tong had also moved constitutional amendments to provide for NMPs in October 1989.[6] He explained the rationale for the amendments at the Second Reading of the Bill[7]:

> "The aim of this Bill is to further strengthen our political system by offering Singaporeans more opportunities for political participation and to evolve a more consensual style of government where alternative views are heard and constructive dissent accommodated. It is part of a broader vision which we in the PAP Government painted in 1984, and which led to the introduction of Non-Constituency MPs, and the establishment of GRCs and Town Councils. It should therefore be seen in this wider context.... we can improve the present system simply by Parliament itself, ie, we, the elected representatives, nominating a number of politically non-partisan Singaporeans who can contribute to good government as MPs. Parliament can consider itself as an 'electoral college' vested with the powers to nominate a number of politically non-partisan Singaporeans to help it in its work. Parliament does not have to, but it is a special privilege it can extend to those Singaporeans who can contribute, but who for good reasons, have no desire to go into politics or to look after a constituency, to enter Parliament. These MPs appointed by Parliament can be people who have distinguished themselves or have special knowledge and practical experience in the professions, commerce, industry, cultural activities, social service, or people from an under-represented group of the population, eg, women."

These two innovations were explicitly designed to introduce non-partisan voices into Parliament. The first NMPs were appointed on 22 November 1990, shortly after the Select Committee on the Elected Presidency had held its hearings. Professor Maurice Choo and Leong Chee Whye were sworn in at the Parliament Sitting on 20 December 1990.[8]

Benefits of Non-Partisanship

The NMP scheme was controversial at the start. I wrote a piece entitled "Some Check is Better than No Check" defending the scheme, which was published in *The Straits Times* on 29 November 1990.[9] I made the point that:

> *"Democracy is not the natural state of man. Put a person in a position of unchecked power and one of two things will happen eventually (1) he becomes dishonest and starts to work the system for his benefit or the benefit of his cronies; or (2) while not being actively dishonest, he becomes intellectually flabby and ceases to think things through with the same thoroughness since there is no one to call him to account."*

Furthermore, I wrote:

> *"Potentially, the Nominated MPs may wield considerable influence. They are beholden to no political party for their posts and can speak their minds...the Nominated MPs do not necessarily have the overthrow of the government in mind when they voice dissent about policies. Given strong personalities, Nominated MPs may exercise influence on public opinion far outstripping that of even ministers."*

◆ The Nominated Member of Parliament Scheme

At the time I wrote this commentary, I had no desire or intention to become an NMP. However, the term of the first two NMPs was cut short when Parliament was dissolved on 14 August 1991 in preparation for the general election. In the subsequent general election on 31 August 1991, Low Thia Khiang of the Workers' Party and Chiam See Tong of the Singapore Democratic Party (SDP) were elected, together with two of Mr Chiam's SDP colleagues, Ling How Doong and Cheo Chai Chen.

A Special Select Committee to pick NMPs was constituted on 15 June 1992, including Chiam See Tong as the only non-PAP member. Having pinned my colours to the mast by publicly supporting the NMP scheme, I felt that I could not cravenly slink away when the call went out for volunteers. During the Select Committee on the Elected Presidency, Mr Chiam had chortled when I crossed swords with then-Brigadier General (BG) Lee Hsien Loong on the necessity for the President to be non-partisan; when it came to the NMP Select Committee Mr Chiam did a *volte-face* and said that neutrality is immoral.

Despite Mr Chiam's reservations about NMPs, the Select Committee chose six of us to be NMPs. We were sworn in on 14 September 1992. Deputy Speaker Abdullah Tarmugi kindly lent me his blazer for the occasion as I had neglected to bring my jacket.

In Goh Chok Tong's speech introducing the constitutional amendments to create the NMP scheme, he had stated that NMPs could contribute in their areas of expertise.

I found myself precipitated into the work of Parliament far sooner than I had anticipated. We were sworn in before lunch. Parliament resumed at 3:00pm to debate the Companies (Amendment) Bill, an area with which I had some familiarity as an academic and member of the board of directors of a listed company. The Bill was committed to the Select Committee for further consideration and I was invited to be a member of that Committee.[10]

My experience illustrates one of the prime advantages of the NMP scheme, viz, the opportunity for a non-partisan Member to present an alternative perspective and even influence the making of law within the area of his or her professional competence. It is true that government and even Opposition MPs can do so, but there is always a certain tension. The major weakness of parliamentary democracy is that the Opposition is trying to displace the ruling party, which itself seeks to retain power. This means that good ideas very often are dismissed out of hand simply because they are brought up by the "other side". A non-partisan NMP's suggestions may be acceptable to both sides since there is no need for party-political point-scoring.

This role may be crucial in regard to policies which are politically controversial. No elected politician likes to commit career suicide by advocating necessary but unpopular measures. Former European Commission President Jean-Claude Juncker neatly summed up the elected politician's dilemma when he said: "we all know what to do, we just don't know how to get re-elected once we have done it". NMPs might help in floating the ideas first and drawing the flak.

Influencing National Policy

Again, my experience has been that this can be done. On 25 July 1994, I introduced the Maintenance of Parents Bill on its Second Reading.[11] The genesis of this lay in an unlikely corner.

In early March 1993, then-Finance Minister Dr Richard Hu gave notice of the impending introduction of a Goods and Services Tax (GST). In the debate on the Budget Statement, I made the point that the GST would be regressive and hit retirees particularly. The rebates and tax cuts offered to offset the effects of GST would cushion the impact on working people, but I pointed out that there was no mechanism to have children share the benefit with their parents[12]:

> "But there is one group in particular that will be hit by higher prices without compensating offsets. I refer to retirees. Working people will get tax cuts. Retirees will not. People who live in HDB flats will get rebates. But retirees who are living in bigger HDB flats, or in private property, benefit not a jot from the package offered by the Government. Not everyone who lives in private property is rich. The middle class lives in this shadowland beyond the warm glow of Government subsidy. ...
>
> What then is the solution? I think we have to step back and remind ourselves that the primary responsibility for looking after retirees should be on their children. When it comes to supporting retirees, I think it is dangerous to start with the idea that the Government must do more and that the Government must give more. While it is good that the Government should be open-handed when it can afford to, Government handouts cannot be a long-term solution to anything.
>
> The onus of helping retirees to tide over GST and subsequent cost-of-living increases should be on their children. I hope we have not reached the stage where people feel that it is the Government's job to support the old. I am confident that most Singaporeans will know where their moral duty lies. Those who benefit from the tax cuts and rebates should pass on part of their benefits to their parents who may not benefit at all, being retired. There are some people who can afford to maintain their parents, but will not. The hon. Members of this House, especially the lawyers and social workers, will, no doubt, have met several

examples of the breed. Right now, there is no mechanism to compel a person to support his parents. He can cut his parents off completely even though it is within his means to support them.

The law provides children with the right of support from their parents. The law provides wives with the right to be supported by their husbands. But Singapore law makes no provision at all for parents to obtain support and maintenance from their children. This cannot be a satisfactory state of affairs. I propose that the Government legislate the right for parents to get maintenance from their children. A parent should be given the legal right to claim maintenance from his children. Legislation of this sort will not affect the vast majority of citizens any more than legislation requiring parents to maintain their children affects them. It is only the small recalcitrant minority who can but do not support their parents who will be affected. Such a law will be in line with our objective to reinforce and entrench good values. Contrary to what some may think, filial piety is not a value exclusive in eastern societies. It is a universal value. 'Honour thy father and thy mother.' The source is Middle-Eastern albeit it rendered into English...

Let me summarise what I have said. Prices defy the law of gravity. They only go up. Government handouts to retirees are a bottomless pit. It is not a long-term solution since there is no guarantee that Government will always be able to afford welfare payments. The onus of supporting retirees should be on their children. Most Singaporeans support their parents. There are some who can afford to do so but will not. The solution is to legislate the right for a parent to obtain maintenance from his children...

In conclusion, let me say that there is no legal impediment to passing such a law. It will cost the Government nothing. It will send a powerful signal as to the type of society we seek to create. If it benefits even a thousand Singaporeans, even a hundred Singaporeans, even ten Singaporeans, I say it is worth the effort."

Then-Finance Minister Dr Richard Hu, in his avuncular way, responded to my speech when he summed up the debate the following day:

"Mr Walter Woon has suggested that legislation be introduced to impose an obligation on children to maintain their parents. This is an interesting revival of a recommendation made by the 1984 Committee on the Problems of the Aged. The recommendation was not taken up then as it was felt that the timing was not right. The issue was again studied by the 1988 Advisory Council of the Aged. It concluded that such legislation was unnecessary as statistics indicated that few parents were neglected by their children. However, if Mr Woon feels that the legislation is now timely, he may wish to move a motion in this House to introduce a Private Member's Bill for Parliament's consideration. If there is sufficient interest in the concept, the Government will be happy to support the proposal."[13]

To tell the truth, I had no inkling that there had been a 1984 or 1988 committee on problems of the aged. Nor did I expect that the Minister would throw the issue back to me. But again, having spoken up, I felt I had to carry the proposal through.

The result was the Maintenance of Parents Bill 1994. There was a three-day debate, at the end of which the Bill was put to a vote. This was one of the very few occasions where something actually hinged on the debate, as the government Whip had been lifted.[14] At the end of the process a division was called; the final result: 50 ayes, 11 noes, two abstentions.[15] The Bill was committed to the Select Committee and eventually became law.[16]

Equally significant was the fact that in the 17-month period between Dr Richard Hu's suggestion that I should introduce such a law and its passing, public opinion had shifted. According to contemporary media reports, initially Singaporeans were generally not supportive, especially the Chinese-educated. By the end of the process, the law had majority support. In a survey by the Chinese press just before the parliamentary debate, a specific question was asked: Should the Bill be passed and legislated by the government? Agreed, 52%, disagreed, 46%.[17]

All this supports the notion that NMPs can have a significant effect on national policy, especially where the government is itself divided. I do not pretend that the process is easy. But the fact that it has been done shows that it can be done; and this is important when we consider how we want our society to develop.

A Final Word

Some people have criticised the NMP scheme as being undemocratic. This criticism is misplaced. The origins of our democratic system go back through Westminster ultimately to ancient Athens.

In Athenian democracy, every citizen was entitled to speak and vote at meetings of the assembly (ἐκκλησία) of the city-state (πόλεις). Indeed it was his duty to do so.[18]

This was democracy at its purest — each citizen contributing to debate on national policy.

In a small way, the NMP scheme is a reminder of the ultimate rationale for democracy, that is, to allow ordinary citizens a say in policy- and law-making.

Editor's Cut: A Q&A with Walter Woon
(This interview has been edited and condensed for length and clarity.)

What is your most memorable moment from your time in Parliament?
Besides the Maintenance of Parents Act, there was the debate on ministerial and civil service salaries. I had spoken out strongly about this at first, but in the end, after listening to the debate on both sides, I decided to give the government the benefit of the doubt — which then caused some people to ask, "Why didn't you vote against it?"

The reasoning was very simple: salaries for political office-holders and salaries for the civil service were linked, and I supported paying the civil service — public servants — market rate, because I was aware, and am still aware, that we are in competition with the private sector for the best people.

Some people have a very fuzzy idea that public service means you should sacrifice for the good of the public, which is total poppycock. I'd seen the lingering effects of the lack of human resource planning in the legal service, and my stint as Attorney-General merely confirmed what I already believed: that if you don't pay people market rate, you're just not going to get good people. To ask people to not only sacrifice their own financial well-being but their families' as well was a recipe for mediocrity.

Paying political office-holders — which was what I had spoken up against — was a different thing, but since the two were coupled, you couldn't decouple them. Since it was a package deal, I voted in favour of giving the government the benefit of the doubt on that point, but people did not understand this because they did not make a sufficient distinction [regarding the points]. So basically, yes, I voted that way despite it being unpopular, but then I would say most people voted according to what they thought was the right thing to do, whatever the pushback.

How did being an NMP change you as a person and/or the work you do?
It was very educational. We live in — well, I wouldn't say a bubble, but we really only know the English-speaking crust of society. Being in Parliament made me aware that the vast majority of people in Singapore don't speak English [as their first language], or don't share the same ideas of what's just or right or moral. This is something that the English-educated, I think, generally do not appreciate so much.

Society has changed since then — I was in Parliament decades ago, for heaven's sake — but perhaps there is still a tendency to assume that the Anglophone world reflects the rest of humanity. This is one of the delusions of Caucasian civilisation: that what they consider to be right and wrong reflects what the rest of humanity thinks.

Being in Parliament brought home to me something I had been unaware of — this assumption that something must be right because all my friends say it is right. No! With the Maintenance of Parents Act, the whole idea that you should use the law ran into emotional resistance amongst the Chinese. But public sentiment also moved during that year and a half. In the end, according to *Zaobao*, around 50-something percent of people felt it should be legislated. So it taught me that, number one, not everyone thinks like the English-educated, but number two, it is possible to move public opinion.

Based on your time in Parliament, what advice would you give future NMPs?
Develop a thick skin. At that time, the press was extremely careful not to criticise PAP MPs, but having non-government MPs was something

new, and I think journalists felt able to criticise people at last. Before, if you criticised anyone in public office, you could expect to be whacked hard but here was a target they could come after. So they had no such inhibitions about us, and about me in particular.

How would you sum up your time as an NMP in one sentence?
It was educational to see how parliamentary democracy works from the inside.

Most people have no idea how the parliamentary system actually works; even law and political science students only have a vague idea. Before I went in, I had preconceived ideas about how things would work or should work which had to be modified in the light of practice. For example, the way that things get onto the papers, how bills are actually debated and passed — I had known in outline how it was done, but since I didn't read Hansard for leisure, it wasn't even theoretical knowledge. Until I helped draft the Maintenance of Parents Act, I had no real idea of the interface between Parliament and the Attorney-General's Chambers. Getting to see the machinery in action and understand how it all works was tremendously interesting.

What more can I say? It was an education in the truest sense. Not just book-learning, but actually getting to experience something.

Endnotes

[1] Full Text of PM's Reply at Walkabout Forum, Singapore Monitor 16 April 1984, p. 6.
[2] Constitution of the Republic Singapore (Amendment No. 3) Bill (no 23/90).
[3] Report of the Select Committee on the Constitution of the Republic Singapore (Amendment No. 3) Bill (no 23/90), pp. B36–39.
[4] Ibid, pp. C52–58.

5   Ibid, pp. viii–x.
6   Constitution of the Republic of Singapore (Amendment No. 2) Bill (no 41/1989).
7   Singapore Parliamentary Debates, cols. 695–697; (29 November 1989).
8   Singapore Parliamentary Debates, col. 669; (20 December 1990).
9   Reprinted as Chapter 3 in "Debating Singapore: Reflective Essays" (Institute of Southeast Asian Studies, Singapore; edited by Derek da Cunha).
10 Report of the Select Committee on the Companies (Amendment) Bill (no 33/92), presented to Parliament on 26 April 1993.
11 Singapore Parliamentary Debates, col. 151 et seq; (25 July 1994). This was a rare privilege as normally only Ministers have the opportunity to introduce legislation.
12 Singapore Parliamentary Debates, cols. 699–702; (8 March 1993).
13 Singapore Parliamentary Debates, col. 833; (9 March 1993).
14 Normally, members of a political party are obliged to vote in accordance with the party line. This means of course that it is inevitable that government bills will pass, whatever views may be ventilated during the course of the debate. When the Whip is lifted, however, members may vote according to their conscience.
15 Singapore Parliamentary Debates, cols. 362–364; (27 July 1994).
16 Credit for the present form of the Maintenance of Parents Act must go to Minister for Community Development Abdullah Tarmugi, whose Ministry proposed the changes that created the necessary mechanism. As I said during my summing up of the debate, as a private member I could not commit the government to establish and fund any new legal infrastructure.
17 Singapore Parliamentary Debates, col. 357; (27 July 1994) referring to a telephone survey conducted by *Lianhe Zaobao* the previous month.
18 Encyclopedia Britannica Online. Retrieved from: https://www.britannica.com/topic/democracy/Democratic-institutions#ref796494

Democracy, Legitimacy and Civil Society

Simon Tay
Nominated Member of Parliament (1997–2001)

> *Editor's Note: Even though I had first met Associate Professor Simon Tay briefly more than 15 years ago in the beautiful black-and-white house at Nassim Road, which Unifem (later called UN Women and which I was on the board of) shared with the Singapore Institute of International Affairs (which Simon chairs), I did not know him personally. Thankfully, he was easy to track down as a law professor at the National University of Singapore for this book. He has impressed me as having found the right balance being an active and respected figure in civil society yet also warmly embraced by the establishment. This essay reveals what might be his fulcrum for this balance.*

In a world where democracy is the norm of governance, anything different is an exception to be questioned. Debates about Singapore's politics are often framed in this context, implicitly or otherwise, and central to the debate is the continuing dominance of the People's Action Party (PAP) — not only the sole political party to hold power in the independent Republic but also the longest serving elected government in the world. Ancillary to this, the role of Nominated Members of Parliament (NMPs) is also debated in terms of legitimacy and effects on democratisation of governance.

I served as an NMP from 1997–2001, when the scheme was still in its first decade, and during the premiership of Goh Chok Tong, in what were called the "Next Lap" years. A second generation of Singaporean and PAP leadership were then taking charge, moving towards a more consultative polity and a gentler, kinder society.

This essay will reflect on questions of the legitimacy and roles of the NMPs in that era and touch on personal experiences to suggest broader points in discussing NMPs and democracy in Singapore. The argument is that NMPs can make positive contributions in questioning the government — both in Parliament and outside — in assisting to bridge consultations between government and citizens and towards the growth of civil society.

In doing so, the NMPs had a place in Singapore at the turn of the century. Arguably, NMPs might play a further role in the progress of Singapore.

Questioning Government

The Parliament I entered in 1997 in the old Parliament House was dominated by the PAP with only two elected Opposition MPs (a drop from the previous high of four). Yet in those days before social media, Parliament served as the key public forum for the discussion of policies and laws and the issues of the day. There was also a growing expectation in society that discussion and inclusion should increase, even if many wanted the decisiveness of government and the unity of the people to continue.

This was something of a conundrum. There was a desire for more consultation and debate of key issues, yet in a Parliament that was very lop-sided in representation. This created an opportunity and need for NMPs to speak up on diverse issues that could reflect questions and points of view that would otherwise not be heard within the House and publicly.

Could and should NMPs question and contest government points of view, beyond what PAP MPs did? Yes, and indeed that was a core rationale to have unelected NMPs at all.

For me, participation in discussions about public and political issues began even before I was an NMP.

I had been a commentator in the media before being nominated and was active in civil society, especially in a group called the Roundtable. Immediately following the 1997 General Election, I co-authored a commentary that argued against a key pillar in the PAP's election strategy to link the Housing and Development Board (HDB) upgrading to their percentage of support in districts, and this had elicited a robust response from the PAP leadership. There is no need to rehash the particulars of these debates; but — like some other NMPs before and after me — I came forward to serve as NMP in the hope and belief that Singapore would increasingly need to accommodate more diverse and independent views. Parliament could help create space and acceptance for this evolution in our country.

On this basis, as an NMP, I sought a range of issues, including those relating to civil society and political rights. One controversy arose concerning the then-new Speakers' Corner in Hong Lim Park. A human rights activist was under police investigation about whether he had held an "illegal" protest there. I pursued the issue by first calling the relevant office holder, then in writing, and then finally raising it in Parliament. I did so not to help the individual person involved (who later stood for elections as an Opposition party candidate) but to uphold the civic right to freely utilise the Speakers' Corner, with the minimum of encumbrance. Soon after, the police dropped the investigation.

As an NMP, there were of course occasions when I supported and voted for laws and policies proposed by the government. There were also instances when I spoke to analyse and suggest ways in which the draft bills might be amended and improved, or to seek clarification about their implications when implemented.

But in considering whether NMPs can and did more than PAP MPs, one marker was whether NMPs did agree and vote against a government bill, and a number of us did. Another marker of difference and independence would be whether an NMP had voted with the Opposition. Not all have found a reason to do so. On one occasion I did so, when the late J. B. Jeyaretnam of the Workers' Party — then a Non-Constituency MP — moved a motion concerning libel and defamation lawsuits in Singapore. While my reasons differed from those argued by Mr Jeyaretnam, I did see merit in reviewing the laws to safeguard possible abuse to stifle criticism and voted in support.

Bridge and Consultation

While being in Parliament, an MP has a role to connect to the wider society — and this includes the NMP, even without a geographical constituency. Could NMPs play a role to help the government connect and dialogue more with citizens, and conversely for citizens to be heard by the government?

This was especially important in those years in Parliament before social media and alternative platforms existed for citizens to express and project their views.

In this context, as an NMP, I took a role in a number of public consultations. Perhaps the most substantive was Singapore 21, a committee commissioned by the government of Prime Minister Goh to look at aspirations of our society as the new century began. This was chaired by Minister Teo Chee Hean, with nine MPs on the main committee, including two NMPs (the other was Dr Lee Tsao Yuan). In particular, I co-chaired the committee on consultation and consensus versus decisive action (with Lim Swee Say, then an MP and later Minister and National Trades Union Congress (NTUC) Secretary-General).

The Singapore 21 (or S21) process involved many engagements with different groups of citizens, and the committee on consultation even more so. At that time, citizen voices were still nascent, even on matters such as the environment, gender and LGBTQ issues. Debates about whether Singapore was our home or simply a convenient hotel and the role of foreigners in Singapore, were also growing subjects of discussion.

Early activists on some of these issues utilised S21 to make their views known more broadly in the S21 process. Many of those debates have grown since. For S21, the formal conclusion was a report to the government that was tabled for discussion in Parliament. My participation in S21 reinforced the possible role of an NMP (and indeed all MPs) to serve as a bridge between the citizenry and Parliament, not just on particular municipal issues but in the consideration of broader and longer-term concerns.

In that parliamentary debate, while the S21 report was adopted by the government, I recall in particular an impromptu intervention by Lee Kuan Yew, then Senior Minister, to cite and then disagree with elements of what I had said about the need for civil society. Details aside, I took from this experience the assurance that, even if their views differed, our highest leaders might be attentive to what an NMP might advocate.

Emerging Concerns: The Haze and Conservation

While S21 was a government initiative, I was also involved in issues that were initially voiced by the public. What role can NMPs have to voice and initiate debate on concerns emerging from citizens?

The answer is far from obvious in relation to localised issues, which can be addressed by MPs with a geographical constituency and municipal functions. But there can be a role for wider issues that affect the nation as a whole. For me as an NMP, in particular, these were the haze and conservation — emerging issues at the time that have grown since in public consciousness.

During the 1997–98 haze, Singapore and the region suffered for many months, in what was an extreme and early episode of a problem that has continued to recur (although in some years and most recently, less severely). In this period, the Singapore Government was cautious in criticising Indonesia about the haze pollution, given the overall relationship with our biggest neighbour, then facing a fiscal and political crisis that ended the long-standing Suharto administration. Newly sworn in as an NMP in Parliament, I however did not feel so constrained.

Many ordinary citizens were affected and upset about the haze, not only in terms of their health, but their livelihoods and their normal course of activities. At the university, I had started the first course on international environmental law and hoped that from this knowledge I could help bring up the concerns of ordinary citizens to Parliament. I was also personally motivated by the birth of my son, Luke, at the end of 1997, given the impact that haze can have on the young.

As an NMP, I initiated a parliamentary motion to call on the Singapore Government to do more to urge and also assist Indonesia to take actions against the haze. This was not initially supported by our government and I could only count on my fellow NMP Zulkifli Baharudin to second the Motion. When the then-Minister for Environment, Yeo Cheow Tong, rose to respond, the government differed on the actions I called for — which included trying to hold the Government of Indonesia and the relevant corporations responsible. But given the public sentiment, the Minister did not seek to oppose or amend, and the Motion proposed was carried.

I did not stop there on this issue. In the subsequent months and following years when the problem returned, nor did I limit my actions and advocacy in Parliament.

In this period, I led the Singapore Institute of International Affairs and Singapore Environment Council to convene the first regional dialogue on the issue among experts and non-governmental organisations. Subsequently, I led a small delegation of Singaporean civil society leaders to Indonesia where we met with their officials, including their Minister for Environment. During an ASEAN meeting on the issue, with Indonesian officials present, I was also invited to make the first non-official presentation on the problem. In this regard, the NMPship assisted my standing to bring these concerns to the attention of governments, and not only to our own.

In the years since, the Singapore Government has engaged their Indonesian counterparts on this issue with greater consistency, and willingness to criticise, when need be. More assistance too is rendered with satellite mapping. In 2014, Parliament passed the Transboundary Haze Pollution Act which can hold corporations liable for the haze, as I and some others had hoped for and advocated. Some two decades on, the problem, even if not solved, is better managed.

Another issue that I consistently raised was conservation, of both natural and built environments. One early intervention I made was when part of the nature reserves was delisted for government use, and I asked for an equivalent block of land to be set aside. I also advocated for greater study of the biodiversity and other benefits of nature in the process of redevelopment.

Another was related to plans to demolish the old National Library that held a place for many from the early years of our country, for the purpose of building a road tunnel. These debates in Parliament linked to concerns being raised in the wider society by citizens and groups such as the Nature Society and Heritage Society (which I knew and engaged in but did not join). I also debated the laws introduced to allow for *en bloc* redevelopment of private strata-title land. Questioning the balance between the rights of homeowners with the wider concern that buildings could fall into disrepair, I ended up voting for the Land Titles (Strata) (Amendment) Bill.

The respective Ministers in all three debates stood firm and with the PAP's bloc of votes, the laws were passed. Yet there were seeds in these debates that have now grown. On the *en bloc* redevelopment laws, the initial regulations on voting were subsequently tightened to raise the hurdle for redevelopment and better protect a minority who might wish to keep their homes. The political and civic awareness about the value of conservation has grown considerably.

Personally, I took another step outside Parliament when I was asked to serve on the Singapore Concept Plan 2000, as one of four co-chairs appointed by the Minister, and the only sitting MP.

Like S21, this process involved a consultation with the public and also experts. Reporting to the Minister of National Development, our recommendations placed a greater emphasis and more deliberative processes to evaluate the merits of conservation. The report also encouraged new development projects to be more distinctive and aligned to environmental concerns. Much of this was accepted by the Minister — the same office holder who had decided on the demolition of the National Library building. The issues of conservation and the environment are now much more broadly acknowledged and acted upon by citizens, corporations and the government.

Concluding Remarks

The vote and choice of the citizen is no doubt a primary concern in selecting their representative in Parliament. But the performance of other roles can also be a legitimating factor.

Given the dominance of the PAP, NMPs assisted with the representation of different interests and broadened the diversity of viewpoints in Parliament. Where that has resonance in the wider society, this increases the acceptance of NMPs.

But to do so, the NMP must seek to be and be seen as independent. There were rumours circulating that some might seek to join the PAP immediately after being an NMP. But for me, I felt that this would not be right for the NMP scheme and my own credibility after serving three terms in that role.

Moreover, for me, I did not believe that it was necessary to join the ruling party to contribute to public debate and life. Subsequent to leaving Parliament, I was happy to serve as chairman of the then-new National Environment Agency (2002–08), reporting to the Ministers (whom I had known from Parliament and also the S21 process) to guide a sizeable statutory board of some 3,500 employees on issues of the environment that I cared for.

I have also continued to work on issues like the haze and the development of economy and polity through my chairmanship of the Singapore Institute of International Affairs, an independent think-tank that plays a significant role in the "track two" diplomacy of ASEAN. Even without a voice in Parliament, I have continued to contribute commentaries in the media on issues of the day. But serving as an NMP at that stage was significant to my hopes to contribute to public life and discourse in my own way.

What next for the NMP scheme for Singapore?

There is an evolving political landscape with social media and growth of civil society, with the increased visibility and seats held by the Opposition. Questions also arise about the 4G (4th Generation) leadership and their attitudes and strategies to evolve their party and Singapore governance. This is especially as they grapple with the pandemic and the stresses that emerge for our economy, our society and our openness to the world. There are those who hope that Singapore will emerge stronger and also better.

The NMP scheme will not be the main driver of this evolution, it was never. But NMPs have been, in my estimate, one of the contributing features in moving Singapore forward from the old days of PAP monopoly — this is not only in the seats of Parliament but in substantive deliberation and the character of public discourse.

Perhaps, subject to evolving circumstances as well as the actions of the current and future NMPs, this special role might still be able to make further contributions to Singapore politics and society.

Editor's Cut: A Q&A with Simon Tay

(This interview has been edited and condensed for length and clarity.)

What is your most memorable moment from your time in Parliament?
As I wrote in my piece, I put up a motion about the transboundary haze pollution. It was a prominent issue in 1997/98, the first years I was in Parliament and we'd suffered from it for many years. I've been an environmentalist since the 1990s — I had studied environmental law at Harvard and later began teaching it — so I felt I had both the conviction and expertise to bring up the issue.

At the time, Singaporeans were upset, but the government, for various strategic and geopolitical reasons, wasn't going to criticise Indonesia very much. So I proposed a motion, with Zulkifli [Baharudin, my fellow NMP's] support, that said Singapore must do more about the haze. I think my position was more critical, whereas the PAP MPs were much more cautious about approaching the issue. But the Motion had been very carefully phrased in a way which was meant to garner the whole House's support; I don't think MPs could've refused it without angering the public.

I will also remember the parliamentary debate that closed off the Singapore 21 public consultation. I had been appointed to the main committee under then-Education Minister Teo Chee Hean and co-chair with Lim Swee Say on the specific issue of the need for consultation. In Parliament, I advocated strongly on the need for Singapore to develop a credible civil society as part of our maturation process and asked that the government allow space for this.

After I spoke, then-Senior Minister Lee Kuan Yew rose to reply, although he was unscheduled. He told the House that he had listened to my arguments but disagreed with me to an extent; one difference was that he believed civil society had severe limits in offering leadership. After listening to SM Lee, I then asked the floor to make a rejoinder, which the Speaker allowed, and with respect, reiterated the need to allow scope for this future development. I learnt in this process that leaders — including Mr Lee — listened and took the debates in Parliament very seriously. I also learnt that there are PAP MPs who take it as a castigation that a minister might disagree with you, whereas there are others who will look at the issue itself. When I see the growth of civil society today, I take a third lesson: that debates in Parliament need to risk being more in step with social developments rather than conforming to the conventional views of the time.

How did being an NMP change you as a person and/or the work you do?
The NMPship came to me early. I was 37 when I entered Parliament; it helped educate me, gave me a wider network and a much more visible public profile. I went on to the civil service subsequently, as well as SIIA, the think-tank I now chair, and I think that helped the government feel more comfortable with me.

Today, with social media, it's possible to have a fairly strong public voice without being an MP or even an NMP, but it was impossible in those days. For people who sought a public platform from which to air their views, I thought NMPship had its uses.

NMPs, to my mind, are active participants in Singapore's growing civil society. During my terms, I focused a lot on this and why it's good for Singapore, but I also thought the government at the time needed to get comfortable with the idea. In that sense, I never tried to be too "in their face" in case they tried to squash things — I wanted them to come round to the idea that civil society wasn't radically opposed to the government, but could help grow and augment how we function.

Based on your time in Parliament, what words of advice would you give future NMPs?
To be honest, I'm not sure the scheme should go on. Times were different when I was in Parliament. Opposition presence [in Parliament] had dropped from four MPs to two, and there was a need to keep debates going — frankly, even then-PM Goh would quietly encourage us to raise our voices and not worry. But today, I don't think Singaporeans need to be encouraged to speak up, even between elections. In fact, the possible danger now is a fracturing of voices.

In my view, Parliament is struggling to be a real focus point of debate on public life in Singapore. Sometimes it runs behind the curve. Moreover, we now have a fairly credible Opposition, and if you look at debates now you might struggle to find NMPs' voices. So maybe...there shouldn't be NMPs anymore. I'm not sure. I *am* sure that times have changed, and they are struggling to get that visibility and public support.

How would you sum up your time as an NMP in one sentence?
Being an NMP was an education for me, and, I hope, a factor in helping to increase my contributions to public policy and public debate. Of course, these are modest, but my time in Parliament made me more able to contribute in the way I wanted to.

NMPs as "Loving Critics" of Singapore

Chandra Mohan Nair
Nominated Member of Parliament (2001–2004)

> *Editor's Note: Unencumbered by partisan rules and free from the Whip, many argue that NMPs' role must be to, unequivocally, provide alternative views, offer challenges to the status quo and hold the government to account in Parliament. Early NMPs like Professor Walter Woon, Dr Kanwaljit Soin, Braema Mathi and Chandra Mohan Nair did not disappoint with their fiery speeches as feisty "loving critics", a term coined by Professor Tommy Koh in October 2019 when he said "Singapore will languish if its lovers are uncritical and its critics are unloving". Chandra Mohan shares his experience of being a loving critic in Parliament because the love of his life believed in him and persuaded him to do it.*

The Constitution of the Republic of Singapore encapsulates the distribution of the state's power, responsibilities and duties to various institutions and individuals for the ultimate benefit of, and in the paramount interests and smooth running of our nation. These include the government, President, Executive, Prime Minister, Ministers, Permanent Secretaries, Attorney-General, Judiciary, Legislature, the Speaker, Members, Non-Constituency Members, Nominated Members of Parliament (NMPs), and the Public Service.

Generally, the individuals who are constitutionally assigned these responsibilities carry out their duties and obligations diligently.

My appointment as an NMP got me closer to the sacred institution of our Parliament and brought into sharper focus the good qualities of my life, including happiness, love, passion, compassion, sacrifice and friendship. As Singaporeans, we must love and cherish our country with all its goodness and caring ways along with some warts, blemishes and shortcomings.

The Singapore I Grew Up In

I was born in Kerala, India. My father migrated from Kerala to Malaya in the 1930s and then to Singapore to earn a living. He experienced World War Two and went back to Kerala in the 1950s. In 1957, he brought my mother, brother and I to Singapore. This British Colony then was hardly an ideal place to call home. It was small, with few decent homes for citizens. My two widowed grandmothers remained in Kerala. How sad to be separated as a family and with little communication, save for letters that took weeks to be delivered.

My dad took care of 11 people in our extended family. We lived in a small two-room flat in Geylang Lorong 3 built by the Singapore Improvement Trust, the colonial predecessor of the Housing and Development Board (HDB).

My life in the neighbourhood and in school was fun with lots of friends, mainly Malays and Chinese with one or two Indians. I learnt Malay, "broken" Hokkien and Tamil. Our intermingling and comradeship with different races and levels of education was memorable.

I witnessed a Singapore filled with poverty, pockets of swamps, gangsters, poor sanitation, problematic supply of water and electricity, transportation, health issues, few schools and industries, British camps, hawkers earning a living legally and illegally, and few farmers. Moreover, it was not governed well, with rules and regulations promulgated by overworked politicians and civil servants whom most people hardly knew or understood. I learnt to survive under these dire circumstances. They forced us to be street-smart and wily in order to survive. What scary and exciting times they were indeed!

My parents, who had very little education, inculcated the importance of education to us as the primary passport to a better life.

The Singapore I Fell in Love With

I was fortunate to be enrolled in the University of Singapore in 1972 and upon graduation in a law class of about 100 students, comprising about 30% Malaysians, was admitted to the roll of Supreme Court of Singapore in 1977 to practise law.

In 1974, I met a fellow undergraduate, Goury Govin, who became my one and only girlfriend. We later married in 1979. She was kind, intelligent, cheeky, spoke Queen's English and was a critic of the highest order about life and current affairs. Goury was a good mother, wise lawyer and a voracious reader who fearlessly advocated for gender equality, fundamental liberties and democracy.

Up until the 1990s, Parliament was controlled by the People's Action Party (PAP), except for two opposition members from the Singapore Democratic Party (SDP) and the Workers' Party (WP), Chiam See Tong and Low Thia Khiang respectively. Few were interested in politics, thanks to the muted political mood then.

It was Goury who persuaded me to consider being an NMP. She knew how committed I was (and still am) to Singapore and the work I do with the legal profession (Law Society, Academy of Law, Board of Legal Education), university alumni (Council of NUS, NUS Society), and various governmental and non-government organisation (NGO) committees to improve society. I was also keenly involved in the sports

◆ The Nominated Member of Parliament Scheme

fraternity, especially in hockey, soccer and athletics. I was then an active committee member of The Roundtable, an NGO which promoted active engagement with politicians and local intellectuals.

I did, and was interviewed in 2001 by the Parliamentary Select Committee, chaired by Speaker Tan Soo Khoon including then-Deputy Prime Minister Lee Hsien Loong and Home Affairs and Law Minister Professor S. Jayakumar. On 1 October 2001, President S. R. Nathan appointed eight of us to be NMPs. The persons nominated had distinguished themselves in the fields of arts, culture, sciences, business, industry, professions, social, community service and the labour movement and were selected to reflect as wide a range of independent and non-partisan views as possible. I served as an NMP in the 9th and 10th Parliaments from 2001 till 2004.

Sadly, my dear wife Goury passed away in September 2000; she did not witness me being sworn in to serve Parliament on 5 October 2001. My children, Valmiki Nair and Dhania Nair, who were then 16 and 15 years old, were with me at the appointment ceremony. They were my ardent supporters and guiding stars who enlightened and inspired me greatly then — a widower at 50 and a newly minted NMP; they have continued to do so since.

Speaking up for Singapore

I was, and still am, a loving critic of the way Singapore is governed. Absolute power can be harmful to society. Since independence, the PAP has had a supermajority in Parliament, which means all bills proposed shall always be passed.

When it comes to loving our country, I truly believe one must be idealistic to dream about the best version of Singapore that we want. But I also realised as an NMP that idealism without actual power did not get me far except to merely debate on issues, dream about doing more good for Singapore and put on Hansard my idealistic suggestions for the powers that be to think about and hopefully translate these ideas into action.

During my time in Parliament from 2001–2004, I discussed a wide range of topics and issues, all of which are recorded in the Hansard.

Dual citizenship for Singaporeans — I asked for liberalisation of this policy so that our people could be more mobile and explore the world to increase the diaspora of Singaporeans.

A Junior Parliament to be formalised in schools and higher institutions — I argued that this would allow our young citizens to debate on national issues with each other, and also that we should invite these "young parliamentarians" to Parliament to hone their debating skills with members of the House.

Accountability of the Corrupt Practices Investigation Bureau (CPIB) — I urged that CPIB should present its Annual Report to Parliament not only to showcase its efficiency and success but also to check on itself to ensure transparency and impartiality.

Legal Profession Act (LPA) and the powers of the Law Society to comment on pending legislation under the LPA — I pointed out that the stifling of this power has dampened the spirit of the legal profession and also taken away the enthusiasm of members of the profession to get involved, especially the 1980s and 1990s; this was a loss to Singapore's intellectual diversity. I argued that this section in the LPA must be amended. No parliamentarian has raised this matter.

Create a Ministry of Peace — I asked why the Ministry of Defence is spending more than 10% of annual budget on military planes, warships, tanks, vehicles and armaments when we should give part of the money to social welfare instead. To my mind, there is a lot of theoretical fear amongst military officers and ministers of defence in ASEAN countries and beyond, of "enemies" lurking around. How sad. We should be promoting universal peace and trust amongst the ASEAN nations.

Reduce the size of the Istana — I argued that too much of the valuable space on Orchard Road is fenced up and underutilised; more space should be given to citizens to use. I proposed that if so much space is indeed required for the Istana then we should move it to another site. I also asked then what was the land cost and returns per year for the last 50 years?

Overseas electronic voting — I asked that overseas electronic voting be made available for all eligible citizens residing abroad so that their fundamental right as a citizen to vote for the MPs of their choice is preserved.

Promote interracial marriages — I suggested that promoting interracial marriages will help bring about a stronger multi-racial society, producing the next generation of Singaporeans with less emphasis on race.

Parliament revamp — I argued that NMPs should be supported well with excellent research by young graduates; this will develop their interest and hopefully lead them to join political parties one day.

More than one Prime Minister — I asked if we should go beyond one Prime Minister and have a few tried and tested ministers share the role and burden at different times in a year or across a period of five years. I proposed that an alternative could be to have a committee of top leaders lead the government because the spread of power is good for the souls of the people in power, and society.

Challenges as an NMP

I had a hectic time being an NMP with my full-time job as a lawyer and active involvement with NGOs and sports organisations. My friends promised to help but they were apparently too busy, so I had to go solo.

There was no secretarial support from Parliament for NMPs. I felt then, in those early days of the NMP scheme, that the treatment that NMPs received was unhelpful and disappointing. There was also no camaraderie; NMPs did not join forces as a team primarily because we hardly knew each other. In hindsight, we should have exchanged notes, discussed our interests and passions and worked together to be more impactful. The then-Speaker and Deputy Speaker of Parliament could have been more involved and made improvements to assist NMPs. Opposition members were also of little help. It was as though we NMPs were left on our own.

However, I do wish to give a special mention to the Parliament librarian, a lovely and kind elderly lady, who gave me much assistance.

Most of the MPs I met appeared sincere and diligent, determined to improve Singapore society. Some quarters, however, felt there was no need for NMPs. A few MPs also hinted that NMPs did not represent any constituency; I responded that I represented Singapore and owed no allegiance to any political party or constituency. I was to serve the nation, this was sacrosanct and paramount.

With the Whip hardly lifted, I feel debates in our Parliament are relatively muted; we must ask for a review of, and changes to, the Standing Orders to allow for more freedom to debate for all elected parliamentarians.

There are some issues I feel strongly about which I did not raise in Parliament. I feel it is important for us to create an Association of

Southeast Asian Nations (ASEAN) university to promote long-term collaboration and interdependence between the countries and their citizens; we should have an ASEAN passport.

The People's Association should be impartial and must serve the people — the perception appears to be too one-sided. I think it is time to change the law so that the leadership is not designated to Cabinet Ministers but by an independent and impartial citizen.

My Enduring Love for Singapore

I care deeply for this nation having witnessed its miraculous prospering post-Merdeka till today. I am proud of how we have shared the economic wealth amongst the people.

When I became an NMP, it was almost a one-party Parliament. I was, and am still, concerned about this power dominance in what is supposed to be a parliamentary democracy.

In my 70s now and a senior citizen, I am finally starting to see more opposition voices in Parliament in recent years, especially with the 2020 General Election. Perhaps the Internet and social media have "democratised" Singapore politics and citizens' political thinking in some small but significant ways.

Hotly contested and controversial when it was first introduced by then-Prime Minister Goh Chok Tong, the NMP scheme is a significant institution that gives opportunities for Singaporeans who are non-politicians to get into Parliament to debate impartially and independently on issues of the day. I do believe that the scheme should be enhanced with more power including support resources and that there be more NMPs than the current limit of nine to ensure the debates in Parliament are more robust and vibrant.

We are still essentially a one-party dominant system with the supermajority held by the PAP; it might take a few more general elections before it becomes a more level playing field. We sorely need leaders who are idealistic, enlightened and just, in addition to also debating well which is relatively lacking in Parliament today.

Our Parliament really needs better debates instead of almost one-sided monologues. We need good and effective debaters who can inspire the nation with ideas and love. Former Prime Minister Lee Kuan Yew set the bar high; in the early years, there were also David Marshall, Lee Siew Choh and J. B. Jeyaretnam, to name a few.

I can see that Opposition MPs and NMPs are trying hard in parliamentary debates, but they just lack the power, parliamentary numbers, research and access to information to debate well. Our schools and institutes of higher learning must play a critical role in developing and inspiring a new generation of debaters!

I would like to urge young Singaporeans to step forward to participate in the NMP scheme, if they are not inclined to become full-time politicians. Many of the changes that we want to see can only be birthed through bills in Parliament and by pushing policy makers to listen to the voices from the ground.

The institution of NMPs might be a small improvement and perhaps, as many believe, may also be a "political" tool to give the perception of alternative voices in the House. However, until a more diverse and well-represented Parliament is upon us, the merits of the NMP scheme and the impact that NMPs can make far outweigh its flaws.

Finally, always the idealist and loving critic, I have this wish list for my beloved country — starting with a review of the Constitution with the formation of a Constitutional Review Body to update our laws to modern Singapore including with respect to fundamental liberties including freedom of speech, assembly and association; the role of the President; the death penalty; granting pardon to deserving prisoners; a new post of Director of Public Prosecutions; the role and necessity of Mayors; and finally, holding a referendum for these crucial amendments to the Constitution so that Singaporeans have a say in the values of this nation.

Editor's Cut: A Q&A with Chandra Mohan Nair
This interview has been edited and condensed for length and clarity.

What is your most memorable moment from your time in Parliament?
During Budget time, every ministry wants to have a certain budget for themselves and get approval from Parliament. In the course of such debates over monetary matters and policy and what [the government's] going to do, you can also raise questions of every ministry.

I raised a lot of issues. I remember that in one year, I think I had the most number of questions in terms of ministries! It was very tough because every time you ask a query in order to give a speech, the Minister will respond and you have to be prepared for that. So in a way, that was memorable for me.

I think a lot of the things I raised were for the sake of debate in Parliament, because, you know, we NMPs don't have any power in that sense; the power lies with the PAP. But I think our role is to raise issues in Parliament for debate and hope that some of those ideas will trigger deeper thoughts on those subjects which will be useful for Singapore's progress. So I would say it was quite memorable to have contributed to that.

How did being an NMP change you as a person and/or the work you do?
First, it has shown me that society is much more than politics. Second, it has affirmed my belief in idealism.

You know, when you're idealistic, your pragmatic ways and standards go up too. Some people will say you must be practical in order to be idealistic, stop wasting your time! But I don't think so. You must be idealistic and work towards raising the level of the pragmatic ways of doing things so that you reach a higher standard, so to speak.

I also realised that friendship is also very important. You might have friends in the proposition and the opposition, but if you mean well and it's the idea that you're interested in, I think it makes you a happier person. I think your soul is more at ease and rests better than, you know, compared to fighting away. That's why I love mediation compared to litigation or going to court.

I think these are lessons you learn when you are facing the powerful. You can read about them and theorise about them, but when you have to do it and you're facing the real problems, I think you mature even more.

Based on your time in Parliament, what words of advice would you give future NMPs?
I would recommend connecting with your fellow NMPs, working together and seeing what can be done and finding others who can help you during your term.

I once raised in Parliament that NMPs should get secretarial support. I remember the leader of the ruling party at the time literally told me to go and look for my own and do my own homework. I think I would have been more professional and presented [issues] better if I had had support from full-time staff. My recommendation was that we should have full-time people who are graduates in, say, philosophy, the humanities, law, economics and so on to do some research — which would be shared amongst all MPs, not just NMPs, so that we can have a good level of debate. This is something I hope the Speaker of Parliament and the government can look into.

How would you sum up your time as an NMP in one sentence?
I would say I was a loner.

I was all alone as an NMP. I had a few colleagues who were fellow NMPs, but we somehow never connected to work together as a team. That loneliness, I think, also made me feel that NMPs could have done better. Perhaps we could even form our own Secretariat with like-minded people who might want to serve [but not as NMPs], and who would provide support instead. They could then, for example, say, "Mister so-and-so, you will present this topic on social welfare…You will present this in law…You will present this on economics, etc." Like a self-organised group to prepare speeches, because those are very important.

Hopefully the ministries find this a worthwhile idea to pursue. [The idea is that] everyone progresses. I think that's very important.

Then and Now, for the Future

Braema Mathiaparanam
Nominated Member of Parliament (2001–2004)

> *Editor's Note: Early NMPs like Dr Kanwaljit Soin (the first female NMP in Parliament) and Braema Mathiaparanam not only demonstrated allyship with civil society as NMPs through their strong and passionate voices in Parliament, they also role modelled the value of more gender diversity in the House. I know both of them personally from different community engagement efforts. Our society has evolved much; social media has changed the political landscape considerably in the last 30 years. In this essay, Braema shares her experience as an NMP in the first decade of the scheme and her perspective of its value through the journey of time, then and now, that ends with a call for a review of a future-ready parliamentary system for Singapore.*

I was first in Parliament from 1 October to 18 October 2001 as the 9th Parliament was dissolved for a general election, following the attack on the World Trade Center in September 2001. I was selected for a second term from the beginning of 2002 to the end of 2004. I am moulded as a person by my experiences at home, school, work (in a few fields), readings, conferences, forums, discussions and observations. I believe in people's empowerment and democracy. Based on who I am and my beliefs, I share my thoughts here on the intent of the Nominated Member of Parliament (NMP) scheme, NMPs' contributions and my personal experience, the limitations of the NMP scheme, and lastly, the need to re-configure the parliamentary system for a Singapore beyond 2030.

Parliamentary Representation

Singapore's parliamentary representation is based on a first-past-the-post voting scheme of having the highest vote scoring candidate securing a parliamentary seat to be an MP. Since independence in 1965, the General Elections (GEs) of 1968, 1972, 1976 and 1980 returned the People's Action Party (PAP) as the only political party in Parliament House.[1] To counter this one-party government of MPs, to liven up debates in Parliament and for security reasons, the government introduced:

- In 1984, the Non-Constituency MP (NCMP) scheme for the top-performing Opposition candidates, to gain, from six to later nine seats in 2010;
- In 1987, the Government Parliamentary Committees (GPCs) of 10 to 11 MPs to function like a "shadow cabinet team" to review work of ministries and offer recommendations;
- In 1988, the still controversial Group Representation Constituencies (GRCs) to be a safety net to ensure minorities — who had historically gotten into Parliament[2] without a predetermined systemic emphasis on race — would not be left out in being nominated as candidates;
- In 1990, the NMP scheme for non-partisan individuals to be nominated and then be selected, based on non-publicly stated criteria, by a Select Committee, for the available nine seats to be independent voices, perhaps even alternative.

These current schemes need to be assessed based on their underlying principles and rationale.

The NCMP scheme is often seen as a challenging process, whereby opposition party candidates who had campaigned and lost well, work very hard and function like an elected MP without the full benefits as an elected MP. It would be easier to scrap the scheme or just have those who have scored 48 or 49% to be full-fledged MPs but place safeguards by limiting fewer seats.

GPCs function as alternative voices amongst backbenchers and raise concerns with Ministers. Nevertheless, when MPs are from the same party, there is a loyalty to the party that can overshadow the cause.

GRCs primarily put minorities on the back heel of equality while simultaneously hindering the growth of opposition political parties, as they become focused on finding candidates according to racial background to have a ready slate for GEs. Race-focused politics in the form of the GRC system takes away more from building social cohesion for a diversely populated Singapore.

As such, each scheme places limits on the function of parliamentary representation even as they disrupt the sameness of having all MPs from one political party.

The NMP Canvas

The NMP scheme began with nominees from varied backgrounds with cross-sectoral interests until the clustering of representation as "functional groups" began. The seven sectors of business and industry, labour, professionals, social and community services, tertiary institutions, civic and people sector, and the media, arts and sports organisations, at one point saw deep engagement by some sectors which held town hall meetings and voted in their best candidate as nominees for selection. But sectoral representation also defined the backgrounds, interests and roles for the selected NMPs, akin to the GPCs' roles, and in congruence with ministries. But people's lives, way of living and thinking, philosophies and changing dynamics in society remain often unpredictable and cannot be compartmentalised into the workable and manageable operational ministries' focus. Thus, in my view, sectoral representation despite the merit of focus, also places, directly or indirectly, limitations on NMPs' interests through such delineations.

Most NMPs over the years made remarkable efforts to stay abreast of many issues in preparation for Parliament sittings. Individually, this is a precarious balancing act of working full-time at paid jobs, being engaged in other mainly volunteer activities, setting time for families, friends and/or recreation, for reading and Parliament. So despite the lack of a constituency, it is still an onerous involvement, especially if one cares about the issues, the bills tabled for discussion, the research needed to make good presentations, meeting communities who wish to engage with NMPs and vice versa, and not losing sight of getting some legislative or policy outcomes on matters close to one's heart, mind and soul.

NMPs have spoken on many proposed bills, lending their voices to support others in Parliament, have filed oral and written questions and been active in question-and-answer sessions. NMPs have contributed by making suggestions, being involved in committees and some have tabled bills or motions — against family violence, for maintenance of parents, repealing the anti-sodomy Section 377A of the Penal Code — showing that NMPs as non-partisan members have the freedom to table a matter that will not lose them any votes or mean dealing with upset constituents. Many worked hard and built up a berth of work. Most contributed, substantively.

My Experience in Parliament

I was nominated by the Association of Women for Action and Research (AWARE) in 2001 to emphasise the lack of women MPs and women leaders in Parliament.[3]

There were few women MPs and in the 9th Parliament it was one woman Minister — Dr Aline Wong — and Yu-Foo Yee Shoon as Senior Parliamentary Secretary, who were working hard, fronting many issues related to women, family, livelihoods, skills, health, housing, women growing older, divorces, sexual crimes and work-life balance. That we have had too few women in Parliament for too long, coupled with women not wanting to be in politics, is our patriarchal embarrassment.

I think this effort by AWARE made some mark as GE 2001 saw more women candidates, which meant more women MPs, in Parliament. Today, some of them are on the front bench and one, Halimah Yacob, is even in the Istana as the President.

I was very active throughout my stint as an NMP. I felt it was my duty to serve since I was nominated by AWARE, and then selected. With help from a research assistant, I kept busy. It seemed I filed the most number of written and oral questions in my term that a Minister said, as my term was coming to an end, how finding answers for my questions took up much time and effort from the civil service.

Henceforth, the number of Parliamentary Questions submitted for written answers ("written PQs") from being limitless was narrowed to five for each sitting. Written PQs are a treasure trove of data, insights into policy and outcome trends.

I filed on motions, made speeches on Ministerial Statements, second readings on bills, Budget statements and at Committee of Supply debates. I realised that my former work as a journalist, a teacher and then in healthcare also signposted me on a number of issues related to community, mechanisms, accountability, training of personnel and development of career paths for staff.

It is equally significant that an NMP's role is not just confined within Parliament sittings.

In December 2002, with others, I began work as a volunteer to found The Working Committee 2, which was later registered as Transient Workers Count Too (TWC2) to champion the rights and well-being of migrant workers when recalled to Parliament for a second term.

It was good timing as the new Minister for Manpower, as part of the Super Seven[4] team, was keen to "clean up" on policies related to migrant workers, making improvements for their safety and well-being. It became an opportunity for my civil society work and NMPship to synergise on key changes needed. As I raised migrant worker issues in Parliament, it also opened doors for us to have discussions with the Ministry's Permanent Secretary and high-ranking civil service officers which offered opportunities to elaborate as well as corroborate on policies and programmes.

Chats with Ministers in the Members' Lounge during breaks were also very handy as I gained insights into the nature of limitations and found ways to collaborate on issues, especially within the labour, education and social service sectors. What was interesting was that Ministers, elected MPs, NCMPs and NMPs also have their own areas of personal interests as well and some did share views that were encouraging on matters of women leadership roles, sex trafficking, migrant workers, social workers' caseloads, to name a few.

I was also preparing before the end of my term to table a draft bill on employment of foreign domestic workers with standardisation of contract terms. Alas, the Bill crafted by a volunteer team of lawyers and researchers was not tight enough, our civil society needed to advocate more at ground-level the need for such legislation and unfortunately there was little time left as my NMP term was to finish by the end of 2004.[5] Instead, the final draft Bill was sent to the Ministry of Manpower as a civil society effort for its consideration. Years later, the Ministry of Manpower's Employment of Foreign Manpower Act was passed in Parliament and came into effect in 2012.

I am happy I became an NMP; I have contributed. The community and civil society were very welcoming of NMPs, valuing our work. I accepted being challenged or "told off" as part of the process, as well as always hoping that the oral PQs I submitted would be answered within the short Question and Answer period, or that the Speaker of the House would see if I raised my hand for follow-up questions or comments.

Has the NMP Scheme Outlasted Its Cause?

I am of the view that the NMP scheme worked well in its formative years when NMPs offered alternative perspectives, shared innovative ideas, suggested solutions, recommended laws, policies and programmes to fill up obvious lacunae and buttressed advocacy on pet interest areas by tabling bills and/or motions.

I cannot place a clear time frame on this, but in the last decade or so, MPs from the PAP and the opposition parties have upped their game in Parliament and there is also a higher level of presence at public events. Additionally, the bar has been raised, as many stakeholders have "must-do" lists which include engaging in varying capacities with elected MPs and the private sector to be in the community seeking solutions, so there are more avenues for independent voices to be engaged on political, economic, social or environmental matters at policy-level innovations.

Social media is a common instrument used by many, including all political parties, to share thoughts and analyses.

Notably, GE 2020 also resulted in 10 Opposition MPs in Parliament. The government also recognised the changing landscape and offered the title of Leader of the Opposition to Workers' Party's (WP) Secretary-General, Pritam Singh. What is tangibly noticeable, for better or worse, is the higher engagement on political matters. This current state of multi-avenue engagement is healthy.

Singapore is on the brink of evolving from a 63-year-old stronghold of an XL-sized majority political party rule in government to multi-party representation, deeper people engagement and a stronger shift towards democracy.

NMPs are dedicated. But isn't it time to probe deeper on relevance and the long-term viability as we look at the future of Singapore, into the 2030s to 2040s?

If the NMP scheme stays unchanged, does it become a convenient inconvenience or an inconvenient convenience taking up the space where more amongst those in politics ought to be in the playing field of democracy? The NMPs' voices are sought after — an attraction — in mainstream and social media but does it become a distraction for elected MPs whose stakes are higher as they are answerable to constituents?

Landscape of Changes

The global economic landscape is one of working in common spaces with a multi-polarity of key states vying to gain economic power. It is no longer just one or two main actors as superpowers. There is greater focus on international foreign relations and negotiations to anchor multilateral collaborative trade agreements, being interconnected to multi-stakeholders and investing wisely in projects to reap benefits.

But there are also global problems such as climate change, increased trading in arms, drugs and people across borders and increased transborder as well as internal conflicts.

Singapore today is highly sophisticated, digitised and literate with people spending hours on internet-enabled processes for work, leisure, reading, writing, knowledge, online activities, administration and online discussions on policies, laws, politics and the environment. Presently there are 4.8 million internet users in Singapore — a more than 88% internet penetration rate — who are online for 8.5 hours per day.[6] Against this backdrop of web-connections, multi-information portals and incessant flow of information, there is also much insecurity as knowledge management is the key to staying ahead and/or being influenced with misinformation.

Change is constantly taking place. Can our current political and parliamentary structure sustain us into the mid-21st century, 2040 to 2050, building up democratic platforms for empowering and engaging people?

The PAP itself shifted its politics from a pre-independence centre-left position to a post-independence centre-right in the belief that the latter was needed to develop Singapore, gain control over workers and be goal-driven. Going forward, in my view, Singapore's model of democracy could reach a stage of becoming a clearer hybrid economic system that combines capitalism and socialism, providing a balance of the two while cancelling out the worst aspects of each model.

To continue being sustainable, we need to ask: Is the current parliamentary representation sufficient or is a re-configuration of our thought process on political ideology, political structures and parliamentary system needed? This reconfiguration process needs to take place now for the future, a future that is core to public engagement, strengthening democracy in Singapore and to continue building on the economy.

Firstly, though the NMP scheme is comfortable and NMPs have contributed over the last 32 years, this scheme dampens the growth of democracy in Parliament. It has to go.

Today, there is growing strength in opposition parties despite them facing damaging reputational blisters. The ruling party is also sharpening its engagement with the people. Civil society is growing strongly, especially as e-networks on social media, despite the restrictive laws. Many amongst the young are politically and socially aware. Opposition MPs are strengthening their interventions in parliamentary debates. People are active on social media.

So why then are NMPs still needed, especially if they are diverting attention from opposition political parties and even the ruling party? The NMP scheme must be phased out.

This can be done over the coming 10 years, that is, over one or two GEs, which administratively means a three-time selection process of nine NMPs on three-year terms. Attention should be more greatly placed on political parties which must work harder to build consistency, reliability and trust with the people so that the electorate have good viable choices at the ballot box.

Secondly, I suggest that an independent task force be set up, hopefully by the government, if not, then as an independent initiative to examine

♦ The Nominated Member of Parliament Scheme

the nature of our parliamentary structure so as to recommend the reconfigurations needed to the structure of our Parliament in another 20 to 30 years.

Could this current form with 83 elected MPs from one party, a smattering of 10 candidates from one opposition party being elected to Parliament, a small number of two NMCPs and nine NMPs be adequate to deal with the changing norms: global economic trends, new social behaviours, in terms of conduct, co-relating with one another and rising expectations of parliamentarians as people are no longer ignorant nor obedient as in the past when they had to wait for information to come by them? What is the safer bet?

The task force could also explore the optimal number of elected MPs in Parliament and number of constituencies needed. It could look at ways to ensure there is diverse and inclusive representation amongst candidates. The roles of MPs could be reviewed too in building harmony and cohesion as consumption of information, digitised workflows and lifestyles are already showing divergent and diverse pathways.

The task force could also assess if Singapore needs a two-chambered Parliament or continues as a one-chambered one. A two-chambered or bicameral Parliament allows for streaming of roles and revisions in governance over town council management, community support responsibilities and enhancing legislative roles with strategic visionaires and policy thinkers.

However, the evidence is not conclusive as yet on whether a unicameral or a bicameral system works better to build democracy and the betterment of people and the environment. Bicameral parliaments exist in countries such as Malaysia, the United States, the United Kingdom, Canada, India and Russia. But single chamber parliaments are also found to be working well in Sweden, Denmark as well as in

China and Iran. Some of these countries are more democratic whilst others are authoritative or communist. The jury is still out there even as studies continue.[7] Incidentally, out of 190 parliaments in the world, 79 parliaments are bicameral and 111 are unicameral, with a total of over 44,000 MPs worldwide.[8]

So what is the best way forward?

Whilst the NMP experience was very useful and most of us contributed well, it is in my view still a spoiler as time passes. For now, I think it has outrun its course. The dynamic changes that we are immersed in mean that it is timely now to plan for our future in the form of a parliamentary system that would prepare us well for 2040.

The teenagers of today will be in their 30s by 2040, and I wonder what we need to do now to ensure that they will participate personally and engage politically as citizens in a Singapore that they can be proud of.

Editor's Cut: A Q&A with Braema Mathiaparanam
(This interview has been edited and condensed for length and clarity.)

What is your most memorable moment from your time in Parliament?
I think the most memorable one was getting "scolded". I've been told off a few times in Parliament and you have to respond in a way that doesn't take away dignity, right? This case was quite funny.

[In this case] I asked that unmarried employers be also given relief from paying levies for employing foreign domestic workers. More often than not, single women who employ a domestic worker need domestic and caregiving help as they are working and also looking after their parents. Levy-reliefs were only given to married couples who employ foreign domestic workers. It was not the Manpower Minister who responded and perhaps because he managed the national budgets, he could not get the essence of the point I was making. I had also asked on another occasion, how were the millions of dollars, collected as levies, spent and if some portion could be paid to foreign domestic workers as their social security. That too did not sit well with the Minister who answered that there was no clear breakdown, other than that it went into a consolidated fund. Levies is a sensitive topic — a trigger. In this instance, after a while, the Minister's response was to suggest that singles ought to get married if they wanted the levy. I was gobsmacked — how did that leap in logic happen? Maybe the point I had made was not clear. Nevertheless, other MPs caught the point and rose to speak up on the point and to validate the suggestion that I had made. I felt that was good enough. Over the years, changes have been made on levy payments, mostly for the better. So I found this memorable, because it was rather amusing and I caught a glimpse, then, of how caregiving work by mainly single females was viewed.

How did being an NMP change you as a person and/or the work you do?
I am very grateful for my parliamentary stint, because you are exposed to a lot more stuff, especially reading materials. A lot of information comes to you in a short space of time; documents just keep flowing. And I try my best to read not just because of Parliament, but for myself as well. It opens many worlds of knowledge to you. It's a very fast and steep learning curve to understanding the rationale behind policies and all that, alongside the search for data, but a lot of it comes through all these documents that you get.

I am totally grateful to the Parliament library folks. They are so eager to help all parliamentarians! You ask them and they will even know which shelf what you're asking for can be found on, and it then lands on your table for you. The level of professionalism was remarkable and I found it so akin to the library staff at *The Straits Times*. It was fantastic support.

Based on your time in Parliament, what words of advice would you give future NMPs?
I believe the NMP scheme is a stumbling block to the development of our democracy, and [we] need to be weaned off [it]. To go back to your question, in that weaning-off period, I feel that NMPs need to take their responsibilities seriously.

I feel for those who are very concerned about the overall well-being of Singapore's society. Engaging well on many issues as possible enables a sterner quality of representation, but it's also a learning process for yourself. You find many in the community, whom you didn't know, were actually impacted by even a small bit of change based on what was discussed in Parliament. And I think, therefore, getting engaged with the community is going to become crucial.

More work needs to be done beyond just reaching out to people via social media, which we have become over-reliant on. Before social media came about, you had to meet people and hear them out, which is more time-consuming. And social media vanguards also function in brigades, and we can miss out touching base with different communities and hear their thoughts if we over-rely on social media, right?

How would you sum up your time as an NMP in one sentence?
This is a difficult question. [I'd say] it was an honour to share perspectives on what is happening within society, in a rational manner, based on evidence and argument.

I thought it was a wonderful avenue that was made available to get what you really want at the end of the day: a change, or a total engagement on why that change is important to the people, to a better Singapore.

Endnotes

[1] Historical notes references extracted from: Tan, K. T. (2013). *The Singapore Parliament, Representation, Effectiveness and Control*. Retrieved from https://www.academia.sg/wp-content/uploads/2020/06/Tan-2013-Parliament.pdf; Hansard; Nominated Members of Parliament, 5 April 2002. Retrieved from https://sprs.parl.gov.sg/search/topic?reportid=012_20020405_S0003_T0004

[2] Baharudin, H. (2021, June 25). Policies like GRC system still needed as S'pore is not immune to racial discrimination: Lawrence Wong, *The Straits Times*. Retrieved from https://www.straitstimes.com/singapore/policies-like-grc-system-still-needed-because-spore-is-not-immune-to-racial-discrimination

[3] Politics and Women, AWARE's Women's Action Website. Retrieved from https://www.womensaction.sg/article/politics

4   The "Super Seven" Junior Ministers, 19 July 2005. Retrieved from http://singaporegovt.blogspot.com/2005/07/super-seven-junior-ministers-in-2001.html
5   Gee, J., & Ho, E. (2006). *Dignity overdue*, Select Publishing.
6   Muller, J. (2021), Internet Usage in Singapore, Statista, 25 June 2021. Retrieved from https://www.statista.com/topics/5852/internet-usage-in-singapore/
7   National Democratic Institute for International Affairs, *One Chamber or Two? Deciding Between a Unicameral and Bicameral Legislature*. Retrieved from https://www.ndi.org/sites/default/files/029_ww_onechamber_0.pdf
8   National Parliaments, https://www.ipu.org/national-parliaments (Accessed on 29 July 2022).

Section 2

∞

(M)erits

PREFACE

MERITS:
A Convincing Case of Contributions

When the Nominated Member of Parliament (NMP) scheme was debated and introduced in 1990,[1] it drew ire from many members of the House. Political commentators and Opposition Members of Parliament (MPs) saw it primarily as a means of deepening the People's Action Party's (PAP) rule,[2,3] while even PAP MPs dissented on the basis that the scheme deviates from notions of democracy.[4,5]

At the time of its introduction in 1990, the scheme provided for up to six NMPs, but a proposal was made to increase this number to nine in July 1997.[6] Introducing a motion in Parliament for the Second Reading of the Constitutional Amendment Bill that was eventually passed to effect the change, then-Minister for Home Affairs Wong Kan Seng said that the NMP scheme was now well accepted by practically all MPs as it had proven its usefulness and worth.

The government intended to expand the scheme "so that more NMPs can be in Parliament to air views which may not be canvassed by the PAP or by the Opposition...so that a wider cross-section of such views can be canvassed and expressed."[7]

This led to further debate in the House that involved evaluating the role of the NMPs thus far, and what the scheme could be. However, as the first batches of NMPs came and went, the utility of the scheme and contributions from such members became clearer to many, as Bernard Chen, former Minister of State for Defence and then MP for West Coast Group Representation Constituency (GRC) had opined. Mr Chen highlighted in Parliament that in the past seven years, he believed that the objectives of the NMP scheme had been more or less achieved, and that many NMPs have in fact "delivered the goods":

> *"As the Leader of the House says, most of them have, although I must add that in addition to making life miserable for Ministers and civil servants, some NMPs even made the Speaker wince by the number of questions that some of them asked, and some of these questions even the PAP MPs would not feel comfortable to ask. But they did make contributions. They had Private Member's Bills."*[8]

Members of the House who initially had misgivings around the scheme, such as Sin Boon Ann (then MP for Tampines GRC), also echoed this, highlighting how they indeed "play a constructive role", "can be relied upon to say things which no opposition MP will want to say" and "can concentrate on the substance rather than the rhetoric of the debate". The member also noted the "sterling performances" of NMPs like Dr Kanwaljit Soin and Professor Walter Woon, who made contributions to legislative changes.

Functional Groups and Formalising the NMP Scheme

It was in 1997 when the first three functional groups of business and industry, the professions and the labour movement were also institutionalised in Parliament and invited to put forward their NMP candidates. These were not included or formalised in proposed amendments to the Constitution and led to a heated debate in Parliament between Dr Tan Cheng Bock, then MP of the Ayer Rajah Single Member Constituency, and Wong Kan Seng during the Second Reading of the Bill.

With only one abstention (Dr Tan Cheng Bock) and one no (Low Thia Khiang), the Bill to amend the Constitution of Singapore was swiftly passed. In 2002, three others — social and community service organisations, tertiary education institutions and media, arts and sports organisations — were introduced. Finally, a seventh functional group, the civic and people sector, was added later in 2011.

Following these changes, other academic and political commentators also weighed in on the expansion of the NMP scheme. Some, like Singaporean writer Koh Buck Song, expressed their concern around the dominance of certain sectors or industries in the choice of functional groups.[9] Others like academic N. Ganesan and MP Irene Ng felt that the NMP scheme served to entrench the ruling party's power and hampered the growth of a viable opposition.[10,11]

In spite of these concerns, many in Singapore and in the ruling party believed that NMPs have a role to play in Singaporean politics. A bill to amend the Constitution was tabled by then-Deputy Prime Minister and Minister for Home Affairs Wong Kan Seng in 2010. This was meant to abolish the original requirement that Parliament must pass a resolution before NMPs can be appointed.[12]

Wong Kan Seng explained during the Second Reading of the Bill that when the NMP scheme was first introduced in 1990, then-Deputy Prime Minister Goh Chok Tong mentioned that each Parliament had the discretion to decide if it wished to have NMPs or not. But with the abolition of the requirements or a resolution, this "will entrench the NMP scheme as a staple feature of all future Parliaments and not a matter to be determined by each new Parliament."[13]

Merits: Key Contributions to Parliamentary Discourse

There was no doubt for many that the NMP scheme was a boon to parliamentary discourse. NMPs have made clear contributions through various means; this included the introduction of Private Members' Bills, filing of Parliamentary Questions to clarify government processes on behalf of the Singapore public, making speeches on the Singapore Budget and weighing in on bills or motions, as well as tabling adjournment motions. This section of the book will highlight some of these contributions in depth from NMPs. This selection is by no means exhaustive as all contributors to this book also share what or how they have stepped forward in Parliament, and beyond.

This section of the book starts off with contributions from NMPs who spoke up about specific issues that have often been neglected in parliamentary discourse, such as digital inclusion, the role of sports in nation-building and the environment.

Lim Sun Sun (NMP 2018–2020) shares her experience in broadening the conversation around Singapore's proclivity for technological solutions and offers balanced and rigorous academic insights on the risks and benefits of digital payments, governance of data sharing, regulation of online falsehoods as well as digital inclusion. **Nicholas Fang (NMP 2012–2014)** writes about how sports tend to take a backseat to more "bread-and-butter" issues in Parliament, but points out that the NMP scheme plays an important role in advocating for sports in Singapore. **Faizah Jamal (NMP 2012–2014)** then describes her experience of being a lone voice in the parliamentary wilderness as someone who was fighting for environmental issues. She describes her discomfort around the lack of discourse over how the Population White Paper would affect the environment as well as the events leading up to her voting against the Motion.

Beyond raising issues that were often neglected or not prioritised in the Chamber, NMPs also played a crucial role in conveying and amplifying the concerns of Singaporeans around policies and bills tabled.

In his chapter, **Walter Theseira (NMP 2018–2020)** discusses his concerns around the Protection from Online Falsehoods and Manipulation Act (POFMA) as an academic, the preparations he had undertaken for an Amendment Motion and his experience dealing with pushback from the government. **Thomas Thomas (NMP 1999–2001)** then draws on his experience as a Labour NMP representing workers in Singapore. He differentiates himself as a non-partisan representative who has enjoyed independence with regard to expressing his views or disagreements with policies by the ruling party, such as the Defence Science and Technology Agency Bill. **Viswa Sadasivan (NMP 2009–2011)** shares his motivations behind being a single-term NMP and why his maiden speech was on the National Pledge. He describes the "baptism of fire" he had undergone following the tabling of the Motion on the National Pledge, and reflects on lessons learnt during his time in the Chamber.

Finally, we then hear from NMPs who write about the need to be passionate advocates for Singaporeans. They share about their own personal journeys that have led them to become NMPs and what reinforced their convictions to speak up courageously for those whose voices may not be typically heard in Parliament.

K. Thanaletchimi (NMP 2016–2018) writes about her own personal journey towards becoming an advocate for workers and their families and her experiences around the process of becoming an NMP. She writes about her maiden speech on vulnerable members of the workforce and how non-partisan views from subject matter experts and passionate advocates like herself can make a difference in Parliament. **Kuik Shiao-Yin (NMP 2014–2018)** then rounds off this section with her reflections on the need for parliamentarians to speak boldly, clearly and with love. She describes her journey of coming to terms with her nomination, her motivations for speaking up in Parliament and how NMPs can make a difference to the people they represent by saying the brave thing, and not just the bland thing.

Endnotes

[1] Singapore Parliamentary Debates, vol. 54, sitting 8, col. 695; (29 November 1989).

[2] Balji, P. N. (2009). A Journalist's Note on a Quiet Rebel. In B. Welsh, *et al.* (eds.), *Impressions of the Goh Chok Tong years in Singapore* (pp. 34–39). Singapore: NUS Press, p. 35. (Call no.: RSING 959.5705 IMP-[HIS]).

[3] Singapore Parliamentary Debates, vol. 55, sitting 15, col. 1013; (29 March 1990).

[4] Wong, A. (1989, November 30). Notion deviates from basic principle of democracy. *The Straits Times*.

[5] Tan, C. B. (1989, November 30). Parliament is no place for Govt to take advice from non-elected representatives. *The Straits Times*.

[6] Tan, H. Y. (1997, July 10). Three panels formed to propose NMP candidates. *The Straits Times*, p. 1; House votes to add three more NMPs, raising the total to nine. (1997, June 6). *The Business Times*, p. 2. Retrieved from NewspaperSG.

[7] Wong Kan Seng (Minister for Home Affairs), speech during the Second Reading of the Constitution of the Republic of Singapore (Amendment) Bill, Singapore Parliamentary Debates, Official Report (31 July 1997), vol. 67, cols. 1497–1499.

[8] Singapore Parliamentary Debates, vol. 67, sitting 5, col. 415; (5 June 1997).

9. Koh, B. S. (1997, August 1). Keep an avenue open for people from all fields. *The Straits Times*. Retrieved from https://advance-lexis-com.libproxy1.nus.edu.sg/api/document?collection=news&id=urn:contentItem:3SJD-MY50-0058-X4YJ-00000-00&context=1516831.
10. Ganesan, N. (1998). Singapore: Entrenching a City-State's Dominant Party System. *Southeast Asian Affairs*, 229–243.
11. Ng, I. (2000, January 29). NMP scheme 'is useful but should be transitional'. *The Straits Times*. Retrieved from Factiva via NLB's eResources website: http://eresources.nlb.gov.sg/
12. Au Yong, J. (2010, April 27). Constitutional amendments passed. *The Straits Times*, p. 1. Retrieved from NewspaperSG.
13. Singapore Parliamentary Debates, vol. 87, sitting 1, col. 53; (26 April 2010).

Lessons from My Extended Classroom: Tempering Technological Utopianism with Circumspection

Lim Sun Sun
Nominated Member of Parliament (2018–2020)

> *Editor's Note: It would be remiss if this book did not address the intersection of politics and technology, and the widespread social implications of our omnipresent narratives of digitalisation, digital transformation and Singapore as a Smart Nation. Always the professor, Lim Sun Sun calls the hallowed Chamber her "extended classroom" in this essay — one where she and I were "classmates" as NMPs in the same term; we also partnered up on an Adjournment Motion which I tabled on closing the digital divide.*

Shortly after I was appointed Nominated Member of Parliament (NMP), I bumped into an opposition politician who remarked somewhat wryly, "I hope you will also reflect the concerns of Singaporeans out there who fear things like facial recognition."

As a social scientist whose life's work has oriented around studying fears and apprehensions people have about technology, along with their gratifications and gains from technological use, I was surprised by his presumption that I would gloss over the former and harp on the latter.

Upon reflection, the fact that I am a professor at the Singapore University of Technology and Design that nurtures future technologists must have led him to believe that I was unequivocally in the pro-technology camp. Furthermore, his assumption that Singapore's intelligentsia unquestioningly embrace technology is understandable, given our country's relentless pursuit of innovation in government, industry and higher education.

After all, Singapore's relationship with technology has long been framed in utopian terms, conjuring visions of blissfully well-connected citizens in futuristic habitats basking in the glow of innovation-driven economic vitality.[1] Indeed, it is often mused that Singapore is also ruled by technocrats who avidly nurture strong synergies between education and industry while investing heavily in R&D and innovation.[2] Within the civil service, policy making relies heavily on detailed scenario planning and forecasting — increasingly informed by big data — to strategise the country's domestic priorities and international positioning.[3,4] From the inception of the first IT Plan[5] to the present Smart Nation blueprint,[6] Singapore has aggressively exploited technology to develop a knowledge-based economy where every sector is augmented with technological solutions, from massive physical infrastructures to pervasive, inconspicuous digital code.

It is precisely Singapore's unbridled zeal for all things technological that led me to recognise the value of my position in Parliament. My research on technology domestication by families and young people has vested me with a deep appreciation for the benefits but also the harms of technology.⁷ I therefore saw my parliamentary term as a prime opportunity to draw linkages between academic research, democratic discourse and policy making. In retrospect, I believe I was able to shed light on a range of issues at the critical intersections of technology and society, as I will further elaborate.

An Extended Classroom

To begin with though, I found it highly ironic that I had been appointed as NMP.

Back when the scheme was first mooted in Parliament in 1989, I was a news-obsessed teen who followed international and local politics avidly. I can still recall fierce criticisms of the scheme as sounding the death knell for opposition politics through anointing critics who were not accountable to the electorate.

The assertion was that NMPs' moderately dissenting voices would translate into meek opposition that would impede democratic debate in Singapore. I remember agreeing with such critiques and questioning the utility of NMPs. Thereafter, as the scheme matured, I observed the contributions of successive cohorts of NMPs with some interest, noting the less typical views they aired given their relative independence and interest to represent the perspective of specific sectors.

Yet I never imagined that I would myself become one.

Nevertheless, when I was nominated by my university in 2018 and subsequently the higher education sector as one of its shortlisted candidates, I seriously pondered over how I would honour the spirit of parliamentary debate, while answering the duty to offer academic insights.

I reflected on my long-term involvement in public service and public education via bodies such as the Media Literacy Council, National Youth

Council and the National Council for Youth Guidance and Rehabilitation. Because Singapore has been technologising so intensely for the past few decades, my research expertise is often sought for salient socio-technical trends and their implications for social cohesion within households and across the community. Besides sharing my insights in these committees, I make it a point to give public talks, write opinion-editorials and field print and broadcast media interviews to raise public awareness about emerging societal concerns. Since I have always strived not to be an ivory tower academic but one who believes strongly in policy engagement and public education, this invitation to serve as NMP held some appeal.

I decided to view Parliament as an extended classroom in which to teach and articulate academic insights that are theoretically grounded and empirically validated, with a view towards informing policy making and public discourse. I thus pledged to weigh in on issues where I felt that academic perspectives would be valuable, especially to counter the instinct towards technological utopianism.

These included resistance to digital payments, governance of the use of big data, investment in digital literacy education, improvement in data sharing practices, regulatory overreach in eradicating online falsehoods, support for gender diversity in the technology sector and accountability in electronic waste. I leveraged my parliamentary speeches to share relevant research findings in a clear and compelling fashion that would resonate with the lay audience and inform parliamentarians.

This goal was important to me because of my personal endeavour to raise the quality of research communication in and by academia. On any issue of national importance, if the public does not understand what is at stake, they cannot make well-informed decisions as consumers and citizens. It is my staunch belief that promoting thought-leadership and public education is a vital role of academics. The rise of online disinformation and the intensifying use of social media have enabled the untrammelled dissemination of false claims by faux experts. Consumers in our increasingly strained attention economy are inundated with information from a plethora of sources and find it increasingly difficult to distinguish attractively-packaged soundbites from academically-informed discourse.

In his thought-provoking book *The Death of Expertise*,[8] Tom Nichols decried that the explosion of online information has paradoxically produced less well-informed citizens who in turn disparage intellectual scholarship and cast doubt on experts. He argues that such ignorance breeds disengagement by the citizenry and undermines the democratic process. In this regard, I consider it more pressing than ever that academics are able to proactively and constructively convey the goals and value of their work to the broader public.

Singapore's unique NMP scheme provides academics with a viable inroad. After all, academic research must not merely reside in journal articles, hefty tomes and data repositories, but must be shared and communicated with the wider audience whose lives it shapes. I committed to doing more within this extended classroom of mine.

This classroom grew larger still when Singapore went into lockdown from April to June 2020 to curb the spread of Covid-19. During this "circuit breaker" period, I was invited by government ministries and agencies, non-profit organisations and other MPs to offer guidance to the public on managing our technology use in the home in light of the sudden switch to work-from-home and online learning.

During these webinars that I conducted via Zoom or Facebook Live, the questions posed by the audience reflected considerable distress around managing children's healthy device use, moderating personal over-reliance on technology and resolving family tensions that had been triggered by technology. Audience members were often reassured when I told them that their situations were neither unique nor unusual and welcomed my suggestions for effective management strategies. I was glad to have these public platforms to tap my academic expertise and provide useful pointers that could help the public make sense of that extraordinary period.

Although I would have likely contributed to such public education efforts as an academic, I do not deny that my NMP position helped to raise my public visibility and draw attention to the causes I champion.

Beyond the Chamber

But every classroom inevitably has its quiet moments. We NMPs experienced those moments acutely, especially during adjournment motions.

All MPs can raise adjournment motions to air issues of their choice. These are only tabled at the end of each sitting, capping what is typically a long and draining day for all members. Hence, once the main business of the day such as the debating of bills has been completed, many members exit in haste to attend to other obligations, leaving the parliamentary chamber dishearteningly hollow. Besides the Leader of the House and the political office holder who must remain to respond to the member's motion, most Cabinet Members would also have left by the time the motion is debated. Raising an Adjournment Motion can thus feel like an exercise in futility because one seems to be speaking to an empty house.

I found myself in that exact position when I tabled a motion titled, "Why Fear the Fear of Failure? Imperatives for Refining our Education System". Drawing upon my experience as a professor and a parent of two school-going children, I chose to make a case for rethinking

Singapore's approach to education. I argued that the achievement orientation underlying our education system, with its intense focus on examinations and grades, instils in Singaporeans an unhealthy fear of failure. I also underlined the fact that on the ground, a small minority of teachers in primary and secondary schools have been known to engage in microaggressions in the classroom where they use questionable naming and shaming tactics to motivate under-performing students.

I explained that such destructive methods of highlighting failure and under-performance can demotivate students and lead them to lose interest in the subject. They can also demoralise students and at worst, inflict long-term damage on their self-esteem. In light of rising concerns about the mental health of young people, I further stressed that we must not dismiss such microaggressions in the classroom but must do our utmost to educate our teachers on their harms. I made a firm call for us to collectively reshape this unhealthy culture of achievement orientation. This necessitates an overall shift in emphasis from relative performance towards individual performance, and where qualitative feedback is prioritised over quantitative metrics.

This was a motion I felt strongly about due to the research I had undertaken for my book *Transcendent Parenting: Raising Children in the Digital Age*,[9] for which many parents had shared with me the aspirations, anxieties, hopes and fears they had experienced in their parenting journeys. I wanted very much to articulate their views to an institution that could make significant and lasting changes to our education system.

And yet I was to deliver my message to a sparsely filled parliamentary chamber, save for my fellow NMPs applauding me when I ended my speech, their enthusiasm making up for the enveloping silence. When I lamented as such to my fellow NMP Arasu Duraisamy as we left the

Chamber together, he said matter-of-factly: "It doesn't matter. You're not speaking to the House, you're speaking to the country."

Right then, his words uplifted me somewhat, but it was only the next day that I appreciated the full weight of their wisdom. Friends, acquaintances and members of the public who had read my social media posts sharing my speech commented positively and thanked me for giving voice to challenges they had endured in parenting their children. Young adults who were not themselves parents sent me private messages to confide that they too had been subjected to humiliating treatment from their teachers that they had steeled themselves to overcome. Clearly, Singapore has made significant strides in schooling our youth, but the psychological toll of a hyper-competitive model continues to haunt many. If through that Motion I was able to reach beyond the Chamber to echo the sentiments of Singaporeans who find facets of our education system wanting, I consider it a contribution to the national discussion of how education can be refined. Reaching beyond the Chamber into the extended classroom, I hope I managed to highlight the importance of making every classroom a safe place for learning and failure.

Joining the Dots

Perhaps one of the most important tasks teachers undertake in the classroom is to join the dots for students — to help them understand how different pieces of knowledge are linked, and the potential initiatives one can generate from drawing such connections. Students bounce ideas off one another, provide mutual critique or affirmation and combine energies to amplify interests and efforts. With the heightened visibility from my public role, greater understanding of policy making mindsets and enhanced access to broader networks of contacts, I found my ability to join the dots and connect like-minded people more effectively.

I experienced this through supporting fellow NMP Anthea Ong's Adjournment Motion on "Closing the Digital Divide for SGUnited: Learnings from COVID-19".

She had proposed this Motion to urge for more resources to be mobilised to help low-income families that were ill-equipped to switch suddenly to work-from-home and home-based learning during the circuit breaker. Knowing of the research I had done on digital literacy and technology domestication by families,[10] Anthea invited me to join her in the Motion. At the same time, my academic colleague Associate Professor Irene Ng from the National University of Singapore, who conducted research on the working poor, was also sensing a pressing need for affordable digital access to be more readily offered to low-income families.

As we had previously collaborated and co-published on low-income workers and their social mobility challenges in a digitalising society,[11] and due to her familiarity with my research on low-income families' technology use, Irene invited me to co-author an op-ed to highlight the urgent need for universal digital access. Our op-ed in Channel NewsAsia[12] would form the crux of my speech[13] in support of Anthea's Motion.

Both our speeches clearly resonated because students, social workers, voluntary welfare organisations and civil society initiatives reached out to Anthea, Irene and me to accelerate the momentum for greater digital support provisions. Irene and I were subsequently invited to share our views at public webinars on the problems of digital exclusion and were approached by individuals and civil society groups who volitionally shared their experiences and proposed solutions.

This groundswell of views and interest spurred Irene and me to embark on further research to understand in-depth the issue of universal digital access in Singapore and more like-minded colleagues and students joined us. Our team captured our findings and proposals in a working paper titled "From Digital Exclusion to Universal Digital Access in Singapore"[14] that we presented to the senior management of the Infocomm and Media Development Authority. These efforts went on to spark further ground actions to raise awareness of the merits of universal digital access, including a webinar to commemorate International Day for the Eradication of Poverty titled "Finding the [WE] in University Digital Access" in October 2021, led and organised by a group of social service organisations including Ang Mo Kio Family Service Centre, Touch Community Services and Engineering Good.

Overall, my parliamentary stint fortified my ability to contribute effectively and meaningfully to such ground efforts at addressing issues of public concern.

Indeed, I feel that more academics of a greater diversity of disciplines should have a chance at serving as NMPs and therefore, I chose not to put myself up for a second term. The more academics who can experience the benefits of the extended classroom, the better it is for academic insights to be more widely disseminated for the benefit of robust public discourse.

The Report Card

Like many classrooms, Singapore's Parliament has had more than its fair share of dull moments. And yet, it has also witnessed epochal events, stirring speeches, controversial bills and legislative innovations, including the NMP scheme.

Although it has fundamental shortcomings that constitutional scholars of democratic political systems will readily call out, the scheme's facility for sectoral representation within Parliament is not without its merits.

In a world overrun with fake news and faux experts that is concurrently grappling with a slew of wicked problems, an avenue for democratic discussion to be more richly infused with academic insights is welcome indeed.

Editor's Cut: A Q&A with Lim Sun Sun

(This interview has been edited and condensed for length and clarity.)

What is your most memorable moment from your time in Parliament?
There are so many! I guess there's the "fear of failure" speech [which I mentioned in my essay]. I felt very strongly about the topic, and prior to delivering the speech, I had actually consulted with parents whom I knew had faced such challenges, so I felt a great sense of responsibility about articulating their views.

Then there was my "bus accident" speech on the Road Traffic (Amendment) Bill, which I made after I got knocked down by a double-decker bus in 2019. It was really funny because I had no intention of speaking on the Bill initially and then my accident happened. I did some research afterwards and realised that many people had, like me, been knocked down at discretionary right turns, where drivers forget or miss pedestrians and just make a go for it. I ended up using that opportunity to help accelerate the conversion of discretionary right turn junctions to non-discretionary ones. Although they were already planning to phase them out over time, I am glad I helped to strengthen calls for the process to be sped up because these junctions are fundamentally problematic and hazardous.

Honestly, though, I can't put my finger on all of them. Some of the memorable moments are really just interacting with other members and the staff in Parliament, and having them tell you things you never expected to hear, or learning about facets of the parliamentary process that you never anticipated.

How did being an NMP change you as a person and/or the work you do?
I'd like to think I'm a little more savvy compared to before I became an NMP. Learning from direct experience how the government machinery works, getting an in-depth understanding of policymaking priorities, experiencing the fierce WhatsApp culture that exists amongst parliamentarians...all this was very eye-opening for me. You develop a better grasp of how you can, from your limited position, try to bring people together to advance initiatives in a more concerted way. Which is not to say that I've got it all figured out, but hopefully a bit more than before!

I'm very much aligned with what I wrote about joining the dots, by which I mean seeing new possibilities for how you can advance a cause, versus as a lay person or civilian academic, when you can only imagine intervening in certain ways.

I don't want to sound too grandiose, because fundamentally, I'm under no illusions as to how much change anyone can effect as an NMP. Even from the start, I don't think I had any lofty dreams that entering Parliament would be a game-changer for voicing my views. But to have this platform for sharing academic insights in the policymaking realm, and having your research read by people who need to read it, is something that I think should be leveraged by academics. As a civilian professor, it's not easy to get a foot in the door, but people are more prepared to speak to you when you have that NMP title.

Based on your time in Parliament, what words of advice would you give future NMPs?
Get to know as many people and perspectives as possible, especially amongst your fellow NMPs. Because of their own professional trajectory

and the different communities they work with, each NMP can have very varied insights on Singapore's populace and on different policies.

For me, it was rewarding getting to meet amazing people from sectors I'd hardly have thought to interact with. For the longest time, I sat next to Louis [Ng], which was great because he has all these unconventional approaches to leveraging the parliamentary process and I learnt a lot from him. Then there were all the people whom I had the good fortune to meet on trips. Covid-19 changed all that for my batch of NMPs when it broke out towards the end of our term, but it was still a great experience.

Also, an MP once told me that you should always consider every bill, whether it intersects with your interests or not. If you've got something interesting to say, even if it's tangentially related, you should just say it so that it goes into Hansard and policy makers will have some form of guidance in the future. I found that a very useful piece of advice, because it made me a lot more creative about looking at bills and where I could intervene.

How would you sum up your time as an NMP in one sentence?
An energising time contributing to Singapore's legislative process, where my personal, professional and national identities collided in surprising ways.

Endnotes

[1] See for example, Ministry of Communications and Information (MCI). (2018). *Digital Readiness Blueprint*. Retrieved from https://www.mci.gov.sg/en/portfolios/digital-readiness/digital-readiness-blueprint

[2] Lee, E. W., & Haque, M. S. (2006). The New Public Management Reform and Governance in Asian NICs: A Comparison of Hong Kong and Singapore. *Governance*, 19(4), 605–626.

3   Quah, J. S. (2013). Ensuring Good Governance in Singapore: Is This Experience Transferable to Other Asian Countries?. *International Journal of Public Sector Management*, 26(5), 401–420.

4   Ting, L., & Tang, Y. (2019). Digital Governance Model for Big Data Era — Based on Typical Practices in Singapore. *Humanities and Social Sciences*, 7(2), 76–82.

5   Teo, T. S., & Lim, V. K. (1999). Singapore — An 'Intelligent Island': Moving from Vision to Reality with Information Technology. *Science and Public Policy*, 26(1), 27–36.

6   Hoe, S. L. (2016). Defining a Smart Nation: The Case of Singapore. *Journal of Information, Communication and Ethics in Society*, 14(4), 323–333.

7   Lim, S. S. (ed.). (2016). *Mobile communication and the family: Asian experiences in technology domestication.* Springer.

8   Nichols, T. (2017). *The death of expertise: The campaign against established knowledge and why it matters.* Oxford University Press.

9   Lim, S. S. (2020). *Transcendent parenting: Raising children in the digital age.* Oxford University Press.

10 See Lim, S. S. (2020, April 8). The joys and frustrations of home-based learning. *Channel NewsAsia.* Retrieved from https://www.channelnewsasia.com/news/commentary/home-based-learning-covid-19-coronavirus-singapore-tips-parents-12618236

11 Lim, S. S., & Ng, I. (2017, February 7). Guard against gig economy creating permanent underclass. *The Straits Times.*

12 Ng, I., & Lim, S. S. (2020, 26 May). Commentary: The case for universal digital access, as home-based computing becomes a post-pandemic norm. *Channel NewsAsia.*

13 Lim Sun Sun, Singapore Parliamentary Debates, Closing the Digital Divide for SGUnited: Learnings from COVID-19 (26 May 2020), vol. 94(2). Retrieved from https://sprs.parl.gov.sg/search/sprs3topic?reportid=matter-adj-1401

14 Ng, I., Lim, S. S., Pang, N., Lim, D., Soh, G., Pakianathan, P. V. S., & Ang, B. (2021). *From Digital Exclusion to Universal Digital Access in Singapore.* Retrieved from https://fass.nus.edu.sg/ssr/wp-content/uploads/sites/8/2021/01/Digital-Access-20210118.pdf

Sports and Institutionalising a Sports NMP

Nicholas Fang
Nominated Member of Parliament (2012–2014)

> *Editor's Note: I did not know Nicholas Fang personally until former NMP Janice Koh introduced us for the purpose of this book as I was most keen to have him on board to share his experience in Parliament championing for elite sports as a former national athlete alongside the official narrative of creating a sporting culture and making sports accessible to the community. In this essay, Nicholas also makes his case for the institutionalisation of a Sports NMP given the lower priority sports occupy in our national consciousness.*

Singapore and Singaporeans have had a funny relationship with sports.

While not a core priority in the practical-minded psyche of most citizens, sports continue to provide a source of entertainment, enjoyment and respite from the daily grind to many people in the country.

At the same time, sporting activities contribute to a healthier, stronger and more resilient population. And when a Joseph Schooling,

Yu Mengyu or Quah Zheng Wen excels on the international sporting stage, sports can be a great source of national pride as well.

Yet there remains tension between sports and other key priorities in Singapore society. Securing a good education, building a career, even securing the nation through institutions such as National Service.

Demands on our time, focus and attention mean that Singapore sports has not featured significantly in terms of our national priorities. This has been reflected in our performance in major games such as the Olympics, where other countries or territories of similar population size have consistently outperformed us over the years.

This is a bit surprising, given that Singapore possesses many of the attributes that are required to build a sporting nation — high standards of living, solid and high-functioning infrastructure, world-class sporting facilities, a Singapore Sports Hub that is among the best integrated facilities in the region if not the world and a history of sporting talents that have appeared sporadically over time. These include our first-ever Olympic medalist — weight-lifter Tan Howe Liang, world-leading swimmer Ang Peng Siong and others who have performed at the regional level.

That we have not had more sporting success can largely be attributed to the lack of a deep sporting culture in the country.

Those who reminisce of the times when the Kallang Roar reverberated around the National Stadium as being the "glory days" of Singapore sports are missing the broader picture — there needs to be a holistic embracing of sports as a viable and attractive pursuit if we are to become a truly sporting nation.

Stepping up

My own sporting journey started as a young child when, like many other Singaporeans with children, my parents signed me up for swimming lessons for water safety. This then evolved into competitive swimming training, although I did not pursue this past the age of 10.

Training and coaching in those days were a little archaic, with coaches depending on old-school tactics such as berating swimmers and in some cases physically punishing young athletes for perceived lack of effort. I cannot say that I enjoyed those sessions much.

After a few sedentary years, I decided to take up fencing and triathlon when I was presented with the opportunities to do so in school and with some friends who happened to be fans of the sport respectively.

After displaying some modest talent at the local competitive level, I qualified for the national teams for both sports and represented the country in various international competitions.

I also competed in modern pentathlon — comprising swimming, running, shooting, fencing and horse-riding — while at university in the UK. Upon retiring as a national athlete in 2009, I went on to serve as a sports administrator, helming the fencing and modern pentathlon federations, serving on the Singapore National Olympic Committee, and was chosen to be the chef de mission for Team Singapore at the 2015 Southeast Asian Games.

This compressed backgrounder about my experience in sports hopefully serves to give a sense of where my interest in, and passion for, sports stems from.

My life and world view have been shaped significantly by the lessons I've learnt through sports. But in 2012, I had not given more thought to advancing the cause of sports further.

That year, in the wake of the 2011 General Election, speculation had begun in the media about the composition of the next batch of Nominated Members of Parliament (NMPs).

The Straits Times ran a story after polling the sports community about who might make a good choice for the Sports NMP role, and my name came up. This spurred me to look more closely at the role and how I could potentially add value.

Once I had decided that it would be something I was interested in, I then had to make a choice on which area I would focus on. Sports was a no-brainer to me, but the "Sports NMP" typically came from a group of interest areas that included media and the arts. I understood that the arts sector had planned to field a strong and passionate candidate, and as such, I decided to submit my nomination as an "independent" who would focus on sports, media, defence and international affairs — all areas I was interested in as well.

The Select Committee charged with interviewing the NMP candidates seemed to appreciate the fact that I could speak on various areas, and were kind enough to select me for that batch of NMPs, along with the arts representative, Janice Koh. I felt it was good that we had both been selected, instead of jostling for a single slot.

Settling in

More will have been written elsewhere in this book about parliamentary procedures and processes, the ceremonial aspects and other logistical requirements which all NMPs are required to learn and adhere to.

Focusing more specifically on my own experience as part of the 12th Parliament from 2012 to 2014, I must say it was an interesting experience. The 2011 elections were considered a watershed for a few reasons, not least of which was the strong performance of the Workers' Party, which clinched a Group Representation Constituency, and also for having the largest number of contested seats and the poorest performance by the incumbent People's Action Party since independence.

With a larger number of Opposition MPs in the House, debates were more hotly contested, and sittings would start to seem increasingly longer in duration. Issues like the Population White Paper became the focus of more attention both inside and outside of Parliament, and parliamentarians were kept busy, especially with the increased focus brought about by social and digital media platforms which were becoming more and more ubiquitous.

Against this backdrop, the work of the NMPs had become relatively more challenging, in my opinion. In earlier terms, the NMPs were often considered the source of alternative voices, given the smaller number of Opposition MPs. But the results of GE 2011 meant that there were now more elected Opposition MPs as well as Non-Constituency MPs and of course the cohort of NMPs.

This crowded space meant that there was less attention on the NMPs by the media for example, compared to previous terms. It also increased the pressure on us to ensure that what we chose to say and speak about were relevant and useful to the broader conversation.

At this particular juncture, there was a prevalent drive towards creating a greater sense of social cohesion and inclusion, which extended to the sporting and fitness arena.

I remember that there were new initiatives introduced to create greater access for citizens to facilities and infrastructure if they were keen to stay fit and get in shape, including the ActiveSG programme which was launched in 2014. This sought to create a national movement for sports and allow Singaporeans to create a sporting ecosystem that provides innovative and experiential sport-related programmes at centres island-wide.

We saw more aqua-aerobics courses for the elderly, Zumba lessons for the musically and rhythmically inclined and various other programmes that would be more accurately described as fitness activities rather than sports.

I felt that I needed to speak up on this and used the Budget Committee of Supply debate over a number of years to highlight the need to keep a focus on what we would traditionally call sports — athletic competition with a view to achieving results at major events.

It was my view that, while encouraging people to stay active was important and can have significant benefits for a society and country, it should not come at the detriment of elite sports.

I may be biased, coming as I do from a competitive sports background, but I have seen first-hand what is needed to produce results at the highest levels of sports. It requires government support, including funding, but also a national infrastructure that brings together a whole-of-government approach that unites the education, defence and other ministries and statutory boards together with the private sector and the broader society to back our athletes in their pursuit of glory.

My fear then was that a swing towards viewing sport through a purely community or mass participation lens would see resources and support being diverted away from an elite sports community that traditionally often complains of being underfunded compared to their competitors in other countries.

I spoke a number of times to highlight the differences in these two approaches, and the need to support them both equally at the very least. Given the relatively low priority that sports occupies in the national psyche, I felt that every effort to develop the conversation around sports issues, regardless of how small, was important.

Just over two years after I finished my NMP term, Joseph Schooling united the nation when he blazed his way over two laps of the Olympic pool in Rio to trounce three legends of the sport of swimming to stand atop the podium as our first-ever gold medallist.

The impact of this superlative effort from the best swimmer of his generation rallied all Singaporeans, and I can still remember the moment when he touched home first and the cheers that reverberated around my neighbourhood and indeed the country. It was a great reinforcement for my belief in the unifying power of sports, and the impact it had in the years to come only served to underline the need to support and encourage our national sports heroes on the global stage.

I wish I could take some credit for Joseph's amazing result in 2016, but the truth is that the seeds of that result had been planted by him and his family years earlier when they made the sacrifice to move to the US so that he could train and compete with the best.

A Question of Culture

The cliché that it takes a village certainly applies when building sporting champions, and the proverbial village in this sense is a deep and abiding sports culture where a broad appreciation for the value of sports is felt throughout society.

There are many elements which go into creating such a culture, including an education system which allows youngsters to experience the power and beauty of sports first-hand, a media ecosystem which extols the virtues of sports and encourages the sporting sector, and of course a strong signal of support from political leaders and policy makers.

The platform that being an NMP afforded me allowed me to do my small part in encouraging the efforts to build a strong sporting culture in our society. It remains a work in progress, but it has been heartening to see subsequent Sports NMPs carrying on what I sincerely believe is a critical effort.

At the same time, there were other issues involving sports that I felt needed to be raised at the parliamentary level to spark conversations and debate that could eventually lead to policy and action.

For example, I had asked in 2013 about the potential for a sports university dedicated to educating and training future generations of sports professionals and administrators. Elevating the sports sector will not be possible without the right talent that is equipped with the necessary skill sets and professionalism to populate the various roles in the industry.

Too often, these roles have been filled by ex-athletes, friends and family, and in some cases sports fans, who may or may not have the requisite capabilities. A formal education process and institution are needed to drive the development of such capabilities.

I raised the suggestion in Parliament, and it was taken on board by the Ministry for Culture, Community and Youth (MCCY), as part of a broader study into the manpower needs of the sports sector. In the end, the decision was taken to work with existing universities and educational institutions to build up the necessary capabilities, but it was an important conversation to have.

Difficult Issues

Another significant issue that I touched on a few times in Parliament was the tension between sports and sportsmen, and the Singaporean institution of National Service (NS).

The need for every Singaporean son to serve two years in the military in defence of the country has been a key aspect of life for every male citizen and permanent resident since NS was instituted shortly after our independence. The key principles behind enlistment are that it has to apply universally and without exception to all.

This of course creates conflict between aspiring athletes, many of whom are either approaching their peak years during the time they have to enlist — typically at the age of 18, or who are entering a period of focused and intense training in order to perform as they leave the junior ranks and enter senior competitions.

Spending two years in the military, with no guarantees of being able to secure time off for their training and competitions, and potentially being sent to vocations which may not be conducive for their sporting development, has traditionally meant the death knell for many a sporting career.

When pitted against the security of the country, the chance to win gold medals seems to pale in comparison. Yet many other militaries around the world, in countries such as the US, Germany and Italy, have sought to leverage on sports by creating units of "sports soldiers", who are essentially professional athletes supported by the armed forces.

The win-win aspect is that these athletes bring glory and publicity to the armed forces when they excel at the Olympics and other competitions, and are also tasked to carry out missions such as conducting resilience and physical training for other units, and also engaging with the public and media where required.

Singapore of course faces different considerations, including a smaller population size and potentially complicated geopolitical neighbourhood, but that should not preclude us from looking at the various options and thinking out of the box to find solutions that work for us.

I realised through the debate around these and other similar issues that the value of an NMP can also lie in questioning and challenging established ways of thinking which may not otherwise come up for discussion and debate, especially in our own specific interest areas.

Entrenching Sports in the House

At the risk of coming across as self-interested, I do believe there is a case to be made for having the role of a sports-focused NMP to be institutionalised, and not just a potential focus area which has to compete with arts and the media for a place in Parliament.

Beyond the critical role that sports plays in modern societies, the benefits of being a truly sporting nation can be seen in many other countries around the world. Communities are united in a common passion, national pride is given another platform to be exhibited, and the flow-down benefits in terms of health and fitness are significant. Sports are also a great way to build a resilient and robust society, given the many lessons to be learnt from training, competing and striving to excel in sporting pursuits.

As I shared earlier, the ability to be heard and represented at the highest level of policy making in Parliament can be crucial in advancing the development and positive growth of sports in Singapore. Having an NMP with knowledge and passion for sports to add to the debate in the House is important for the broader sports sector.

At the same time, the signal of having a Sports NMP as a fixture of Parliament would send a strong message to athletes and all who are passionate and committed to sports that their endeavours and passion are relevant and important to the country as a whole. With many of them sacrificing much to fly our flag on the global sporting stage, such encouragement can go a long way to sustaining their efforts.

Beyond the conversations in the House, I also truly enjoyed the opportunities afforded to me during my time as an NMP and beyond. I was invited to speak to young people at various occasions and ceremonies, and I tried to make the most of the chances to share more about the importance and role of sports in our society. I was also invited to sit on various committees, including one that was responsible for a review of the Singapore Sports School, where I could tap into my personal experiences as well as those gleaned in Parliament to make small contributions wherever I could.

Having shared a brief account of my experiences as an NMP, it is my sincere hope that more individuals with a deep and abiding passion for sports will step forward and serve in the same capacity should the opportunity arise.

For many of us, sports have enriched our lives in significant ways. The chance to serve as an NMP and to use that position for the betterment of the sports we love is hopefully something that future generations will embrace wholeheartedly.

Editor's Cut: A Q&A with Nicholas Fang
(This interview has been edited and condensed for length and clarity.)

What is your most memorable moment from your time in Parliament?
The moment most memorable to me isn't actually a sports-related one, but the debate around the Population White Paper post-2011. We started to see the composition of the House change a little bit with more Opposition MPs. The introduction of the White Paper followed on very quickly from that year's election, and it was very heavily debated in the House.

To me, it was interesting to observe the shifting nature of the debate and seeing, you know, some of the back-and-forth between the ruling party and the Opposition, and how some of these things took on a life of their own and spread out into the public sphere. I don't know how many Singaporeans watch Parliament with any great interest, but in my time, certainly no-one could say "oh, I want to see what's going on" and turn it on, right?[1] But [being there] allowed me to see how debates are going to be shaped.

How did being an NMP change you as a person and/or the work you do?
I don't think it has necessarily changed what I do, but it gave me insight into the policy side of the House. It showed me how politicians must juggle a lot of demands, [and are] quite often thrust into very difficult positions with a lot of expectations placed on them. And more importantly, it gave me insight into the difficulties of policy making.

If you consider something like the Bukit Brown debate, people were actually very upset. If you looked at all the different vested parties, you would realise that there were maybe three or four different groups who were diametrically opposed to each other, and if you told the policy maker or the Minister or whoever that your job is to make everybody happy, it's not possible because everyone's running directly counter to each other. You can't make everybody happy. So when I listened to the debates and the explanations, the questions being asked and the responses…you realise that the answer is not really that clear. That was a big takeaway for me.

Based on your time in Parliament, what words of advice would you give future NMPs?
First of all, you genuinely have to be very passionate about an issue or issues that you want to speak up about. If you have that passion, you would typically have some background knowledge, experience, understanding and awareness of that particular sector or industry, so you don't need to do too much homework. You basically just need to learn how the parliamentary process works, you know, all the administrative stuff. And then you have to apply yourself to making an impact.

If you do it because you think "it looks good on my CV", there might be somebody else who would appreciate it more and could make a bigger difference. Of course, it doesn't necessarily follow that someone would have a harder time even if they didn't go in for the right reasons, because you see NMPs whom you don't really recall saying a single word and just cruise for their whole term. It's a personal choice, of course, but in that case you're wasting the position, you're wasting the opportunity. So do it for the right reasons.

How would you sum up your time as an NMP in one sentence?
I will say it was a very, very hectic time, but exceedingly rewarding.

I'm saying this from the point of view that our Parliament doesn't actually sit for very long. Other countries' Parliaments sit every day for one month straight. Nowadays the sessions run a bit longer, but ours used to be one, maybe two days a month, except for the Budget period. Then there's the prep work you have to do to make sure you know what's going on. I didn't hire a legislative assistant, so I did everything myself. I talked to people and made sure I understood the issues so that I wouldn't say something stupid in Parliament, and then there was preparing speeches and questions and all that, so it was a bit hectic.

Maybe it's just my personality, but I'm interested in a broad range of issues — there are media rights and freedoms, sports, defence, security and international affairs, and so on. I did hold myself back a little bit because I didn't think I was qualified to comment on every single issue, but I found it all very interesting.

Endnote

[1] Live-streaming of Parliament was introduced in early 2021.

Speaking for the Trees in Parliament

Faizah Jamal
Nominated Member of Parliament (2012–2014)

> *Editor's Note: I was very clear I wanted Faizah Jamal in this section on "Merits" from the onset because she was the first Member of Parliament to speak up boldly and passionately for the trees and the environment which paved the path for many MPs, including myself, to carry this torch after her. She, along with Laurence Lien and Janice Koh, made waves when they voted "no" in a call for division for the parliamentary debate on the Population White Paper in 2013. I knew Faizah many years ago; we were both part of a spiritual practice group on self-awareness. This essay takes us into her thoughts and emotions through the White Paper debate and a fiery expression of her continued conviction to speak her truth.*

"All those in favour say Aye...."

Just as the all-too-predictable majority voices were to reverberate in the House, Low Thia Khiang of the Workers' Party (WP) rose, and said, "Madam Speaker, I call for a division."

Amidst a puzzled buzz in the House, Speaker Halimah Yaacob called for the Serjeant-at-Arms to ring the bell and lock the doors. The Serjeant-at-Arms' voice boomed dramatically in the House, "Doors locked, Madam!"

As the Speaker called for members who supported Mr Low's request to stand, my first thought was, "Thank goodness for Constitutional Law class all those years ago in law school!"

Not even a regular Member of Parliament (MP), never mind the Nominated Members of Parliament (NMPs), would have heard those words too often in a House dominated for so long by the same party.

At that moment, I thought, "If I don't stand up now, I can never look at myself in the mirror, or look my children in the face, ever again."

So I stood up.

I could not see who else was standing. All the Opposition MPs and NMPs were either behind me or to my left. I resisted the temptation to turn around and see who else was standing because I thought it would not be a very MP-ish thing to do.

To this day, I wish I did!

That choice of standing up to support the call for a division was not just the single most defining moment of my short two-and-a-half years in Parliament; it was also one of the most memorable moments in my life.

Putting My Hat in the Ring

The Nature Society of Singapore had been approached to consider putting in a name for the nature conservation and advocacy community, under a new platform — the "Civic and People Sector".

"We at Nature Society would like to nominate you for the Nominated MP position," they told me in a phone call.

"Why me?" was my incredulous reply.

Like all Singaporeans, especially after the watershed 2011 General Election, I had my own armchair criticisms of the political scene but being in Parliament had never been on my radar.

I told my two children I would not agree if they did not think I should do it.

"You mean you get to teach them all the environment stuff you taught us and your students? Say 'Yes', Mama. We can totally see you in Parliament!" they said, as if being in the highest law-making body of the land was the same as facilitating problem-based learning environment education classes.

So I put my hat in the ring.

At the interview, when asked what I would wish for as NMP if I had three wishes, I cheekily said, "Only three? EIA laws, EIA laws, EIA laws," and explained why. I did not know it then, but demanding Environment Impact Assessment laws was to become a recurring theme in many of my speeches, including at the Population White Paper debate.

In the middle of class on 2 February 2012, my audible gasp of "Oh my God" alarmed my students. I had received an email from the Parliament Office confirming that I had been selected.

My work of raising consciousness among young people, not just about the environment but also about being politically aware, had just taken on a whole new level.

I was terrified.

Speaking for the Trees

> *I speak for the trees,*
> *for the trees have no tongue...*
> — *The Lorax, Dr Seuss*

From the outset, I was very clear that I would not be a spokesperson for the Nature Society, with its narrow focus on biodiversity and nature conservation.

◆ The Nominated Member of Parliament Scheme

In my media statement, I announced that I wanted to seek greater consultation, openness and transparency between the authorities and the public generally, specifically with regard to nature and heritage areas, and to raise awareness on how nature can enrich lives.

Realising early on that there had been little or no mention of environmental and nature concerns in Parliament, I knew I had to speak in the language the agencies and Ministers understood if I were to justify my presence in the highest law-making body of the land.

Having been sworn in just before the Budget Debate in February 2012, the newly minted NMPs were thrown straight into the deep end. My maiden speech, a lesson in environmental consciousness, set the tone not just for the rest of my term but gave an insight into the kind of person I was, and still am.

I would weave environmental concerns into every speech to every government agency or ministry I addressed — natural spaces as preventive healthcare and mental wellness (Ministry of Health), nature and environment education as important components of school curriculum and character-building from preschool to tertiary (Ministry of Education), nature as eco-tourism (Ministry of Trade & Industry), nature as "natural capital" (Ministry of Finance), our unique easy access to biodiversity-within-a-city as a source of national pride (Prime Minister's Office), and of course, the very obvious biodiversity arguments to the Ministry of National Development.

I even went as far as to address "nature-as-healer" with its much-needed transcendental quality for a materialistic society already so disconnected from itself, and in danger of losing its soul.

I did not care that some friends had suggested that I stay away from referring to anything "spiritual". I retorted that if my students had found our nature walks connected them to something bigger than themselves, then that was what I was going to relay to policy makers.

I even included the lessons my Orang Asli friends taught me in my numerous forays into the Malaysian forests, on the art of walking lightly on Earth, in my speeches.

The Call for Division

A few months into my term, I was beginning to despair.

Almost all my "environmental" questions were listed near the bottom of the long list of Parliamentary Questions (PQs) submitted. With more Opposition MPs than ever before, a very active bunch of NMPs, and Question Time being only 90 minutes in each sitting, my questions never quite got to have their time in the sun. To my mind, there was a hierarchy in the perceived importance of our questions, no matter how pressing the issue was to the individual MP.

Then came the 2013 Population White Paper, touted by then-National Development Minister Mah Bow Tan as "the most important document regarding our future since independence".

Yet it was undoubtedly one of the most contentious policies ever debated. The public made their criticisms heard online and offline. The parliamentary debate on the Population White Paper took place barely a week after it was announced. In fact, I noted in my speech the irony that while the White Paper said "Singaporeans form the core of our society and the heart of our nation", it was not even part of the "Our SG Conversations" that had been happening then, nor any form of public consultation. I suggested that the government first repair the trust with us, the citizens, that had been broken.

♦ The Nominated Member of Parliament Scheme

It was not lost on me that this debate was my greatest opportunity to weave the web of life into what was, to me, an uninspiring piece of policy making.

The White Paper was debated over two weeks in February 2013. Even MPs from the ruling party expressed reservations. However, for the most part, arguments were based on economic grounds with banal words like "productivity" being bandied about.

I was perturbed that so few members saw what was, to my mind, something fundamentally wrong with the White Paper.

The WP's Sylvia Lim had just spoken against the White Paper, like all her WP colleagues did, when my name was called by Speaker Halimah Yacob. Noticing that the Prime Minister and many Cabinet Ministers were in the House, I rose to speak with trepidation.

I expressed my astonishment that, amidst all the number crunching and the exhortation for Singaporean women to be mothers, no one had taken into account the impact that the White Paper would have on a bigger mother — Mother Earth.

It was deeply disturbing to me that in order to meet the needs of a projected growing population (that 6.9 million magic number!), *inter alia*, the Cross Island Line (CRL) was to run through the Central Catchment Nature Reserve, typically understood by its very name to be inviolate.

> *"In these areas also are some rare and endemic species, found not only nowhere else in Singapore but nowhere else in the world. Not for nothing are they given the 'nature reserve' status. And yet the CRL proposes to cut through these precious forests. Perhaps because they do not seemingly contribute to GDP growth?"*

While the CRL-through-our-nature-reserve was an important component of my argument, I went further. I questioned why issues of food, water and energy security, with the projected increase in population by 2030 given our country's heavy dependence on imports, were not even raised.

I began my speech with a quote from Antoine de Saint-Exupery, "If you want to build a ship, don't drum up people to collect wood and don't assign them tasks; teach them rather to long for the endless immensity of the sea", taking a dig at the government's "most important document since independence".

I ended with a lesson from the ancient Egyptians' death ritual. They would throw away the brain and keep the heart, because to them the brain was worth nothing; it was the heart that mattered. I used this as an analogy for how the government had been good at making decisions based on linear thinking, but fell short of that which comes from the heart, from empathy and compassion — particularly for the non-human species.

So I said, "I cannot in all good conscience, endorse the White Paper."

After my speech, I was mildly amused to hear the Speaker commenting, "Now I know what the ancient Egyptians did."

An NMP sitting behind me leaned over and said, "Did you realise when you ended your speech, there was a stunned silence from the front bench?" No, I did not notice because I was too busy recovering from the fact that I had just said "No" to my government in the highest law-making body of the land!

Disappointingly, no other MP mentioned anything relating to the environment nor saw any problem with the CRL-through-our-nature-reserve.

◆ The Nominated Member of Parliament Scheme

During tea break at the Members' Room, a couple of Ministers came up to me. One of them semi-jokingly said, "How about we give you more land if you give us more babies?" to which another said, "Eh, that would be 'transactional', that's not good!", referring to what I had said in my speech about the government being transactional in treating citizens like economic digits.

That said, I did not feel any pressure to vote differently when the time came, maybe because in the bigger scheme of all things GDP, my views did not count for much anyway — after all, I was a mere tree hugger!

As we flocked back to the Chamber, an amendment to the White Paper Motion was tabled by People's Action Party (PAP) MP Liang Eng Hwa. I pondered whether this would affect my vote, and decided that all my environmental arguments remained.

I listened intently to Prime Minister Lee Hsien Loong's speech, and as he teared up, my cynical self said, "I need more than tears to make me change my mind."

Unsurprisingly, the majority voted "Yes", including four NMPs, while the 13 who voted "No" were all nine WP MPs, Non-Constituency MP Lina Chiam and NMPs Laurence Lien, Janice Koh and myself. NMP Associate Professor Eugene Tan abstained from voting. Eight people were not in the House, with PAP's Inderjit Singh's absence from voting, despite a very critical speech, being very noticeable and much talked-about for weeks after the debate.

Immediately after the news broke, numerous calls came from the media for why I had voted "No". With headlines ranging from "Nature forgotten, says NMP" to "White paper encourages society with no heart" to my speech being described as "laden with fiery pot-shots", people from friends to random strangers shared my full speech which I had posted on my Facebook page. Even my children, then 17 and 19, told me their friends had also shared it with their own family and friends.

My response to the media storm and public interest was to simply post a quote on Facebook: "Speak the truth even if your voice shakes."

Whither the "Environment NMP"?

It has now been more than eight years since that eventful vote. I can hardly recognise the environment and nature discourse landscape now, in politics and in public.

In 2021, MPs from both sides of the House spoke up for Dover and Clementi forests. Even PAP MP Christopher de Souza, calling for the preservation of forests in his constituency, claimed in his Facebook post that he is a "nature lover".

My silent response to this is "Where were you eight years ago, when our nature reserve was under severe threat from the government?" I would have welcomed some solidarity instead of being the lone voice in the wilderness.

When part of the Kranji forest was destroyed, apparently without NParks' knowledge, many people, beyond the usual suspects, were up in arms demanding accountability from the authorities.

So, whither the "Environment NMP"?

Firstly, while I represented the "Environment" civil society then, there was and is still no such official platform; I was put up through the "Civic and People Sector" platform.

Secondly, I have never believed there should be one.

In my speech at the debate on the Presidential Address in May 2014, I exhorted *all* MPs to speak on the environment because it is the right thing to do.

◆ The Nominated Member of Parliament Scheme

> *"All members of this House should be concerned and ask why something as inviolate as our nature reserve, on which we draw free eco-services that make our very existence that much more meaningful, is to be desecrated in the name of infrastructure."*

As I mentioned many times, "No environment means no business, no arts, no sports, no economy."

Would having such a specialised NMP have value in today's political landscape where MPs from both sides of the House are now speaking up on the environment?

Further, an "Environment NMP" would have to step up even more and be ready to speak up on issues beyond environmental concerns.

Even eight years ago, I felt compelled to raise "non-environmental" issues, such as the plan to get rid of Sungei Road Thieves Market, the NLB "Penguingate" saga and the abysmal rates of breastfeeding in Singapore compared to our neighbours, which earned me titters in the House from some male MPs.

"Wah today got breastfeeding lecture in Parliament," they said to me during the break, to which my sharp response was, "What's so funny? Your wives don't breastfeed?"

More recently, despite the seriousness of the Foreign Interference (Countermeasures) Bill (FICA), only two NMPs took part in the debate. Although both expressed reservations, they ultimately abstained rather than vote against it. (It is interesting that at this debate, Leader of the Opposition Pritam Singh called for a division like Low Thia Khiang had done at the White Paper debate.)

A young lady active in nature advocacy asked me why in the FICA debate, as with the Protection from Online Falsehoods and Manipulation (POFMA) debate, some NMPs abstained instead of voting "No", despite making their discomfort known in their speeches. I had no answer for her because I too am puzzled; it is not as if there was no precedent in the history of the NMP scheme.

In a *Straits Times* article dated 24 May 2014, "What next for the NMP scheme", Tham Yuen-C, Mariam Mokhtar and Rachel Au-Yong said, "Take the current batch of NMPs. Some among them have already made history by being the first NMPs to not just speak against government initiatives, but to vote against them, too. Three — Ms Faizah Jamal, Ms Janice Koh and Mr Laurence Lien — voted against last year's White Paper on Population..."

Incidentally, I had also voted against the "Little India Riot" Bill.

Who Gets to Tell the "Environment" Story?

Over the last eight years, under Minister Desmond Lee, much to his credit, NParks has practically taken over the narrative on all things nature and environment including using the government's powerful machinery to galvanise 25,000 young people each year under NParks' Youth@SGNature initiative.

Words like "natural capital", "environment impact assessments", "free eco-services", etc., which I introduced in my speeches, are now common parlance by civil servants in their prepared speeches for Ministers.

Lately, not a day passes that the mainstream media does not mention the overused term "sustainability" in reference to what Ministers and agencies are doing.

If that is not taking over the narrative completely, I do not know what is.

For me, the Nature Society has lost much of the shine that drew me to it in the first place (cue the first-ever petition in 1991, which I was involved with, against the government's plan to turn Lower Peirce Reservoir into a golf course).

With its older demographic and a leadership that has remained largely unchanged for over 10 years, the Nature Society is no longer the go-to organisation for young people interested in nature advocacy. Many have told me they do not resonate with the Society, and some have started their own groups.

Walking My Own Road

Someone asked me if my parliamentary experience had changed me.

Only insofar as it reaffirmed my belief to speak my truth even if my voice shakes. That same voice also made sure that I wrote every single speech myself. How else would I get to speak my own truth?

I set out to plant seeds. I would like to think I have manifested that.

Even if just one politician were to heed my call for a life beyond GDP, as I had said in my White Paper speech, that would be enough. I did not need a second NMP term.

> *Traveler, there is no road;*
> *only a ship's wake on the sea.*
> — Antonio Machado

Editor's Cut: A Q&A with Faizah Jamal
(This interview has been edited and condensed for length and clarity.)

What is your most memorable moment from your time in Parliament?
It would definitely have to be that White Paper debate. There was just so much going on, and it was so much more serious than speaking to my students! The issues were so personal to me. After Speaker Halimah Yacob mentioned my reference to the Egyptian ritual, during our break at the Members' Lounge afterwards, people kept coming up to me and telling me, "Wah, Speaker commented on your speech." I didn't really know how to respond to that so I just said, well, maybe she enjoyed learning about the Egyptians!

And of course the moment when Low Thia Khiang ran up and called for a division, and we had to vote on that. In that instant, I realised the enormity of standing up for what I believe in.

How did being an NMP change you as a person and/or the work you do?
I think the question should be the other way around — how did the person I am affect my work as an NMP? I don't think being an NMP changed me as a person. Growing up, I was often told I was the black sheep of my family because I've never been the sort to just be okay with things. I didn't always know how to express it when I was young, and that can be so frustrating.

I guess [being in Parliament] did show me that sometimes, things you say can make a difference, although till today I don't know how true this is. I don't know how much impact I had on local environment discourse. Terms like "natural capital" and "eco-services", which I used in my maiden speech, are trendy today. Minister Desmond Lee has talked about them, government agencies have talked about them. I don't know if my speeches had any role to play in this or if they were already thinking about these things, but basically, what I was calling for was more than "save the forests". It was about living a more conscious life, a life beyond GDP and for deep reflection on what it means to be Singaporean.

Based on your time in Parliament, what words of advice would you give future NMPs?
Times are so different now, I don't know that whatever advice I could give would be of any use!

I think that because there are so many intricate issues coming up now, it can be very difficult if you're not on top of things. I think there can be a danger that in order to be seen and heard, people might talk about issues that they don't have a real affinity for or understanding of. You might just become a loudhailer for someone else's cause, which I don't think is right.

This said, [as an NMP], if you just talk about issues that concern your sector, you're not going to be very useful at all. You have to up your game and be out there, asking the really tough questions, because otherwise, why are you there?

When you say "No" to things you don't believe in, or speak up for the things you do, you give others permission to do the same. Maybe not the next day, maybe 10 years down the road, but the energy that comes from speaking your truth will help other people speak up for the things they care for. And it doesn't even have to be in Parliament, you know? I mean, NMPs, we're not politicians — we're just average people who were given a very privileged opportunity to speak up.

How would you sum up your time as an NMP in one sentence?
In one sentence? Wow. It was a wild ride.

Actually, that's putting it really mildly. It was a wild, emotional ride. I basically did everything on my own. I wrote my own speeches and did my own research. I was an adjunct lecturer then and I had the time to do all this, but imagine coming home at the end of the day and still having to do all this work. I was fortunate that my batch of NMPs was quite close and supportive of each other. Most importantly, I couldn't have done it without emotional support from my children — they'd come meet me for tea after Parliament sittings and I'd be ranting and raving about how things had gone. It was tiring and emotionally draining, yet also enriching and fulfilling.

POFMA: Duty, Conscience or Both?

Walter Theseira
Nominated Member of Parliament (2018–2020)

> *Editor's Note:* To my mind, the POFMA Amendment Motion that Walter and I jointly tabled with NMP Irene Quay in May 2019 is a noteworthy part of the NMP story. The widespread public disquiet and discontent with POFMA and its "chilling effect" was touted by many as unprecedented, perhaps prompting the Minister for Law and Home Affairs to pen a CNA commentary, "NMPs agree on all major points of Falsehoods Bill", a few days before the parliamentary debate ostensibly in response to our motion for amendments (even if the headline seemed odd since our proposed amendments clearly meant we did not agree on some major points of the Bill!). In this essay, Walter recounts the motivations and process behind the Amendment Motion yet also reflects honestly on his learnings from this.

When I was appointed as a Nominated Member of Parliament (NMP) in September 2018, I had hoped to spend my term helping to bring academic insights into policy debates. Like many other academics, I felt that public debates were becoming increasingly polarised, fact-free arenas where personal attacks and ideology were replacing reason and evidence. I wanted to contribute to a more progressive and fact-based political discourse. I was not thinking of getting involved in the meaning of fact, falsehood and whether the government should have powers to restrict speech in the public interest. But these questions were central to the Protection from Online Falsehoods and Manipulation Act, or POFMA, which passed into law on 8 May 2019, after a contentious two-day debate.

POFMA deserves much more than a brief article, and I admit shortcomings in this piece. This story also belongs to my fellow NMPs tabling the Amendment Motion, Anthea Ong and Irene Quay, and to the stakeholders from civic society who contributed to our Amendment Motion and to the broader public debate around POFMA.

While I did not relish being identified with POFMA,[1] ironically, a bill criticised for restricting democratic liberties stimulated an intense democratic discourse in Singapore, and showed that NMPs could add value to our democratic institutions. For these reasons, I offer this piece as part of the NMP story.

Grave Concerns About POFMA

The POFMA Bill was introduced to address the problem of fake news that continues to harm democracies worldwide. The government's solution was to give the Executive powers to take limited actions against any statement published or communicated online that was false and against the public interest.

I believed that the Bill, as drafted, was imbalanced in how it granted discretionary powers to the Executive, and presented a real risk of political abuse by some future government. I did not think the government framed the Bill with the intention of taking political advantage, but I did think it erred on the side of granting itself excessive discretion. Because online falsehoods can be fast-moving and dangerous, I agreed that the Executive should have discretionary powers to stop or prevent a crisis. But there was no systematic oversight inherent to the Bill that would regulate use of these powers, except for appeal to the High Court, which was in the Bill itself insufficiently documented.

As a social scientist, I also found the way the Bill approached questions of fact, in the context of public policy and science, to be problematic. Academic research progresses by overturning older stylised facts or theories when better data or methods are discovered. The text of the Bill, which granted powers to the Executive to act against deemed falsehoods, sat uneasily with the process of scientific inquiry. What people think of as scientific facts are often just reliable estimates based on theory and models.[2] Would the Bill mean that public debates on science might be clouded by the possibility the Executive might intervene to declare a contested finding a falsehood?[3] And would it undermine the basis of scientific education, which aims to give students the tools to discover and discern facts critically, rather than to accept as dogma what authorities declare to be facts?

A group of Singaporean academics[4] had circulated an online open letter to the Minister for Education outlining their concern that the Bill would discourage critical research, and dissemination and discussion of that research, in and on Singapore. I knew some academics had experienced pressure when publishing articles critical of government policy or issues in Singapore. Reasonable academics accepted that the government — indeed, anyone — had a right to challenge their work. But challenges had to be based on evidence, rather than on Executive discretion that simply declared a finding to be false. After all, the astronomer Galileo Galilei was once condemned for promoting heliocentrism, or the theory that the Earth revolves around the Sun; a fact now taught to every child! Science, and the pursuit of truth, always risked opposition from authorities who might find some facts inconvenient.

Preparing for the Amendment Motion

I did not form these impressions the day the Bill was introduced at the First Reading. I knew some legislation on online falsehoods was forthcoming, and the precursor to the Bill — the Select Committee on Deliberate Online Falsehoods[5] — had been controversial.[6] But there was no reason for me to pre-judge the Bill.

Bills are introduced or passed in almost every Parliament sitting. Few are preceded by a briefing to NMPs, and fewer still are conducted by political office holders. So when the NMPs were invited to a special briefing, the morning of the First Reading, held by Senior Ministers of State Dr Janil Puthucheary and Edwin Tong, that signalled the Bill would be important. The Ministers assured us that the Bill was narrower in scope than present laws addressing online communications and less restrictive in powers and application. I remember agreeing with their views. I had no reason to doubt their assurances.

My concerns started shortly after the First Reading, when voices from civic society, academia, the media and more started raising questions about the Bill. I started digging into the Bill itself. It soon became clear that I would have difficulty agreeing to pass the Bill in its present form.

I thought the government would want to address the controversy on the Bill, while retaining the policy objectives of being able to deal with online falsehoods swiftly. NMPs might be helpful to address these concerns, as neutral parties with the standing to raise concerns in Parliament. The question became how to do so.

The standard approach for MPs was to raise questions and concerns during the Second Reading debate — the "Q&A approach". This was not ideal. The government would typically address MPs' questions by clarifying the policy or legislative intent, but without making any changes to the actual text of the Bill.

Another avenue was to raise concerns outside of Parliament, through public and private discussions in my capacity as an MP. But a pattern was swiftly developing where Ministers were quick to support constructive suggestions on the Bill or to argue that concerns were unfounded, but refuse to give any indication the legislation needed amendment.

I thought a third approach might be best — to propose constructive amendments to the Bill or to encourage the government to do so. Anthea Ong had been thinking about the same and we quickly agreed to collaborate.

Although neither of us had proposed amendments to legislation before, and we had no legal background, Anthea brought with her a formidable set of allies, including legal experts with case experience on public administration and constitutional law. Together with inputs from other stakeholders, we started work on a set of amendments that might address specific concerns while maintaining the policy intent of the Bill.

We also agreed on a three-pronged approach.

First, we had to anchor our amendments around concerns for good governance and safeguards against the abuse of executive powers. These were objectives that we thought all stakeholders had in common, and which would resonate with Singaporeans.

Second, we wanted to bring in support from other NMPs and MPs. Although we were not sure if we would be able to get other MPs to support our amendments, we still tried and hoped they would at least speak on similar governance concerns. NMP Irene Quay joined in our motion for the amendments.

Third, we hoped to work with the government, whether through the Ministry of Law agreeing to adopt the amendments in whole or part, through the Ministry putting forth its own amendments to the Bill to address our concerns, or through referring the Bill to a Select Committee after the Second Reading for additional review.[7]

Deliberation, Doubts and Duty

After consulting closely with the government, it became clear there would be no acceptance of our amendments. We also realised support from other MPs would be minimal. While other NMPs and People's Action Party (PAP) MPs might express concerns in their own ways, we could not count on them to vote for our amendments. We also realised it might not serve the interests of NMPs as an institution, nor that of our stakeholders, for the issue to appear politicised, and so chose not to work with the Workers' Party (WP) MPs.

Although the government was keen to seize the common ground offered by our amendments — which accepted the principle that online falsehoods required the Executive to have powers to act in the public interest — we knew that if we persisted, the government would publicly oppose our amendments. History suggested that this process could be very robust.

I realised that my character and integrity might be attacked by some critics, given that my concerns with the Bill could be disingenuously equated with support for online falsehoods. This prospect gave me some pause, even if Anthea was undaunted and charging ahead.

Margaret Thatcher famously kept a copy of Charles Mackay's poem, *No Enemies*, as a reminder that enemies are the evidence of a political career well lived. But I did not relish the thought of dying on the wrong hill. I was prepared for critics to argue that I was mistaken or out of my depth.

More problematic for me was the view that the NMPs moving amendments were playing the role of useful idiots. Some in the government believed that certain groups opposing the Bill intended to weaken the government's legitimacy and harm Singapore's interests. We could be seen as giving ammunition to such critics of the government. Nobody likes to be thought of as an idiot, useful or not, and it would do no good to have our concerns conflated with those who might be working against Singapore's interests.

Finally, some might believe we were motivated by vanity or political intent. The Bill was attracting huge domestic and international interest. I had to ask myself whether my own vanity played a role in my decision to speak up on the Bill.

These thoughts were in the background as I prepared for the debate. But I had to do my job. It fell to myself, and my fellow NMPs, to do what we thought right at the time.

The Parliamentary Process and Exercising My Vote

In my experience, MPs typically enter the Chamber knowing how they want to vote and why. While pre-judgment may be a mortal sin for judges, it is entirely normal if not expected for MPs today. Parliamentary matters are complex, and MPs need to form their positions carefully before the debate. Political parties, moreover, make collective decisions, so they can whip their MPs to vote accordingly (it is noteworthy that Irene Quay and Anthea Ong both asked for the Whip to be lifted for this Bill).

Parliament is not a Court of Law, and the role of debate in a modern parliamentary system is not to introduce evidence or arguments *de novo* to fellow MPs, as it might once have been. It is, rather, to put those arguments on the public record. MPs are often accused of "playing to the gallery" with their speeches, but the debate is now meant to persuade the public at large, rather than their fellow MPs or the government, whose positions should have been secured in advance. Indeed, in the POFMA debate, the votes that were in real suspense, and potentially persuadable, were our own — and those of our fellow NMPs.

The details of the debate are in the Hansard. After two gruelling days, as expected, we had failed to persuade the government to adopt any of our amendments, to introduce their own amendments or to send the Bill to a Select Committee. The Minister for Law had been straightforward. He pre-empted the debate by addressing and dismissing our amendments in his opening speech, and government MPs backed him up.

The House was packed at a time when most MPs would normally have left for their Meet-the-People sessions or other duties, showing the government — and Opposition — regarded this vote to be critical. Given the government's dominance in Parliament, the outcome was guaranteed. The only question was whether we would have to — or want to — put our votes on the record.[8]

I was ready to vote in favour of the Second Reading. The Second Reading signifies that Parliament agrees with the main principles of the Bill, and I was satisfied that there was public interest in the principle that the Executive should have new powers to deal with online falsehoods. I was not convinced by the WP's position of rejecting the Bill on the basis that the Executive should not be given such powers at all, although I could see merit in a hybrid arrangement where there was an urgency test for the Executive to act. Further, I did not think our amendments clashed with the main principles of the Bill, but rather, sought to ensure that institutional oversight would be integrated into the Bill to limit Executive discretion.

Passing the Second Reading would bring the Bill to the Committee Stage, where we would have to decide whether we wanted to force a vote on our amendments — which we would lose — or withdraw them in peace. This was not a simple administrative matter. Although our amendments were tabled as a unified set of proposals, in practice, they would require eight different specific amendment clauses to be voted on!

By procedure, bills and amendments thereof, are considered line by line in the Committee Stage. When there are no amendments, the Chair takes one voice vote that Members agree that each line, as originally proposed, stands as part of the Bill. However, when amendments are proposed, the literal nature of "line by line" consideration comes into effect.[9]

We were tying up most of Parliament and the Cabinet. It was well past dinner-time, and everyone was tired and hungry. It would be expedient to withdraw the amendments since we would lose anyway.

But Anthea, Irene and I felt that on balance, the record should reflect that we saw no reason to withdraw our amendments, and the government saw no reason to accept them. In this case, it was better to be fired than to quit.

With all our amendments disposed of, the final question was at hand: Should we vote in favour, against or abstain?

The WP had followed through with their opposition to the Bill by calling a Division for the Second Reading and directing their MPs to vote against the Bill. They duly called a Division for the Third Reading. The Division bell started ringing. There would be no refuge in the toilet for me.

I could not vote for the Bill, given that our amendments had been rejected. But would voting against the Bill signal agreement with the

WP's that the fundamental basis of the Bill was so seriously flawed that it should not pass into law? The WP had a principled set of objections, and they spoke for many Singaporeans who had fundamental disquiet with handing the Executive far-reaching powers. But I did not think the Bill should be rejected out of hand, and I thought it would not serve the interests of NMPs, or that of the stakeholders concerned with the Bill, to be identified with partisan politics.

The Speaker ordered the Serjeant-at-Arms to lock the doors. I voted to "Abstain", and felt immediately relieved; it was the end of a very long day and I had made the right choice, even though it may not have seemed like much of a choice to many.

Conclusion and Postscript

As I write this, more than three years have passed since the passage of POFMA into law. It seems that the feared chilling effect of POFMA on online discourse has been subtle. Online debate, criticism, and sadly, routine transmission of online falsehoods, have continued seemingly unrestrained, particularly during the Covid-19 crisis.[10] However, it may be premature to conclude that POFMA has had no effect, and high-profile falsehoods have been corrected. It may be a joke to suggest that one might be "POFMA'ed" for expressing a view online, but it has a touch of gallows humour, particularly among persons with a public presence.

I have also asked myself whether I could have done more to ensure that POFMA was crafted as good legislation. A lacuna in POFMA soon arose. In an appeal against a POFMA direction, does the Executive or the appellant have the burden of proof in showing whether a statement is false or misleading?[11] Different judges of the High Court came to conflicting conclusions on the matter, requiring the Court of Appeal to

◆ The Nominated Member of Parliament Scheme

resolve the matter. I think I, and Parliament, could have done better. If the burden of proof, at least at some stage and in some form, should lie with the appellant, this should have been stated in the legislation and defended in the debate, rather than argued by the Attorney-General during appeals.

Entering the battle of Trafalgar, Admiral Lord Nelson signalled the fleet: "England expects that every man shall do his duty." But war criminals, too, claim that they are merely doing their duty.

By any standard, POFMA was one of the greatest political battles fought in Singapore in years, and all MPs sought to fulfil their duty in the way they thought best for Singapore. But MPs owe many duties: to themselves, their constituents, their political party and to Singapore. What should MPs do when they find that one or more of these duties conflict? And what of NMPs, who owe duties only to their conscience and to their vision of what is right for Singapore?

I do not think I am a war hero, and I certainly hope to not be considered a war criminal. What I do hope is that any other Singaporean, placed in my position as an NMP, would have felt it their duty not to shy away from the political battle, and to participate to the best of their ability and according to their conscience.

Editor's Cut: A Q&A with Walter Theseira
(This interview has been edited and condensed for length and clarity.)

What were some memorable moments from your time in Parliament?
There was one debate where I slipped up and said what I actually felt, which isn't always advisable in Parliament. This was the Second Reading debate on the Fire Safety (Amendment) Bill in 2019, and Senior Parliamentary Secretary Sun Xueling had just wrapped up her reply speech. I had spoken earlier on the Bill. So I asked a clarifying question. I remarked that many MPs had asked the Ministry to consider mandating or subsidising various fire safety interventions — but based on the reply speech, I didn't think the Ministry was going to take up those suggestions at that point in time.

That caused a bit of a stir! Not from the SPS, to her credit, but from the backbenchers. Because I was giving voice to what many backbenchers — PAP, WP, NMPs — had felt. In every Second Reading debate, backbenchers line up to offer criticisms and suggestions to the Ministry. Invariably, the criticisms are parried, while the suggestions may be discussed but are not given any commitment from the government. The Bill passes.

I understand why. The government's job in putting a bill to Parliament is to get it passed as smoothly as possible, just as the backbencher's job is to take the opportunity to raise the concerns of constituents and stakeholders. No Minister wants to agree to extra work for their Ministry during the debate. Even if they think backbenchers' ideas have merit, well, those ideas need to be carefully considered by the Ministry outside Parliament. And some ideas do get taken up that way. But it does give backbenchers the feeling, sometimes, that nothing comes of what they said during the debate. So I had just blurted out what the backbenchers were feeling at that time!

♦ The Nominated Member of Parliament Scheme

How did your time in Parliament change you as a person or influence the work you do?

It was a rewarding, but very difficult learning experience in what responsibility means as a representative of something much bigger than yourself. As an academic, I had to deal with students, colleagues and other stakeholders — but I was only responsible to a limited group of people. If I accomplished anything, it would usually only benefit myself, my research projects, maybe my students or colleagues. It was a very self-centred life!

All that changes if you're in Parliament. Regardless of the actual power you have — which I have to tell people, is not a lot — what you have is influence, and that makes a difference to people's lives.

So I had to remind myself that in what I was saying and doing, I wasn't just representing my own views, but also, those of other stakeholders. I had to ask myself if what I was going to do might harm or help them. And I had to be as open as possible to hearing people out, even or especially people who disagreed with me, because I might learn something important or useful, and I might be able to explain to them why I was saying or doing something.

I don't know if I have carried all these lessons on my return to private life, but I hope that I have become more mindful that what I do and say matters to people beyond myself. It's also important to not be paralysed into inaction by the fear you might offend some interest as well — the important thing is to act when needed with integrity and responsibility, but be open to engaging your stakeholders, including those who disagree with you.

What advice would you give future NMPs?

You are in Parliament as a representative of something much larger than yourself. NMPs might not be elected, but you have stakeholders nonetheless. And even though NMPs are largely selected from functional groups, you may find you have stakeholders you never knew existed. Although our NMP system might guide new NMPs into thinking they should only speak up for their functional group, the problems that Parliament has to consider and the responsibilities of being an MP, go far beyond that. So at some point you have to define just how far you want to go as a stakeholder representative and how involved you want to be.

Of course, the country will run itself without you, because we have professional politicians and leaders who are not waiting for you to act in Parliament. But the key is to ask yourself if you are in a position to add something valuable, unique or which would otherwise be missed, to Parliament.

You also have to be responsible for anything you say, do, or don't say or do. That also makes it difficult, especially if you face a conflict between the demands of your stakeholders, and your own personal conscience or — let's be frank — your personal prospects.

As a former NMP, I would say that only you can judge whether you've done your duty according to the best version of yourself that you want to be.

How would you summarise your time in Parliament in one sentence?
I served according to what I felt was my duty at the time.

◆ The Nominated Member of Parliament Scheme

Endnotes

1. Please refer to Appendix D for more on NMPs and their engagement in Parliament.
2. For example, the unemployment rate or income level is based on statistical estimates, although these figures are usually understood as facts. Researchers can and do dispute such facts when new evidence or methods are used.
3. Unfortunately, some research I did suggested reasons for concern. Ministries would sometimes label claims they disagreed with as false, even when the claim was more a matter of interpretation than a statement of fact. I discussed this in my speech in the Second Reading debate on the POFMA Bill on 8 May 2019, available in the Hansard.
4. This effort was led by Professor Linda Lim at the University of Michigan, Associate Professor Chong Ja Ian at the National University of Singapore, Associate Professor Teo You Yenn at the Nanyang Technological University and Professor Cherian George at the Hong Kong Baptist University.
5. The Select Committee on Deliberate Online Falsehoods is a select committee of the Parliament of Singapore that was formed on 11 January 2018 to examine and report on the problem of deliberate online falsehoods and to recommend strategies to deal with them. See their findings and report on https://www.parliament.gov.sg/sconlinefalsehoods
6. Some academics were of the view that part of the Select Committee hearings was used to attack historian Dr Thum Ping Tjin's academic integrity; he had submitted evidence, including an academic paper, that was highly critical of the government's record on the truth, and the government had responded robustly.
7. It was common for ministries to request that NMPs discuss their speaking points prior to Second Reading debates. The unspoken understanding was that this facilitated parliamentary exchanges where NMPs could put critical views on the record, and yet receive replies from Ministers that addressed the concerns raised in a measured and well-balanced way. We thought the same process could be extended to concerns on POFMA.
8. Some might think parliamentary voting is a tense affair where the outcome goes down to the last MP holding on to some matter of great principle. This makes for good television, but in reality, almost all parliamentary business is conducted with a simple voice vote, where no individual MP's vote is recorded. The Speaker or Chair puts the question to the Chamber, once for the Ayes, and once for the Nays, and calls the outcome based on whether the Ayes or Nays are louder. Just as in a firing squad, no one will know if you fired the fatal shot.
9. The Chair is required to first affirm by vote that Members support each line as originally proposed, up till the line where an amendment is proposed. Then, a new vote is taken to consider the amendment. This repeats for every amendment proposed, and because bills often contain the same language in different sections — for example, in POFMA, the same language is used covering appeals to the Minister for different sections of the Act — an amendment which addresses all cases where the same procedure is used must be voted on each time, even though it may be obvious whether Parliament agrees or disagrees with the general principle of the amendment after the first vote.
10. Singaporeans have been quite vocal with their criticism of the government. One viral satire portrayed the two Ministers leading the Multi-Ministry Task Force as Captains of a ship on a "Cruise to Nowhere", captioned "Two Captains, No Direction", referencing flip-flops

in Covid-19 policy. There has been no POFMA Direction issued against that poster, even though the Ministers are not in fact Captains of any cruise ship. This is in line with the assurances given by the Minister for Law that "The suggestion that satire is covered by POFMA is erroneous".

[11] See Singapore Court of Appeal Case No 96 of 2021.

Dilemmas and Challenges for the Labour NMP

Thomas Thomas
Nominated Member of Parliament (1999–2001)

Editor's Note: It is widely known that the NMP representative for the labour sector is never contested as the internal contest happens within the union movement until they pick one. Many have often wondered how the Labour NMP and PAP Labour MPs differ in speaking up for workers and their rights. In this essay, Thomas gives us more than a glimpse into this difference, specifically mentioning how the Labour NMP is not subjected to the Whip and sharing examples when he held opposing positions from his fellow Labour MPs during his term.

I had the honour to serve as a Nominated Member of Parliament (NMP) in the 9th Parliament from 1 October 1999 to 18 October 2001, representing the Labour Movement over two terms. I was nominated by the Central Committee of the National Trades Union Congress (NTUC), of which I was a member. My second term lasted for 18 days before Parliament was dissolved for general election in 2001.

Unions and Politics

Unions have been involved in politics since their formation in the late 18th century. They were formed in Europe to protect workers from exploitation during the early days of the Industrial Revolution. Factories had started mass production, which enriched capitalists through the exploitation of workers. Rural folks moved to cities and industrial sites to work in these factories. Workers toiled long hours under appalling conditions with very poor wages. Children were exploited to lower the cost of production and achieve higher returns for factory owners.

To make conditions more tolerable, workers organised themselves into trade unions. They collectively bargained to improve working conditions and wages. Governments gradually recognised the unions and put in place regulations to make them legal entities and to protect union leaders.

These became bigger unions, organised national centres of unions in countries and globally to gain improvements and recognition. In addition to industrial relations channels, they supported sympathetic politicians and formed political parties to represent their interests. With universal suffrage, unions used the vote to balance the power between capital and labour. The British Labour Party, for example, was the child of the British labour movement. Social democratic parties in Europe are another example of political bodies with strong trade union links.

Unions and Singapore Politics

In Singapore, trade unions were illegal under the British colonial government until 1940 when the British enacted the Trade Union Bill, which was not fully implemented until after the Second World War. The Malayan Communist Party established close relations with many unions

◆ The Nominated Member of Parliament Scheme

and used them for political purposes while giving voice to grievances of workers.

In Singapore, unionists were part of the government from the early days and had always been represented in the Legislative Assembly and Parliament.

Lim Yew Hock, Singapore's Second Chief Minister from 1956 to 1959, was a trade unionist. He was a clerk and one of the founders of the Singapore Trades Union Congress. Half of the founding members of the People's Action Party (PAP) in 1954 were unionists; the unions were part of the anti-colonial struggle to give dignity to workers and the people of Singapore by deciding on their own destiny.

Some rank-and-file unionists became office-bearers. They raised issues and contributed to the passing of many progressive laws that gave workers and citizens a better quality of life. The close working relationship between the unions and the political leadership contributed to industrial peace, productivity growth and attracted investors to create better paying jobs.

As the NTUC grew in membership, financial strength and as owners of sizable social enterprises, professionals and elected PAP MPs took more leadership positions. The number of rank-and-file members moving to Parliament reduced while the movement of leaders from PAP to NTUC grew. All union leaders have to stand and win elections for union positions. This means they will have to win the support of workers. For that, the professionals in the union need to know and understand grassroots aspirations and concerns.

Additionally, since the late 1970s, many PAP MPs have served as advisers to unions. So practically all the ruling party MPs have links to the unions and issues for workers.

NTUC and the PAP have a "symbiotic relationship". Similar arrangements exist in many other countries, like the British Labour Party drawing support from the British Trades Union Congress and unions; in Europe, social democratic parties have close links with the trade unions.

Labour MPs and NMPs

In this context, how could the Labour NMP be different from the elected MPs from the Labour Movement? Will NMPs bring additional value for workers?

When PAP MPs moved into the unions, one concern was whether it was to control the unions for the Party or to give voice to workers' concerns and aspirations at the highest levels of policy making. Would MPs without previous union experience be acting as representatives of the PAP or representatives of union members? Would they win the support and confidence of union members and grassroots union leaders?

The rank-and-file union leaders and members generally welcomed the NMP scheme. The NMP route was an opportunity for rank-and-file unionists to continue representation in Parliament, a voice that did not consider party interests or positions.

NMPs are not subject to any party whip.

Making the Point

During my term, I was able to act independently. I was not told by anyone from NTUC what position to take on any particular matter. While I used the NTUC library resources for my speeches, I received no staff support nor any help in crafting my speeches. Other rank-and-file union leaders and my contacts in other circles were my sounding board. Sometimes, they would approach me formally or informally on issues. I had raised some of them directly with political office-bearers as I felt this was the best way to help these members. I found the Ministers and others helpful. If they were not able to help, they usually explained the reasons.

During my term, I had not been "censored" by any Minister. In fact, I had received calls on some of the questions I raised to give me some background and on "sensitivities" that I had not been aware of. Some of the issues had links beyond the shores of Singapore. The feedback and the seriousness and respect given to the questions were good and I appreciated the effort.

My guiding principle had been my own beliefs and values system. I was also aware that NTUC and the PAP have a "symbiotic relationship", I had supported many of the government initiatives as part of the NTUC leadership.

While I could express my views, even if it was against the official position, I had to be aware that I was neither a member of the ruling party nor the Opposition. I had to be focused on the issue and be neutral.

In addition to being a unionist, I had been active with the Consumers Association of Singapore (CASE), serving as its Vice-President then as well as in the co-operatives and social sector. I focused on issues that I felt comfortable with that would add value to Singaporeans.

I had been able to submit Parliamentary Questions at almost every sitting during my term.

Industrial Relations

Through debates and questions, I tried to promote the position of workers.

Singapore has done well in many areas. At the same time, there are also many other areas I felt we needed to change and progress faster.

These include changes to labour laws and ratification of the International Labour Organization's (ILO) core conventions, as in the ILO Declaration on Fundamental Principles and Rights at Work. This Declaration was adopted in 1998 and covers core conventions on forced labour, child labour, non-discrimination, freedom of association and collective bargaining. Every country was to be assessed on the implementation of these conventions regardless of their status on ratification. This also meant that all businesses were expected to comply with the conventions everywhere they operate.

DSTA Bill — Taking a Stand

One example of speaking my mind and being aware of the sensitivities of Singapore politics was my speech on the Defence Science and Technology Agency (DSTA) Bill (21 February 2000).

While I supported the strengthening of national security, I raised concerns on how staff matters were managed. I felt some aspects of the Bill did not give the "right signal that people are valuable, can be trusted and can be treated as such". I specifically questioned the amendment that empowers the Minister to compel an employee to carry on working even if he or she has tendered in their resignation. I did not hold back in my speech.

> "When employees are unhappy, they normally express it by voicing out their complaints. In most places, when they are not heard, they leave. So we say that you either voice it or if it cannot be heard, you just leave and exit. This Bill puts restrictions on both. And I ask: is it really necessary? Are we sending the right signal? Is our existing law not adequate to handle differences that may arise between an Agency, or for that matter, any

> *employer, and its employees? Someone who wants to leave and he is asked to carry on is an unhappy worker which will not contribute to the morale and general work environment of the workplace. So why is he leaving? And if there was a union, he could articulate his concerns and aspirations of workers which can be addressed early, wisely and reduce the chance of a trade dispute arising."*

I further questioned the amendment in the Bill that looked to prohibit employees from going on strike or taking industrial action, that to my mind ran counter to our existing legislations including the Criminal Law (Temporary Provisions) Act, the Trade Disputes Act, the Trade Unions Act as well as the Industrial Relations Act.

> *"...The Industrial Relations Act in Singapore therefore has comprehensive provisions for collective bargaining, conciliation and arbitration of trade disputes. These provisions have given us industrial peace with justice. It has served us well. Why does the Agency not want to use the existing laws instead of imposing new and seemingly unnecessary restrictions on trade unions and workers?"*

Finally, I felt that I needed to speak up for workers and whether we were giving the right signals.

> *"The Singapore worker is widely broadcast as the number one workforce in the world and the Singapore trade union movement as a responsible one that is not afraid to put national interests before that of sectoral interest. Our legal system governing*

employment is ranked high by investors. We have a track record to show our responsibility as a movement and its workforce. Only last year, Singapore workers accepted a wage cut without any social unrest. I ask: in these provisions of the Bill, is the Government giving a different signal in its trust and faith in the Singapore workers and the Singapore unions? Is there enough confidence in our present legal system?"

PAP MP Hawazi Daipi, as an employee of NTUC, supported the Bill. *The Straits Times,* in the column *From the Gallery*, stated that my speech was the most substantive of the day but did not cover a single word on the speech anywhere in the paper. NTUC, in their newsletter, published both my speech and that of Hawazi's in full.

Protecting Workers

Coming from a trade union background, most of my questions were related to workers and their families.

Given the changing employment trends, I asked for the Trade Unions Act (22 February 2000) to be amended to make it easier for unions to represent, including workers who are not classified as employees. I urged that we must take proactive steps to enable the trade union movement to bring these workers of "atypical employment" situations (e.g., part-time work, short-term and casual employment, agency work, self-employment, work-from-home, contract work and unemployment), within our existing industrial relations system to reduce social tensions and enhance social cohesion. It is good to see that two decades later, these issues are being addressed in giving self-employed and gig workers greater protection.

For the amendments to the Companies Act (13 November 2000), I spoke on the inadequate protection for workers regarding judicial management which was silent over monies owed to workers.

I had also raised questions on the protection and welfare of temporary, casual and contract workers (9 May 2000), the non-contribution of Central Provident Fund (CPF) for some workers, and portable medical benefits for workers.

Speaking up for Civil Servants

The concerns of my public sector union friends motivated me to raise questions regarding civil servants. Among them, I urged the government to classify all civil servants as "employees" under the Industrial Relations Act (12 March 2001) to give them access to better representation by trade unions.

Representation was also made to adjust pensioners' allowances, as salaries were low when they retired and the amount was not reflective of living costs many years after retirement.

Foreign Workers

I also touched on foreign workers during the Budget sessions and in questions to the Minister. I questioned about agents and high recruitment fees, the indebtedness of these workers, living conditions, passport retention by employers and non-payment of wages by unscrupulous employers who cancel work permits and force them to leave the country against their will. The Ministry of Manpower had been supportive and also explained how they were working to improve the system. Questions on treatment of domestic foreign workers were also raised.

I voiced my concerns about local workers being replaced by foreign workers and the suppression of wages by cheap foreign labour.

Fair Trading Act

During my term, I was involved in making representations on the introduction of the Goods and Services Tax (GST) given that I had been Vice-President/President of CASE from 1989 to 1992. In 1993 I appeared before the Select Committee and asked for more consumer protection legislation as the existing legislation was inadequate. I pushed for stronger protection for consumers and a Fair Trading Act during Budget debates. The Act was introduced in Singapore in 2004.

Final Words

Labour NMPs face a greater challenge when it comes to expressing workers' views without echoing the ruling party or sounding like the Opposition. Overall, as part of NTUC, they are part of the ruling establishment and are in agreement with many current policies. Yet from a grassroot unionist's point of view, every matter is not perfectly aligned. There will be areas to change or improve on. Eventually, Labour NMPs can only contribute to better policy making with additional inputs and alternate views on issues. Parliament has to reflect the diversity of views of Singaporeans while enabling the party with the mandate of the people to implement the manifesto that citizens voted for.

I wish I had more resources and time to prepare and participate in the legislative process. NMPs had no legislative support then, and still do not. But I thank the staff of Parliament for their support, the librarians were amazing at getting information for me.

The experience of being an NMP was a highlight of my life. I learnt many things, especially on how the legislature works. However, the discussions and debates in the Members' Room were more interesting and heated at times than in the Chamber! I enjoyed the comradeship of MPs from all sides. Regardless of party positions, I could see that they worked hard for their constituents and Singaporeans.

Editor's Cut: A Q&A with Thomas Thomas
(This interview has been edited and condensed for length and clarity.)

What is your most memorable moment from your time in Parliament?
There was no eureka moment that stands out. Most of it was actually quite routine!

I guess things in the Members' Room could be quite interesting. Before sessions started, we might meet and have lunch, and those moments were quite awakening. Sometimes that's where the real debates happen. One of the things you realise is that people might sing the same song but not always to the same tune. You could see people were not guarded — that's where you see PAP MPs speaking their minds, maybe even sounding more opposition than the Opposition! They didn't treat me as an outsider, maybe because of my NTUC background, but there was quite a lot of free discussion.

One of the things which did surprise me was how the Opposition members then — Low Thia Khiang, Chiam See Tong and J. B. Jeyaretnam [who was there for a while during my term] — did put up good points, but I don't think their views were always fairly represented by the media.

I am also grateful to a few experienced MPs who advised me and gave feedback on my speeches, questions and views. I was touched by them wanting to help an NMP better understand the workings of Parliament.

How did being an NMP change you as a person and/or the work you do?
It didn't really change anything, except that I got more experience, exposure and got to know more people. Being an NMP was just like additional work to my other union roles, so when I finished, it was just back to life as usual.

I just hope the views I expressed were considered by policy makers. That would have been an achievement.

Based on your time in Parliament, what words of advice would you give future NMPs?
Don't expect to change the world. To be very blunt, I don't think NMPs have clout. If the party in power has a supermajority, they will be able to carry out their agenda. But the key part is that if you do put in your views, I think some of the Ministers do listen and might take your feedback into account even if they don't accept everything.

I think it's important to be able to give alternative views and suggestions, otherwise Singapore will just have groupthink. It's not fair to our citizens if everyone only thinks along one line.

How would you sum up your time as an NMP in one sentence?
It was an experience getting to be a part of legislating, and to see and meet other MPs and policy makers, at close range. It takes some time to understand and get into the rhythm of Parliament. The faster we learn, the better we can contribute.

There is so much hearsay that goes round. You get impressions of people from a distance, based on what you've read about them or been told about them, but it may not be reflective of who they are.

I found a lot of people to be very dedicated and competent. Of course, people come from all sorts of different backgrounds and see things quite differently from a grassroots unionist like me. There are some people who follow the script and assume you have nothing new to add to their knowledge, but there are also those who will try to understand your point of view and ask you questions which make you think, even if they disagree with you. That's when you know they are trying to make good policies.

A Baptism of Fire

Viswa Sadasivan
Nominated Member of Parliament (2009–2011)

> *Editor's Note: Viswa Sadasivan holds the distinct honour of compelling then-Minister Mentor Lee Kuan Yew to "bring this House back to earth" in one of his last speeches in Parliament. Mr Lee's rare intervention in 2009 was in response to Viswa's maiden speech and Motion to affirm the tenets in the National Pledge when debating government policies and his question on whether it was time for Singapore to move beyond race and treat everyone as an equal. Viswa tells his side of the story in this essay, offering his observations and learnings on what happened with this debate, and beyond.*

"...the basis on which the Nominated Member has placed his arguments is false and flawed. I thought to myself, perhaps I should bring this House back to earth...I think it is dangerous to allow such highfalutin ideas to go undemolished...."

I felt my stomach churn as I watched Minister Mentor (MM) Lee Kuan Yew saying this in reference to my speech. He had not spoken in Parliament for more than two years. His words were sharp and unmitigated. I had to remain composed and focus on the substance. It was a test of my conviction and motivation as a Nominated Member of Parliament (NMP). You could say it was a baptism of fire.

It was my maiden speech in Parliament on Tuesday 18 August 2009. I was barely a month old as an NMP. I spoke for an hour on a Substantive Motion which read: "That this House reaffirms its commitment to the nation building tenets as enshrined in the National Pledge when debating national policies, especially economic policies".

Inviting Debates as an NMP

I was 49 years old when I became an NMP. I had spent all my adult life engaging on issues and policies and helping to open up space for meaningful discourse between the government and the public. This I did as a broadcaster and as a leader in the government's Feedback Unit in the 1980s and 1990s, hosting forums and dialogue sessions. These experiences deepened my understanding of ground sentiments as well as policy considerations and dilemmas. For discourse to be meaningful we need honesty, knowledge, sensitivity and, most importantly, trust.

When I was sworn in as an NMP in July 2009, I had already decided that I would not seek a second term. This would allow me to speak without inhibition on issues that would have a big impact on Singaporeans and Singapore. My interests and expertise lay in socio-political issues, national security and education.

I soon realised that there were only three ways an MP can speak in Parliament. The first is by raising questions for oral or written answers from the government. As there is a one-and-a-half-hour guillotine time for this, there is not much scope for deep engagement on issues here. The second is by speaking on bills. This means that one comments on someone else's, usually the government's, agenda.

The only way you can engage deeply on an issue of your choice is by tabling a motion. I realised that motions were rare in the Singapore

Parliament. The reason for this, I believe, is that you would need to make a substantive speech and be prepared for a robust debate on it.

If you are an NMP or an Opposition MP, you will most likely face a many-to-one debate with an avalanche of rebuttals from several back and front bench MPs over a two-day period. This can be highly intimidating and daunting, especially if you aren't adept at public speaking.

My experience as a broadcaster/TV anchor, a debater and a discussion moderator helped with confidence. I knew that my age, experience and knowledge would be a bonus. After careful consideration, I decided at the outset that I would table three motions during my two-and-a-half-year term as NMP.

Why the National Pledge

I chose to talk about our National Pledge in my maiden speech. Right from the days when I used to recite the Pledge in school, the words resonated with me. It bothered me that we would merely rattle off the words during the morning assembly; it was a mindless, pointless routine. Yet, to be honest, and sadly, it did not bother me enough to do something about it.

In 1989, I did an on-camera interview with the late S. Rajaratnam, Singapore's first Foreign Minister. It was an epiphanic moment. The interview was for a documentary I was producing, titled *The Ninth of August*, to trace the circumstances that led to Singapore's separation from Malaysia. Towards the end, Mr Rajaratnam became quite emotional as he shared how he came to draft the Pledge. He talked about his deep belief in a "Singaporean Singapore" not divided by race, language, religion or socio-economic class. I asked him if that wasn't too utopian. He disagreed, stressing that this is what exceptionalism means — committing to an ideal even though it appears unattainable.

I came away from the meeting inspired, but with a heavy heart. I understood why S. Rajaratnam was a giant of a man. I could also see why he was disheartened. To him, years of an almost absolute emphasis on economic growth and pragmatism had placed nationalistic ideals on the backburner. What he said about exceptionalism made me feel guilty. It is the Pledge, not the Constitution, that defines us as one people. Yet we pay so little attention to its carefully chosen words.

In July 2009, I decided that my maiden speech as an NMP would have to be on the National Pledge. I explained the reason in my speech:

> "I was invited by BG Tan Chuan-Jin, Chairman of NDP Ex-Co 2009, to write a piece on what the national pledge means to me…it defines who we are; what we aspire to remain regardless of the realities of a fast-changing world; it is about what we stand for — our credo…We need to commit to ensuring that every time each one of us recites the national pledge, we say it with commitment. For this, we must ensure all citizens understand it beyond the words. Most importantly, we in Parliament must lead the way by demonstrating that no national policy or Bill will be passed if it goes contrary to the letter or spirit of the pledge."

There was another reason why I chose to speak on the Pledge: It provided an effective platform to discuss a broad range of policies. I de-constructed the Pledge. The speech covered the value of being "citizen(s) of Singapore", policies and initiatives that go against the "regardless of race, language or religion" tenet, what it means to be a "democratic society based on justice and equality", and what the pursuit of "happiness, progress and prosperity" entails.

♦ The Nominated Member of Parliament Scheme

A significant part of the speech was devoted to economic policies and their strong correlation with social cohesion considerations. It was probably the first time Singapore's high Gini coefficient was highlighted in Parliament:

> "According to figures from CIA World Factbook, Singapore ranks as one of the highest in the world in terms of income inequality...Based on 2008 figures, Singapore has a Gini coefficient of 48.10 — which is much higher than other countries in Asia including China, Malaysia, and the Philippines. In fact, it would appear that Singapore is closer to many underdeveloped countries in the Gini Index...If indeed happiness and quality of life are higher order goals and economic growth and jobs are a means to achieving those goals, then we should ask ourselves if we need to rethink how we are managing things...."

The speech dealt with issues I intended to raise during my term in Parliament. The maiden speech was a curtain-raiser of sorts.

I was also determined that my first motion would be passed. I was confident that a motion highlighting the importance of the Pledge would not be dismissed. All the more if the speech was debated in August when the euphoria of National Day celebrations was still in the air. It had to be an August speech.

The Baptism of Fire

After a few iterations, the Speaker of the House cleared the wording of the Motion. The day I was waiting for, 18 August 2009, came sooner than I was ready. It was a packed chamber and the mood was sombre. It dawned on me reading the words of my motion in the

Order Paper that this was it. At 4:30pm, the Speaker called out my name. I proceeded to deliver my maiden speech for a whole hour, uninterrupted.

I ended the speech with a call for greater faith in our people:

> "...we are at a point of inflexion — an opportunity to change; to reverse some trends and attitudes that are detrimental to our progress, indeed our survivability, as a nation...We need faith. Faith in our people's capacity for good judgement. Faith that Singaporeans will not abuse what is given to them, the privileges, the choices...I say to the Government and to this House, let us take a chance on our people, on ourselves. Let us act on the firm belief that our national pledge will serve as a bright shining light that keeps us on track. We have reason to believe that we will succeed if we are faithful to the pledge that was crafted 44 years ago with passion, conviction and foresight by our founding leaders in their infinite wisdom."

There was a deafening silence the moment I ended my speech. I could not fathom it.

Then a barrage of rebuttals rained upon me. Seventeen MPs including Ministers rose to speak, one after another, in response to my speech. With the exception of two MPs, all were critical. I found it interesting that they all had copies of the text of my speech in advance, but I did not have any of theirs in spite of asking for them. I had to listen intently with the hope that I heard it right and my hastily scribbled notes were legible!

What took me by surprise and was disconcerting was that the PAP MP who seconded my motion spoke against key aspects of my speech.

♦ The Nominated Member of Parliament Scheme

Michael Palmer, a decent man and a good MP, had an enlightening conversation with the party Whip:

> *"I feel I must express my disagreement with three issues that he (Viswa) has raised. First, he has raised the accountability of the Government to the people. As an elected Member of this House, we are always accountable to the people on the ground… Second, I do not agree that there is a climate of fear among our people. In fact, my experience on the ground has shown the opposite…Third, I cannot agree that this Government does not listen in response to the concerns of the people. In my view, the opposite is true…."*

Somewhere during the delivery of my speech, MM Lee Kuan Yew came into the Chamber. He did not look pleased. Parliament adjourned at 6:15pm. I was parched. As I was drinking a tall glass of water in the Members' Room, I heard MM Lee's booming voice at a distance. I could not quite make out what he was saying. It was evident he was upset with my speech and possibly with me.

The following day, Wednesday 19 August 2009, the debate on my motion resumed at 3:00pm. The House was full.

My good friend PAP MP Zainudin Nordin was the first to speak. He proposed an amendment to my motion. As this was being debated, MM Lee walked into the Chamber looking deeply upset. His hair was visibly dishevelled. As the MP was speaking, there was a flurry of activity around where MM Lee was seated. Leader of the House, Wong Kan Seng, Deputy Leader of the House, Mah Bow Tan and PAP Party Whip, Lim Swee Say were getting instructions from MM Lee. House Speaker Abdullah

Tarmugi was looking on, somewhat befuddled. He called for a 30-minute recess. As I walked into the Members' Room, I sensed tension in the air.

Back in the Chamber, at 4:25pm, MM Lee rose to propose an amendment to the amendments proposed earlier by Zainudin Nordin. MM Lee said that the Pledge was "an aspiration":

> "Mr Rajaratnam had great virtues in the midst of despondency after a series of race riots when we were thrown out during Independence. And our Malays in Singapore were apprehensive that now that we were the majority, we would in turn treat them the way a Malay majority treated us. He drafted these words and rose above the present. He was a great idealist. It came to me; I trimmed out the unachievable and the Pledge, as it stands, is his work after I have trimmed it. What is it, an ideology? No, it is an aspiration. Will we achieve it? I do not know. We will have to keep on trying. Are we a nation? In transition."

The final amended Motion read: "That this House acknowledges the progress that Singapore has made in the 50 years since it attained self-government in 1959, in nation building and achieving the aspirations and tenets as enshrined in the National Pledge, and reaffirms its commitment towards achieving the goals and ideals of our Pledge when debating national policies."

I voted in support of the amendment as it did not contradict my original motion. I did acknowledge, categorically, the progress we made and attributed this to the government.

At 6:30pm, right after the amendment was passed, Deputy Speaker Matthias Yao called out my name to conclude the two-day debate by responding to the various speeches. There was no preparation time. All

I had were hand-scribbled notes. I stood my ground on the points raised by MM Lee without being disrespectful:

> "While Minister Mentor Lee highlights the realities that we have to be cognisant of, I am sure he would agree with me that the day we stop believing in the aspirations and working towards them, is the day we cease to make real progress…It was precisely this commitment to the aspirations of equality that drove our government to ensure that ethnic minority groups and their needs would be given special attention. It may sound paradoxical but moves like affirmative action are indeed motivated to attain the aspirations of equality…I am deeply concerned about the level of rootedness and the latent threats to harmony…For this, we need an emotional anchor or a collective reflex for which I am confident our national pledge would serve as a reference point."

The debate made headlines in the mainstream media. The coverage was more than what I would have liked. I had interview requests from several international media agencies, all of which I declined, as I felt this should remain a domestic discourse. In the online space it remained the most debated issue for a decade. I felt I achieved what I wanted.

The Pledge has come to take its rightful place in our consciousness. This made the experience in Parliament worth it. The debate had an uncanny prescience.

Lessons from the Chamber

The two-day debate in Parliament taught me, firstly, the importance of being bold and rigorous when choosing what issues to raise and preparing for the debate. There is a certain power in speaking on larger issues that may not be top-of-mind with the people but are matters of high consequence.

Secondly, I realised that what kept me going and gave me much-needed confidence was the awareness that my motivation was right, and I had a clean conscience.

Thirdly, it is so important that we do not go in seeking a fight or battling it out. This trips you up and is likely to make it self-fulfilling. Let us assume the best of people, even those whom you think are adversaries, and strive to persuade. Our propositions need to be more "yes-able", and in tone, more aligned. Intellectual rigour, moral conviction and humility need not be at cross-purposes.

These lessons provided clarity of purpose as they boosted my confidence. They provided the impetus for me to speak on two more motions as an NMP.

On 19 July 2010 I spoke on an Adjournment Motion that read, "Looking beyond GDP as a measurement of a country's well-being." Then on 24 November 2010, I spoke on a Substantive Motion urging a comprehensive review of pre-school education in Singapore, highlighting serious faults in the system. I talked about the critical importance of early intervention in ensuring that education continues to remain a social leveller and does not end up exacerbating inequality.

Till today, I have friends and acquaintances telling me that I was unfairly treated in Parliament when and because I raised issues of consequence. My honest response is that ruling party MPs can afford to be less combative and vitriolic when debating arguments presented by Opposition members or NMPs. However, I choose to see this as par for the course. It was the right of the PAP MPs and of MM Lee to rebut

♦ The Nominated Member of Parliament Scheme

the points I raised, and robustly. I was not denied my right to the final word in the debate. It is democracy at play, and it is work in progress.

The last time I met MM Lee Kuan Yew was in Parliament House on 16 September 2010. MPs were celebrating his birthday. I wished him accordingly. After a brief pause, as an aside, he asked, "Still giving trouble?"

Reciprocating the spirit of the question, I said, "I try my best, MM."

With a half-smile he said, after another brief pause, "It's more important to be respected than liked". This is the last thing I heard from MM Lee in person.

I understood the significance of the baptism of fire.

Editor's Cut: A Q&A with Viswa Sadasivan
(This interview has been edited and condensed for length and clarity.)

What is your most memorable moment from your time in Parliament?
I wouldn't call it memorable, because memorable sounds like something you look back on with a smile, but the most unforgettable experience was really the confrontation with MM Lee regarding my maiden speech. I did expect pushback, but I didn't expect that he would be livid. Nobody had expected him to be present, let alone speak. And then the day after my speech, the newspaper had his photograph and mine next to it.

That sent a shiver down my spine, because it's really not the kind of publicity you want. It felt different from the times I'd gotten my knuckles rapped earlier in my career. I was almost 50 by then, so I couldn't claim that I was "blur" or ignorant or anything like that. I also had some measure of public profile or following by that time and if any of your motivations get called into question, the repercussions can be very, very serious. It's not a game for sure. I had some friends, senior people in government, who told me very seriously afterwards that I should consider migrating because I was finished here.

So I wouldn't call it memorable, but it wasn't totally negative either. What I learnt from that episode was that if you believe in something and you want to stand for it with a clear conscience, just do it. We must also know when to let it go.

How did being an NMP change you as a person and/or the work you do?
The episode happened less than a month into my term as an NMP. It made me realise that I should keep speaking up, but I needed to be selective about it. There had to be seriousness of purpose; I couldn't do

it for anything and everything. That was the first thing. Second, I realised that there are flaws in the system that inhibit healthy debate, and I told myself that I had to do whatever I can, even after leaving Parliament, to push for freer discourse from which we all can benefit.

The last thing was I realised that sometimes, the way you say or do something can be more important than what you're saying. The manner, tone, all of that matters. If you go in looking and sounding highly aggressive, your ideas won't find acceptance. And this isn't just about Singapore or Parliament; it's the nature of things. If you sound confrontational, it becomes a contest, but if you want discourse, tonality is important.

I learnt that there are some things which naturally lend themselves to being raised in the Chamber, but there are a lot more which should be discussed over coffee and biscuits in the tea room. The topics you bring up in speeches are the ones you want Singaporeans in general to think about, to create awareness of, but when there were specific issues I wanted to find solutions to, I would do it in the Members' Room. Decision-makers can be a lot more receptive when you're talking to them in private. If you want specific, practical solutions, take it offline.

Based on your time in Parliament, what advice would you give future NMPs?
Whatever you do as an MP or NMP, you've got to do for the larger good and not use the stage that's given to you for personal gain. That's the main thing.

Second, if you want to bring about change, you've got to come up with propositions that are usable. You need to speak from your heart and with conviction, but you don't necessarily want to be confrontational.

That gives you time in the limelight, but it may not give you the outcome that you want.

It's not the same as mincing your words — it's about finding a way to put across something that would otherwise be unpalatable. Being able to present sophisticated, complex ideas in a balanced yet honest manner is an art, and once you've acquired that skill, you need to use it. In negotiation parlance this is a "yes-able proposition".

How would you sum up your time as an NMP in one sentence?
It has renewed my faith in the system and made me even more determined to speak up till the end.

When I made my speech, the outcome could have been a lot worse for me. The government wasn't pleased, sure, but I didn't face the kind of repercussions that many of my friends thought I would face. I didn't get called up by the Committee of Privileges or get sidelined and have my business contracts cancelled. MM Lee had just as much right as I did to stand up and speak his mind. That's democracy. But of course, I think the system is quite far from perfect, which is why I'm determined to keep going.

NMP as Advocate, or Advocate as NMP?

K. Thanaletchimi
Nominated Member of Parliament (2016–2018)

> *Editor's Note: I met K. Thanaletchimi when I was still an NMP as she and I were asked to be part of this video series of NMP interviews by the Parliament Secretariat. Thana, as she prefers to be called, was enthusiastic about my idea to initiate an NMP alumni group and immediately offered to help. I invited Thana to be part of this book so she can share about her journey as a worker's advocate and NMP in the most personal manner for advocates and activists from all walks of life to be inspired that the NMP platform is unmistakably an advocate's platform.*

The Nominated Member of Parliament (NMP) scheme was introduced in 1990 for the appointment of non-elected parliamentarians to provide alternate, non-partisan views and advocate on cause-based matters that represent the views of various civic groups in society.

I was in my early 20s when the scheme was first introduced. As a Young Activist with Young NTUC (National Trades Union Congress), I was given lots of opportunities to speak up and be heard as an advocate for workers and their well-being.

But never would I have imagined that I would one day be given the prestigious NMP platform in Parliament to do exactly what I have been doing since I joined the Union movement at a tender age.

How It Began

My passion to speak up for underprivileged and lower-wage workers has to do with my humble beginnings.

My parents barely made ends meet. They struggled immensely to raise their three children, with me being the youngest. Life was never easy. I gave tuition classes to supplement my parents' income when I could. I had so many questions about wage parity, recognition of hard work and the caregiving needs of workers for their families. I pondered how the rage of poverty can overwhelm one's passion and dreams and lead them into a downward spiral of hardship and grief. Will we be able to redeem ourselves, will we be able to break away from this rage? So many questions crowded my young mind. I was resolved to find a path that would give me an opportunity to surface the ordeals of workers and their families.

I became President of the house union of a restructured hospital in my early 30s. This led me to leadership positions in the Healthcare Services Employees' Union (HSEU) and subsequently in NTUC.

When I was first approached by a senior leader in NTUC who informed me that I had been nominated for the role of NMP representing NTUC, I was truly perplexed and hesitant.

My initial response was "Not me!", then "Why me?" before asking myself, "Why not me?". I experienced trepidation and uncertainty, but I was ready to take on this journey because the fire of passion in me was flaring. Workers are, and will always be, the centre of all things I do in the Union, so yes, why not me?

Family as My Pillar of Strength

However, I still needed more time to consider the nomination given my commitments, including family. I wanted the blessings of my elderly parents who needed my presence and support at home. I did not want to give them any less attention; my family means the world to me.

I also needed my siblings' support, especially my sister who has been a pillar of strength to the family. She provided much support to my parents when I was preoccupied with serving my union members, representing workers and indulging in community work.

My parents raised me well despite such adversity; my sister has been my backbone and my late nanny always taught me to be helpful to others at all times. I was at peace when I had assurance and support from my loved ones.

I knew that I was given this opportunity to represent my constituents (workers) to the best of my ability. I knew that activism comes from the wholehearted devotion to serve others rather than self, to be worthy of servant leadership. I also felt some degree of calm and certainty as I had the support of the rest of the Labour MPs.

So I said yes to the NMP nomination.

The NMP Application Process

My parliamentary journey began in 2016 with preparing a write-up on what I wished to speak about in Parliament, if appointed, for the formal application. In my view, an NMP should be someone who is passionate in serving others and true to his or her purpose and beliefs; someone who can feel the heartbeat and pulse of those who are being served, especially on issues that matter to society and Singapore's future.

I have been working on advancing the interests of working people from all ranks on the issues that matter most, including jobs and the cost of living. I have a special interest in two areas: women and healthcare affordability.

With more than 20 years of union experience, I have gained deep insights into the issues that trouble ordinary working people, including employment rights and workers' dignity as well as adequate opportunities to enhance one's skills, relevant to the needs of industry sectors. As a full-time employee myself, I am constantly learning through my regular engagements with workers, including issues facing women at work. It is also clear to me that different generations of the workforce have different expectations and aspirations.

I set out to raise the following issues:

- Making every employer a family-friendly employer.
- Doing more for the female workforce, especially to support procreation, employability and employment so that all three can coexist harmoniously.
- Providing better support for single mothers, especially for those in employment, and ensuring access to social support groups in every workplace. I am a firm believer that an emotionally stable worker is a creative and productive worker in all aspects.
- Leveraging on SkillsFuture to better equip working women as well as those who wish to enter the workforce.

My hope was to help improve the labour participation rate for women significantly.

♦ The Nominated Member of Parliament Scheme

I also championed issues for the healthcare industry, which is close to my heart, including:

- Attracting and incentivising more Singaporeans to work in the healthcare sector, with special efforts to attract locals to the Intermediate and Long-Term Care Sector (ILTC). This will enable a gradual reduction in the reliance of foreign healthcare workers and raise the standards of care delivery with technology being an enabler;
- Constantly innovating and redesigning jobs to equip healthcare workers with better skills and better career opportunities for all levels of workers, whilst leveraging the latest technology to support continuous employment for all ages; and
- Sustainable and affordable healthcare for all Singaporeans, now and in the future.

These concerns were highlighted repeatedly by workers during my engagements with different cohorts and still remain. Creating a conducive environment for workers to be productive, cultivating the desire and hunger for lifelong learning within each worker and changing the mindset of employers and workers are all works in progress in this highly competitive environment.

I was determined to leverage the deep and regular engagements that I have with workers to add value to parliamentary debates, calibrate policy thinking from a non-partisan perspective and contribute in some way to shaping the policies that affect the heartbeat of working people, all for the good of the nation and Singapore's future.

The Path to Parliament House

On 19 February 2016, NTUC submitted my nomination as a veteran union leader to the Special Select Committee of Parliament as the Labour NMP-designate. Less than a month later, at 10:10am on 9 March, I was seated in front of the Special Select Committee at the Select Committee Room in Parliament House for the selection interview.

I did not do much preparation because I wanted to be true to myself and to the panel that I was sincere in my cause and determined in my advocacy for the workers. I spoke from my heart in answering various questions that were posed to me without hesitation or stammering, because I had more than 25 years of exposure and experience as a veteran unionist.

I still remember vividly my excitement being on the grounds of Parliament House for the first time in my life. I was proud to be a Singaporean, and felt such a strong sense of civic duty and societal activism. I still do.

On 17 March 2016, I received a letter informing me that the Special Select Committee of Parliament had recommended me to the President for appointment as an NMP. Yes, I was successful in my application, one with a strong backing from NTUC!

On 22 March 2016, President Tony Tan presented me with an Instrument of Appointment at the Istana. The Speaker of Parliament was also present to witness the ceremony.

I was humbled by the appointment as I felt the real work that I had wanted very much to do had just started. My aged parents were there at the Istana for the first time in their lives. I could see the pride and

♦ The Nominated Member of Parliament Scheme

joy illuminating from their eyes, even though they shared little about their feelings. I vividly remember my father, who suffers from Parkinson's disease, pushing himself to walk up the stairs in his zeal to be there for his daughter and to witness every memorable moment in the Istana.

Immediately after the ceremony, the NMPs proceeded to Parliament House for a short lunch hosted by then-Speaker Halimah Yacob, now the President of Singapore. With her were Deputy Speakers Charles Chong and Lim Biow Chuan, Leader of the House Minister Grace Fu and Government Whip Minister Chan Chun Sing.

Thereafter, the friendly Parliament staff talked us through the rules and regulations that a parliamentarian should know and must always practise. There was such an information overload; the orientation stretched till sundown and I was more than exhausted!

The feeling of insecurity set in for me soon enough, for I was not sure of the process and yet had to prepare my maiden speech for the upcoming Budget Debate. The saving grace was the reassuring Parliament staff and my fellow NMPs who were also in the same struggle of trying to comprehend the dos and don'ts at that time. I was delighted to learn then that a handful of NMPs had been re-appointed for a second term, so there was this unspoken support that they were ready to give to us. We immediately set up a WhatsApp group to help each other navigate this parliamentary journey together that lasted almost three years.

The Maiden Speech

The parliamentary staff were extremely helpful in guiding us NMPs as we prepared for the Budget Debate. We received the Budget 2016 Guide to Budget Proceedings and other reference materials which were very useful as I began to prepare for my maiden speech.

I decided to focus on workers, as the Budget called upon the partnership of all Singaporeans to work together in new ways to transform our economy and build a caring and resilient society. I spoke about the vulnerable workforce, workers in transition, inculcating the culture of lifelong learning, small and medium-sized enterprises (SMEs) building the Singaporean core and the plight of middle-income earners. I highlighted these issues and concerns as well as recommendations with questions that needed to be addressed as whole of the government and society.

The vulnerable workforce included lower-wage workers, women workers and mid-career individuals who took on new jobs and needed more help. Retirement adequacy continued to be a challenge for lower-wage workers, and more so for women. Statistically speaking, women are expected to live longer than men; this means more retirement savings are needed so that we can age gracefully with peace of mind, with dignity and vitality.

Many older women in Singapore have not worked in the formal economy or have suffered from a gender wage gap in their earlier working years. For this group, the Silver Support Scheme served as a good supplement to their retirement income in addition to the existing support schemes such as MediShield Life and the Pioneer Generation Package.

It is important that women are given fair opportunities at the workplace, while continuing to care for their families at home. The family unit is the basic building block of a thriving nation. Our families give us support and keep us grounded, and women continue to play a larger role in families. However, striking a balance is not easy and more needs to be done for women workers to ensure equal opportunities in placement and career progression. Women should be given stronger support so as to be able to pursue different definitions of success. Women should not be fearful of "sacrificing their careers" for their family if they are given the right to request for flexible work arrangements or given equal opportunities when they are back to work.

Once I got over the initial challenges with the maiden speech, I got into a good flow with subsequent speeches. I spoke on matters pertaining to the Ministry of Health (MOH), the Ministry of Manpower (MOM) and the Ministry of Social and Family Development (MSF) for time allotted during the Committee of Supply sessions.

NMPs can raise Parliamentary Questions (PQs) for oral or written replies. I had the opportunity to ask several Ministers questions and raised follow-up supplementary questions for clarifications. I also had the honour and power of voting in the House on bills and other matters, including the constitutional amendment on the Reserved Elected Presidency. The parliamentary debate on this Constitution Amendment Bill was such an eye-opener for me!

No Regrets Doing My Best

It was a roller-coaster ride juggling family, work and union responsibilities as well as my parliamentary role. However, I do not regret my NMP experience. My philosophy in life is to devote myself to the fullest in whatever I undertake so as to attain fulfilment and a sense of satisfaction at the end of the journey. My passion in being the voice of the workers, championing their plight, challenging norms and actively engaging in debates has made my advocacy as an NMP even more meaningful.

Prior to becoming one, I had always thought that an NMP's role was not significant. But nothing beats hands-on exposure to better appreciate the importance of non-partisan views, perspectives and contributions.

Sceptics of the NMP scheme may have differing views on this but I stand firm that non-partisan, subject-matter experts, especially people who are driven by passion without expecting anything in return, need to be applauded for volunteering their time and effort in advocating for causes that they strongly believe in. One can live, breathe and even die for their passion.

I have much admiration and appreciation for the many NMPs before me. I had always felt it would be useful if we could put together the collective wisdom of these NMPs, their experiences, their fears, their courage and their feelings for future NMPs to use as a "guide", so I hope my essay in this book goes some way in doing that.

The perspective of an NMP as an advocate or an advocate as an NMP is like looking at a glass and asking whether it is half-filled or half empty; the answer lies in the eyes of the beholder.

It was an extraordinary journey, a memorable experience, a treasured exposure and a legacy that, I hope, survives the test of time.

Editor's Cut: A Q&A with K. Thanaletchimi

(This interview has been edited and condensed for length and clarity.)

What is your most memorable moment from your time in Parliament?
There was the time when Parliament had to vote on a bill regarding the Elected Presidency. I remember thinking to myself then that there was a moment of tension in the air when debating and voting, you know? The whole debate was exciting.

Also, one of the things I enjoyed most was filing and asking PQs. I was able to file PQs and get responses from the various ministries, which I thought was good because I got answers directly from the Ministers or ministry-appointed people. If there was a need for any clarification, I could even ask supplementary questions because sometimes the original questions led to many other questions. I got replies right away, and if certain things were not done, I think the various ministries would look at it and see how they could enhance certain processes or act on suggestions, so that was good.

How did being an NMP change you as a person and/or the work you do?
I believe my attitude towards policy making and the way our policies are refined, and my impression of how certain things can or cannot be done, has changed.

When we're not in the scene, we tend to grumble and say oh, why can't this be done, this is so silly and all that. But when you're in action as part of the policymaking body, you come to understand the process better. You understand the constraints better. And you know the challenges of winning the hearts of the majority and the people [I say majority because there will always be pockets of people who won't be happy with you].

I think my character hasn't changed as a result of my NMP experience, but the two-and-a-half years certainly made me more mature in my understanding of policy making.

Based on your time in Parliament, what words of advice would you give future NMPs?
I would say to always have a learning mindset. You know, no one is perfect. Even though you might already have a certain reputation outside of Parliament, you're always learning each day in the House. I think it's important to always try to understand others' perspectives and not just try to get others to understand yours. If you're stuck in your own mind and just think that what you believe has to be believed by others, then the parliamentary process will be an uphill task for you.

I guess one last message would be that when you're in Parliament, you're debating on issues. No one should take it personally, okay? But when you're outside Parliament, everyone is your friend. I made a lot of friends during the two-and-a-half-years in Parliament, and I never regretted letting those friendships bloom. It's important that you separate issues from your personal relationships. If you do that, everyone is a friend. Even Opposition MPs and PAP [People's Action Party] MPs are friends. So build friendships, don't burn bridges and address issues as they are.

How would you sum up your time as an NMP in one sentence?
It was an exciting journey and an inspiring experience.

Speaking Personally, Clearly and Kindly

Kuik Shiao-Yin
Nominated Member of Parliament (2014–2018)

> *Editor's Note: I reached out to Shiao-Yin after I was appointed; we met for coffee at the basement of The Adelphi the morning of my first sitting in Parliament! Her speeches struck a chord with many, including her earnest and compelling final speech urging parliamentarians to speak plainly to engage with the public, especially the youth. In this essay, Shiao-Yin shares personally and kindly about her doubts and challenges as an NMP and takes us through a journey of authenticity and courage as she renews her call for NMPs of the future to speak our truths in love.*

Stories and Politics

In 2014, when I was asked to consider being a Nominated Member of Parliament (NMP), my first response was "No."

I was 37 years old, just emerging from my turbulent 20s and entering the messy middle stage of life. I was honestly struggling with what it meant to be a better leader, personally and professionally. So there were multiple stories I told myself that caused me to question whether someone like me actually had a place in Parliament:

I am not a lawyer. I am not an economist. I am not a civil servant. I am not an academic. I am not expert enough. I am not political enough.

The stories we tell ourselves are powerful because we do not think of them as stories, we live them out as facts. And the most powerful stories that shape our reality are the ones that begin with "I Am/I Am Not".

To help me reconsider my "No", I cold-called a few former NMPs for advice. It was one former NMP in particular who had a huge influence on my eventual choice to step into Parliament.

In her conversation with me, she drew a circle in the air to symbolise how there must be a communication loop connecting the people working at the top, to the ones working the middle and then, the ones on the ground. She shared that sometimes communication breaks down and the circle becomes incomplete. She believed that NMPs are well-placed to step into that gap to bridge the necessary parliamentary conversations.

Her unique reframe invited me to see beyond my "I Am Not" stories that excluded me from Parliament. Her story helped me see my "I Am" stories that could be surprisingly relevant to the institution:

I am creative and a writer. I can connect the disparate dots of what is happening into lines that can be heard.

I am a teacher. I know how to simplify what appears complex and deepen what appears simple to anyone curious to learn.

I am a struggling, imperfect leader. I know how complex, lonely and unknowable that journey is. I can empathise with any

> leaders in the House and beyond, facing those challenges. I can acknowledge how difficult it is to solve wicked problems.
>
> I am a person on the ground in many forms — a mother, a wife, a person of faith, a small business owner, a voter and more. I am also a friend to different people with different identities, issues and interests. What matters to them can matter to me too. If I tell their stories on their behalf, they might know they belong in this House too.

Why are these "I Am/I Am Not" statements or identity stories important?

Our identity stories are the psychological cornerstones upon which we build our worlds and shape the worlds of others. They are also political because they can compel us to include — or exclude — ourselves from certain arenas, rooms, positions, issues and institutions where decisions are made.

Some of our excluding stories might be written by ourselves:

> I am not good enough for them.
> I am not good enough as them.
> I am not good enough.

Some of our excluding stories might be written by others — a familial, cultural or political inheritance.

Regardless of where our excluding stories came from, what matters is that we recognise these stories have political consequences. Missing voices from the decision-making table means missing conversations, missing data-points, missing observations — and thus, missed opportunities.

If not for NMPs and other parliamentarians speaking on behalf of them, certain voices might never be heard in the House: single mothers, divorcees, people with mental health struggles, the arts community, the media industry, athletes, the LGBT community, low-income households and so on.

A system becomes healthier as a whole when we bring more of our Self to the table and — in turn — bring others to the table as well. If we want a resilient political future, we need more diverse young people to engage wholeheartedly with the system. This can happen if we embody a more inviting political culture: one which sees us in our wholeness, acknowledging our adequacies (not just our inadequacies) and accepting our differences (not just our similarities).

This culture can be created over time if we learn to increasingly speak personally, clearly and lovingly about the truths of our convictions to each other.

On Speaking Personally

> *Who am I?*
> *Whose am I?*
> *Why am I here?*
> *Who doesn't get to be here?*
> *What if the persons living through those issues were actually sitting in the chamber with us?*
> *How would they want me to sound on their behalf?*
> *What if they were standing at the podium instead of me?*
> *What would they say if they could stand where I stand? How would they say it?*

In the three-and-a-half years as a parliamentarian, I learnt to begin preparing my speeches by first asking myself more deeply personal questions. These allowed me to speak more personally into issues that might have first seemed removed from me.

To me, speaking personally means the ability to put one's Self and other people's Selves — their personhood — at the core of our communications.

Often, speaking personally can be mischaracterised as showboating, oversharing, emotional manipulation or an excuse to be loose with facts. If taken to the extreme, that may be so. But if done in moderation, it provides the necessary human connection to counteract the cool detachment of pure institutional objectivity.

Speaking impersonally, even when we are representing public institutions, bores our listeners. This is not about entertainment. "Boring" is the emotion we feel when something seems irrelevant and thus, uninteresting to us.

I remember back when I was a teenage student, Parliament seemed like this far-away institution. Listening to adults speak there bored me. That is not a healthy perspective, but it was true then for me. And I think this is still true for many young people as well.

It is dangerous when a majority of young people find Parliament boring because it means they find Parliament irrelevant. They do not see yet how the passing of laws shapes their lives and the lives of others.

Thinking back on what helped me cross my own bridge in 2014 from being a politically indifferent youth to one willing to engage as a parliamentarian, it was the personal stories of others that gave me the conviction.

As an outsider, I listened to speeches by past NMPs like Janice Koh and Laurence Lien because they chose to express their personal convictions, interests and values in their public narratives rather than stick to impersonal observations and clichés. And because they chose to reveal parts of themselves in their speeches, I could better see parts of myself in an institution and issues that would otherwise seem far too removed from me; I could "identify" with the system at last.

I appreciate parliamentarians like Low Thia Khiang, Kok Heng Leun, Lee Bee Wah and Louis Ng who chose to speak personally, so that their real voices and real interests were unmistakable. I found that regardless of whether one disagreed or agreed with their perspectives, they were heard: their audiences in the Chamber and beyond actually could take in what they were saying and contend with it, mull over it or appreciate it. The issues they raised did not go unheard.

To me, whenever we have a policy debate, it is always a personal debate whether we like it or not. These are someone's personal lives, personal choices and personal sufferings we are talking about. To talk about any issue that deeply affects people in an impersonal, detached way dishonours them. This also undermines the people's ability to trust that our institutions are sincere in their care for people, not just key performance indicators (KPIs).

What are the challenges of speaking personally? Speaking personally is uncomfortable because not all will accept or appreciate it. It was clear to me that not everybody in Parliament could relate to what I personally had to say or how I personally expressed it.

When the Administration of Justice (Protections) Bill was tabled for debate in Parliament, I hesitated about whether to speak on it because I felt I did not have sufficient legal training or expert knowledge of the implications of this Bill. But there were young people who cared about it deeply — and on the other end, there were also young people who were totally indifferent and felt the former were making much ado about nothing. I wanted both views to be represented in Parliament for the sake of building public understanding. But trying to represent both ends can also provoke those who feel very strongly about one side to denigrate you as being too compromising.

♦ The Nominated Member of Parliament Scheme

Still, the call to speak personally is not about pleasing others. It is about learning to be your own person, staying true to yourself and people you represent. If it means feeling alone from time to time, then that is the necessary momentary price that must be paid for something of long-term value: a sense of true belonging, not the counterfeit of "fitting in".

An NMP may sometimes have to stand profoundly and uncomfortably alone at the podium. The existential challenge for most NMPs is that we enter the House as a lone individual, independent from any political party and unmoored from any singular institutional point of reference. Without strength of numbers, safety of resources or the assurance of party loyalties to back you up, you can really struggle to speak up about things you suspect nobody else in the House cares much about or is prepared to speak up for. I struggled.

But the NMP scheme as an institution cannot learn and grow if individual NMPs just stay comfortable. The desire to belong is deeply human. But rather than immediately hooking ourselves up to our preferred political bandwagons so we can feel comforted, NMPs must lean into the opportunity of being unbound by party lines or ideologies to exercise their autonomy to speak on behalf of ourselves and those who are not represented in the House. If it deeply matters to me and the people I represent, then I must step into that political no man's land and bear the brunt of aloneness for a while.

It is way too easy to say the bland thing instead of the brave thing. There is the pressure of speaking in front of powerful people; of knowing that every word I say in Parliament is recorded forever in the Hansard; of knowing my words are instantly streamed out for mainstream media to truncate and for social media to interpret, dissect and distort.

Understandably, some choose to stay blandly impersonal because it attracts less attention and criticism, but it is costly. Bland political speeches robbed of personal voice or emotional affect come off as insincere and inauthentic. They can sow just as much distrust and invite just as much cynicism unto the institution of Parliament as showboating and grandstanding from the extreme other end of the spectrum. People lose trust in Parliament if all they sense from the individuals there are "model answers", stonewalling responses and stereotypical phrases.

On Speaking Clearly

Beyond speaking personally, we must learn to speak clearly.

National issues with multiple players to navigate, multiple perspectives and multiple emotions are not easy for anyone to digest. The public and Parliament's ability to see, connect and empathise with what is going on in the country and the world is affected by how skilfully parliamentarians think, write and speak about issues. So to me, a parliamentary debate must be about using words to create clarity, helping people see what they previously could not see in an issue.

In this sense, public speaking and speech-writing is a core skill and an ethical responsibility that parliamentarians must embrace and not outsource as far as possible. Using words effectively, we can draw mental connections, regulate emotions and open new possibilities. The words parliamentarians exchange (or do not exchange) in the House help frame the public's understanding of policies as well as the government's understanding of the people.

Even the most pragmatic parliamentarian must appreciate how words are necessary for clarification of intent and coordination of action. The more confused our words, the more confused our intentions, and the more confused are our follow-up actions.

So it surprises — and disappoints me — whenever I see any parliamentarian (or aspiring parliamentarian) dismiss the skill of speaking and writing. Some pride themselves on how they are more about doing "deeds" vs saying "words" and taking "action" rather than making "speeches".

But words-deeds and speech-actions are classic polarities — two seemingly contradictory but actually interdependent concepts that need each other to deal with their excesses. All talk and no good action leads to disillusionment, disappointment and disenchantment that must be counteracted with clearly defined action steps. All action and no good talk leads to confusion, misunderstanding and uninspired, disinterested people. This can only be counteracted with clearly defined, articulated conversations.

The call to speak personally and clearly in the House is not for creating public spectacle. It is for supporting public sense-making. An electorate that grows bored and indifferent to what is spoken in Parliament grows ignorant, cynical and blasé about what goes into national decision-making.

If we think public understanding of complex issues is vital, we must invest the time to personally write and deliver speeches on these issues in a way that compels people on the street to not just pay attention themselves but to pass it on virally to others.

Speaking Kindly and Lovingly

But if we speak personally and clearly without love, all our words will come to nothing.

Politics is essentially about power. When we make political speeches, we are expressing our power, aligning with power, addressing power, navigating power, offering power — even requesting for power. As the great political contender Martin Luther King Jr. once shared:

> *Power without love is reckless and abusive, and love without power is sentimental and anemic. Power at its best is love implementing the demands of justice, and justice at its best is power correcting everything that stands against love.*

When we state our honest opinions personally and clearly, it is our act of power. But speaking out our hard and necessary truths can separate, divide, fragment and break. People may experience our presentation of truths as a form of violence with an intention to wound. This is how we may win the battle of debate and lose the war for the hearts and minds of the people.

My personal rule of thumb in life, as in Parliament, is this: the harder the truths we want to table, the greater the love we must prepare to offer alongside.

According to the theologian Paul Tillich,[1] love is our intention for "the unity of the separated". As we speak our difficult truths, in the moment there might be hurt and separation experienced, but if we are clear that our intention is truly togetherness at the end of the day, it can create sufficient safety for the pained to still stay connected.

And this is something that NMPs have the agency to accomplish. As non-partisan representatives of the people, we are not bound by majoritarian pressures or party whips. This means that more often than

◆ The Nominated Member of Parliament Scheme

not, our desire to speak personally and clearly, especially on less popular issues, must be accompanied by a desire to love deeply.

I spent weeks writing every single speech I delivered in Parliament because I wanted to make sure that everything I said was as true, as fair and as kind as I could make it — to fellow parliamentarians, leaders in the House and to the people outside of it. I wanted every speech to be personal and clear. I wanted to explore whether it was possible to speak in Parliament in a tone of loving-kindness and intentional unity even as we speak on disagreeable issues. As NMPs, without the pressures of political rivalry and party lines, we have a special duty to embody the possibility of disagreeing while still choosing to love each other as fellow citizens, rather than see each other as political enemies.

A quote from a former parliamentarian that always encourages me is former MP Chiam See Tong's reflection: "I am actually not a brave man. But I love Singapore and I love Singaporeans." It speaks to what I have experienced and want to experience.

The complexity of issues and passions triggered by these issues from every side can make us scared to put ourselves in the line of fire. I was not brave. I felt intimidated when I had to decide whether to speak about contempt of court issues, poverty issues, Presidential Election issues, the Oxley controversy and national reserves issues. Of course I feared making mistakes, offending others and attracting unwelcome attention. But love moves us out of fear. I could only speak when I reminded myself that I want to practise loving people as equals, worthy of respect and dignity: be they strangers, would-be "enemies" or critics. Love can give us back our voice — and our power.

Love's desire is never to further splinter apart the separated nor to further fragment the brokenness of a system. Love seeks to bring together the separated and heal the lines of division. Tillich's definition of love has helped me to see that anyone who claims to engage in political discussions out of patriotism and yet leaves the electorate more separated, fragmented and disunified is not actually acting out of love for country but personal delusion, ambition or ego.

Final Words

The central theme of all my parliamentary speeches had been a call to build trust by deepening a sense of unity across our system — even in our differences.

I wanted us to lean in and listen to the stories the politically disengaged tell us (and themselves) about who they believe they are and who they are not. As we listen with genuine curiosity, we pick up what we must speak and how we need to speak it. Where there is indifference, speak personally. Where there is confusion, speak clearly. Where there is separation, speak lovingly.

According to Charles Feltman,[2] trust is established when we convey four things: competency, reliability, sincerity and care for the other. When we speak personally, we convey our sincerity of why we are there. When we speak clearly, we convey our competency and reliability in observing what is to be done and how it can be done. When we speak kindly, we convey we care for who is before us — and that our differences do not necessarily divide us.

I ended my NMP stint with a plea for parliamentarians, present and future, to speak plainly to engage with our youth.[3] If we, NMPs, listen well enough, we might actually hear how their stories are our stories too.

Editor's Cut: A Q&A with Kuik Shiao-Yin
(This interview has been edited and condensed for length and clarity.)

What is your most memorable moment from your time in Parliament?
I actually really enjoyed my time with my second batch of NMPs! It sometimes felt like we were the naughty students in the room. It was memorable and surprising because I didn't think I could have fun in Parliament.

Seriously though, I think the delight was in finding other people in the House who cared about similar things and were willing to talk about them seriously in the Chamber, but didn't take themselves too seriously outside Parliament. It was delightful because, frankly, not everybody you meet in there is an open book. Some people were very serious or very political in who they decided to be friendly with, so it was difficult to make friends with everyone.

How did being an NMP change you as a person and/or the work you do?
I came out of my stint in Parliament with a clearer sense of who I am and my identity as a voter and as a Singaporean.

I was constantly surprised by having a diversity of people randomly come up to share that they had heard my speeches. I thought my speeches were quite long and sometimes quite complex, so I didn't expect them to travel far. But I got emails, Facebook messages, chats with random taxi uncles, passersby at cafes, and most memorably, a cai png hawker who talked to me about my speech as I was lining up at his stall, while all these office workers wondered what he was going on about! That changed my perspective on how consequential it is to put your personal voice into the room and to speak your truth in a way that connects with other people's truths. I learnt not to just speak on my own behalf but on behalf of others whom I could identify with or wished to identify with.

It changed my confidence levels because I didn't think what I shared would connect that much. I learnt people don't just hear the words that you say: they hear your embodiment of the words. They hear the emotional affect. They hear who you are and who you want to be. That is all part of communication.

Another surprising by-effect was that I got more in touch with my anger. I'm not a person who gets angry easily. I still don't, but it's easier for me to get angry now. I think that's a natural consequence of becoming more in touch with who you are, your identities and the values you stand for. When you are clearer about your boundaries, you are more aware of what's okay or not okay and why. If nothing matters to me and I don't identify with anything, then there's nothing to be angry about. But once you start to care more about your values and identities and try to identify with others, you will naturally get angry when people and things aren't taken care of.

Based on your time in Parliament, what words of advice would you give future NMPs?
Don't apply to be an NMP for the sake of applying. Check in with your own intentions first, because if you take a seat in the House, you are, in effect, denying someone else a seat. If you're going to occupy that space, why are you occupying it? Who do you intend to be in that position? Whom do you occupy it for? If it's just to represent yourself, please don't apply, but if your intent is to be a voice for people who matter to the system or cannot be represented in the House, you'll be going in there

with hundreds or thousands of people behind you. But please don't go in there just to network or keep quiet to earn a point for your resume. It's insulting.

How would you sum up your time as an NMP in one sentence?
I tried to speak the truth about what matters — and to speak it with love.

Endnotes

[1] Tillich, P. (1954). *Love, power, and justice: Ontological analyses and ethical applications* (Vol. 38). Oxford University Press, USA.

[2] Feltman, C. (2011). *The thin book of trust: An essential primer for building trust at work*. Thin Book Publishing.

[3] Ng, K. (2018, June 24). Speak plainly and from the heart to connect with people: NMP Kuik Shiao-Yin. *Today Online*. Retrieved from https://www.todayonline.com/singapore/speak-plainly-and-heart-connect-people-nmp-kuik-shiao-yin

Section 3

∞

(P)ossibilities

PREFACE

POSSIBILITIES:
An Evolving Institution in a Changing World

When the Constitution was amended in 2010 to make Nominated Members of Parliament (NMPs) a guaranteed fixture in Parliament, it appeared, at least on the surface, that years of wrangling over the scheme might finally be put to bed.

It had not been an easy road. At its inception, the NMP scheme was considered such a gamble that then-Deputy Prime Minister (DPM) Goh Chok Tong had been prepared to build a sunset clause into the eventual legislation. While the suggestion was rejected at the Select Committee stage,[1] this was replaced by a requirement for Parliament to pass a resolution before NMPs could be appointed.

After 20 years, the experiment was finally deemed to have proved itself. Noting that the merits of the scheme had already been "extensively debated", then-DPM Wong Kan Seng spent only a few short paragraphs on his case for entrenching it. NMPs past and present had played "valuable roles in enriching the debate and discussion on national issues," he said, adding, "I believe that the NMP scheme has become an accepted feature in this House."[2]

By at least one measure, the public seemed to have come round to NMPs as well. In a 1992 commentary, the former editor of *The Straits Times*, Han Fook Kwang — then a journalist at the same paper — argued that the real measure of the scheme's success lay in how many applications it received. Winning the vote in the House had been the easy part, he argued; "The infinitely more difficult bit is winning the ground outside Parliament so enough people believe in the scheme and are willing to give it a shot."[3]

Leaving the question of what is "enough" aside, more people have certainly been willing to toss their hats in the ring. Only 10 applications were received for the 1992 batch of NMPs; by 2009, this had risen to 46. (Sixty-one applications were received for the sitting batch of NMPs at the time of writing — the highest number ever.)[4]

These developments — increasing applications and making the scheme permanent — indicate a measure of acceptance for the NMP scheme. And yet, accepting something is not the same as embracing it. Neither the debate around the NMP scheme nor the disquiet surrounding it has ever truly gone away. Meanwhile, the institution itself, despite having evolved in some respects, has remained static in others.

Same Arguments, Different Context

Commentaries analysing the relevance and utility of the NMP scheme tend to surface every few years, particularly at the appointment of a new batch of parliamentarians.[5] While the debate arguably tends to be limited to political circles, in several respects, the arguments for and against NMPs have changed little since 1989.

Arguments in favour of the scheme now fall along two main lines: that NMPs (a) boost democratic representation by being able to represent people on the margins of society and (b) being uniquely positioned to raise issues which are too controversial, sensitive or otherwise politically toxic for political parties — including the Opposition — to take on.[6] Meanwhile, critics continue to point to NMP's lack of democratic accountability, the lack of transparency in the selection process and the arbitrary nature of the functional groups. Similar to how Opposition MPs viewed the introduction of the scheme as a ploy to hobble them, observers like Emeritus Professor Garry Rodan have suggested that the NMP scheme aids the People's Action Party (PAP) in the long run by "obviating the formation of alliances" in competition with PAP interests.[7]

What *has* changed is the political landscape in which the NMP scheme now exists — and, by extension, the arguments around what roles NMP should play in this shifting climate. Recalling then-DPM Goh Chok Tong's claim that the NMP scheme should be viewed in the wider context of Singapore's political maturation, especially its accommodation of dissenting or alternative views, some argue that the scheme is losing its relevance in light of both greater Opposition gains (most notably in the 2011 and 2020 General Elections), leading to more robust debate in Parliament and the growth of civil society.

Notably, even former NMPs have expressed ambivalence over the scheme's future.[8] Several former NMPs, among them Siew Kum Hong, Dr Kanwaljit Soin and Associate Professor Paulin Straughan, have either called for the scheme to be abolished or questioned its credibility and usefulness. Speaking to the press in early 2021, Mr Siew suggested that the scheme was now moot. "The problem it seeks to address is now gone," he said.

How Much Has Really Changed?

Ironically, these developments suggest that, much like in the scheme's earliest years, there remains little consensus over what role NMPs should play in the legislative and political matrix. Despite then-DPM Wong's comments in 2010, the House was not entirely in favour of making NMPs permanent.

The Workers' Party (WP), represented by MP Low Thia Khiang and Non-Constituency Member of Parliament (NCMP) Sylvia Lim, maintained its opposition to the scheme during the 2010 debate. In a blog post the year before, WP member Gerald Giam (who would subsequently go on to enter Parliament, first as an NCMP and later as an elected MP) opined that NMPs had been "handicapped" to be "pretty much no-action, talk-only" by virtue of the constitutional limits on their role.[9]

Although all the PAP MPs voted to support the Bill, a handful, including Hri Kumar Nair and Irene Ng, either suggested the selection process needed to be reviewed or disagreed with making NMPs permanent. MP Ho Geok Choo, although supportive of entrenching the scheme, sought clarifications over how NMPs' role needed to evolve:

> "The NMP scheme served its purpose well when it first started, primarily to encourage and stimulate more alternative, non-partisan views in a period where views were not so forthcoming. I remember many of them, past and present, who have contributed to the plethora of views in their respective areas of interests. But today, many avenues are available....The views and ideologies from sectoral interest groups to VWOs are proliferating like wildfires. Sir, has the original role of NMP

evolved over the years and, in light of the proliferation of more avenues for expression of views, how will the NMP role change to be more effective?"[10]

Today, observers like former NMP Associate Professor Eugene Tan — one of the contributors to this book — note that NMPs are squeezed from all sides: by increased Opposition presence in Parliament, a more diverse slate of PAP candidates and growing civic engagement in national discourse, placing them "at risk of becoming mere pedestrians" if they do not "up their game".[11]

Meanwhile, despite a series of gradual changes to the scheme in form over the years — lengthening NMPs' terms to two-and-a-half years, increasing the number of NMPs, including more functional groups and making the scheme permanent — other elements have remained relatively unchanged in substance and practice since its introduction.

As many critics of the selection process have noted, only the broad contours of its Select Committee's decision-making process and considerations are known. The full list of applicants is also not published.[12] Although some sectors of civil society, most notably the arts and environmental groups, have instituted processes for choosing their nominees, these have not been adopted by other sectors. In most cases, the various functional groups do not disclose their official nominees.

Although they are paid an allowance pegged to 15%[13] of the elected MPs' for their contributions, NMPs still do not receive any official secretarial support or research assistance, despite needing to contend with the increasingly complex slate of issues facing Parliament today. And while NMPs have joined forces amongst themselves on occasion, cross-parliamentary collaboration with their elected colleagues remains rare.

To Boldly Go

Proponents of the NMP scheme might say the institution has made great progress, and indeed contributed greatly to Singapore's progress, since it was introduced. Less charitable takes might suggest that however far it has come, it has wound up where it began: as a divisive intervention whose utility and purpose remains murky.

We do not know how history will look on the NMP scheme. This book, as a collection of "witness accounts" from the very people involved, is not in a position to judge this. Nor does it purport to state conclusively what should be done to or about the scheme. Rather, what this section offers is a slate of reflections and suggestions from seven NMPs, past and present, about the breadth of possibilities for how the scheme might yet evolve. Drawing on their own experiences in office, the contributors in this section consider the place and operations of the NMP scheme in Singapore's broader political landscape as well as a world of increasing volatility, complexity and uncertainty.

Opening the section is **Laurence Lien (NMP 2012–2014)**, who makes no bones about his stance: that the NMP scheme should be made irrelevant. Reflecting on how his early ambivalence towards the scheme has evolved, he asks what it means to be "non-partisan", and argues that the scheme's successes have been contingent on broader failures in Singapore's democracy. **Dr Shahira Abdullah (NMP 2021–present)**, the only contributor who is also a current NMP, likens her stint in Parliament so far to going "deeper than the deep end". Drawing on her lessons over the last year, she writes about the challenges of being thrust into her role as well as pushing the limits of her "Youth NMP" label.

Former Arts NMPs **Janice Koh (NMP 2012–2014)** and **Audrey Wong (NMP 2009–2011)**, in a co-written piece, take us behind the scenes of the arts community's "town hall" process of choosing its nominee and explore its benefits and limitations in depth. In his essay, **Mahdev Mohan (NMP 2016–2018)** discusses his experience working with four NMP colleagues to move the *Education for Our Future* Motion, drawing on the group's experience in coordinating its efforts to make suggestions for how future NMP-led motions can be strengthened.

Eugene K B Tan (NMP 2012–2014) brings insight from his work as a constitutional law scholar to his reflections on his term in office, taking the opposite view to his batchmate Laurence: that NMPs' non-partisan role remains significant, particularly in light of how their votes can be read as bellwethers for the positions of ordinary Singaporeans. Finally, **Anthea Ong (NMP 2018–2020)** writes about bringing her agenda of causes and speaking for marginalised and under-recognised communities during her term, inverting the more common question of whether unelected voices are needed in Parliament to ask instead: Are elected MPs enough in a majoritarian democracy?

Endnotes

[1] Report of the Select Committee on the Constitution of the Republic of Singapore (Amendment No. 2) Bill (no 41/89) (Presented to Parliament on 15 March 1990).

[2] This said, the House was not united on the issue. MP Low Thia Khiang (Workers' Party) voted against the Bill, and Non-Constituency Member of Parliament (NCMP) Sylvia Lim (WP) spoke against it. Several People's Action Party (PAP) MPs, including Irene Ng, Ho Geok Choo and Hri Kumar Nair, also either voiced objections to the NMP scheme or queried aspects of it, though all the PAP MPs voted to support the Bill eventually.

[3] Han, F. K. (1992, June 6). Real test of NMPs lies in quality of the candidates. *The Straits Times*, p. 33.

[4] A list of the number of applications for each batch of NMPs can be found in Appendix D.

[5] See, for example, Tham, Y. C., Mokhtar, M., and Au-yong, R. (2014, May 24). What next for the NMP scheme?. *The Straits Times*; and Lim, J. (2021, January 25). The Big Read: 30 years of NMP scheme — are non-partisan, unelected voices still needed in Parliament?. *Channel NewsAsia*. Retrieved from https://lkyspp.nus.edu.sg/docs/default-source/ips/st_what-next-for-the-nmp-scheme_240514.pdf?sfvrsn=e236710a_2 and https://www.channelnewsasia.

com/singapore/big-read-30-years-nmp-scheme-are-non-partisan-unelected-voices-still-needed-parliament-429426

6. Abdullah, W. (2016). Electoral Innovation in Competitive Authoritarian States: A Case for the Nominated Member of Parliament (NMP) in Singapore. *Japanese Journal of Political Science*, 17(2), 190–207. doi:10.1017/S1468109916000037

7. Rodan, G. (2018). Nominated Members of Parliament in Singapore. In Rodan, G. (ed.), *Participation without democracy: Containing conflict in Southeast Asia* (pp. 70–92). Cornell University Press.

8. See, for example, the essays by Braema Mathiaparanam and Laurence Lien in this book.

9. Giam, G. (2009). *In opposition to the NMP scheme*. Geraldgiam.sg. Retrieved from https://geraldgiam.sg/2009/05/in-opposition-to-the-nominated-mp-scheme/

10. Ho Geok Choo, speech during the Second Reading of the Constitution of the Republic of Singapore (Amendment No. 2) Bill, Singapore Parliamentary Debates, Official Report (26 April 2010), vol. 87, sitting 1, cols. 88–89

11. Eugene Tan, quote in Lim, J. (2021, January 25). The Big Read: 30 years of NMP scheme — are non-partisan, unelected voices still needed in Parliament?. *Channel NewsAsia*.

12. This was only done once, during the first appointment of NMPs in 1990.

13. Retrieved from https://www.psd.gov.sg/faq/remuneration-for-ministers-and-members-of-parliament

Make the NMP Scheme Irrelevant

Laurence Lien
Nominated Member of Parliament (2012–2014)

> *Editor's Note: I first met Laurence Lien in 2009 when he was CEO of National Volunteer & Philanthropy Centre, looking for a CEO for the then-new Community Foundation of Singapore. He is best remembered for saying in Parliament that Singapore is in "social recession" and that a "social reset" is needed. Laurence does not hold back in recounting the personal challenges of being an NMP and offering his observations on the limits of the scheme. He argues for a "social renaissance" where there is greater citizen participation and community ownership, a future when NMPs are no longer needed in Parliament.*

I have always been ambivalent about the Nominated Member of Parliament (NMP) scheme, from its inception.

My mixed feelings came about because while I saw the need for more independent voices in Parliament that are not constrained by partisan positions, I also had doubts about the purpose of the scheme and whether NMPs are actually able and willing to be independent.

Part of it was my anger that the main motivation behind its introduction appeared to be the hope that the NMP scheme would help arrest the increasing support for Opposition candidates.[1] Part of it was the petty annoyance, as I was a civil servant in the 1990s and 2000s, to have had to take on additional work to craft responses for the political bosses to counter points made by the NMPs.

Hence, when I was asked by Stanley Tan, my then-Chairman of the National Volunteer & Philanthropy Centre (NVPC), whether I wanted to be an NMP in 2011, my first response was to reject it. He was helping the social service sector administrator find its nominee. I was then the CEO of the NVPC and concurrently the CEO of the fledgling Community Foundation of Singapore (CFS) — two jobs for one salary — and my children were all still young. Time was not what I had, and my conflicting feelings about the scheme had not abated.

Stanley, being a guy who can sell vegetables to a lion, convinced me to reconsider. I then took some time to reflect, and this was in the immediate context after the 2011 General Election (GE 2011). Many had then considered GE 2011 — when the first Group Representation Constituency (GRC) was lost by the People's Action Party (PAP) — to be a watershed event. Social issues and the relationship between people and the PAP Government were in focus. These were the exact issues that I cared deeply about, and the 2011 post-GE climate seemed most favourable for such discussions.

After prayerful discernment and spousal consultation, I decided to take up the challenge, to be the voice for the social sector. Being an NMP would give me a platform to focus attention on the social realities on the ground — be it an ageing population or the income divide — and talk about what I see as fundamental issues such as community ownership and the need for the government to do less and let Singaporeans do more in some areas.

Looking back, I had a fulfilling term, filled with highs and lows. Unfortunately, based on my own NMP experience and observations in the years after my term, many of my apprehensions of the NMP scheme remain unresolved. Let me share some of the more substantive experiences. I will highlight three points and then end with my view on the future of the NMP scheme.

The Role of NMPs

Many NMPs in my term were credited with raising the quality of the discourse and had made citizens sit up to listen.[2] What surprised me was the number of citizens who in fact followed parliamentary exchanges. People were looking to politicians, public intellectuals, civil society advocates or anyone for that matter, who would either give voice to their concerns or provide different ways of framing pressing national issues.

In my maiden speech, during the Budget Debate in 2012, I raised how Singapore was facing a "social recession" where there was a weakening of individual resilience, loosening of family bonds and decline in community cohesiveness, and I argued for the need to review Singapore's social compact. I thought I was mainly addressing the frontbenchers. But the term "social recession" caught on, and people still remember it today, perhaps because they thought it captured their feelings on the prevailing conditions. The multiple feedback encouraged me to frame my subsequent speeches at Budget Debate 2013 and 2014 as a trilogy, where I introduced the need for a "social reset" and a "social renaissance", respectively.

In my view, effective NMPs should not be just individuals with substantive virtues and expert knowledge who depend on the power of logical discourse to prevail. They should also be leaders or facilitators of a mobilisation exercise, one which shows that the issues raised clearly resonate with many people and require action to address them. Otherwise, why should the Singapore Government take the NMPs' arguments

♦ The Nominated Member of Parliament Scheme

seriously, since it already believes it has a talented corps in the Singapore Public Service who would have already heard, considered and examined most, if not all, important ideas? If the value of the NMPs' contributions was solely the power of ideas, these proposals could much more easily be provided outside Parliament.

By role definition, NMPs are politicians, although supposedly non-partisan, for the purported purpose of elevating the quality of parliamentary debate. But Parliament is not meant to be only a talkshop, but also a platform to make legislative decisions that directly impact the lives of people in Singapore. If NMPs were to have moral legitimacy, they would need to be representatives not just of issues but also of people.

But how will NMPs decide when they are unelected and pigeon-holed into state-conceived categories on whose behalf they are supposed to be speaking? And if NMPs were to be effective in the political process by engaging their perceived constituents, do they lose their independence, perhaps to the extent of becoming embroiled in an ongoing conflict between self and the groups in society that may try to use the NMP to further their narrow agenda?

The Power of NMPs

One reason that NMPs suddenly have an elevated status when they enter Parliament is because they have real power and are not advisors who merely talk with no influence on actual voting.

NMPs can vote in Parliament on any bill or motion, with a few exceptions like a bill to amend the Constitution, a finance-related bill or a vote of no confidence in the government. NMPs also have the same power as elected MPs to request answers to direct questions made to the government (in the form of Parliamentary Questions and

Supplementary Questions), to put substantive issues on the agenda for debate (in the form of motions) and to use the bully pulpit to bring attention to issues.

One might wonder whether NMPs have any real power practically, with the PAP continuing to have the supermajority in the Singapore Parliament since 1959. More bluntly, for more than 60 years, every single vote in Parliament has been a foregone conclusion in Parliament even before it is taken.

However, an NMP's power and influence are not just determined by the (in)ability to determine the actual outcome of any parliamentary vote. Whenever there is a contentious bill or motion, it is always obviously clear how the ruling MPs and the Opposition MPs would vote. For a much clearer barometer of what the general population is thinking, one might look at how the NMPs would debate and vote, if the NMPs were driven by the nature of the substantive issues and not in fact partisan.

A case in point was the controversial Population White Paper that was hotly debated in Parliament in January 2013. Although it was formally endorsed by Parliament with a resounding 77 votes to 13, citizens paid significant attention, relatively speaking, to the NMPs' speeches and votes, particularly when a division was called by the then-Workers' Party (WP) leader, Low Thia Khiang.

The spotlight was on the rarity of NMPs voting against a motion or bill put up by the PAP Government for a vote. There were a total of nine NMPs. Three NMPs, including myself, voted against the Motion, even though it was substantially amended as put forward by a PAP MP at the end of the debate. A fourth abstained and a fifth was absent, while the remaining four NMPs voted in favour of the Motion.

Even though I had already indicated in my speech that I did not support the Population White Paper, it was an entirely different proposition to go through the deliberate process of voting, after the division was called, with blaring sirens and locking doors amplifying the already tense atmosphere. A highly relevant question was how NMPs should even think about how to vote? On whose behalf were we voting? Can it be purely out of personal convictions and beliefs?

In the end, I voted from my own perspective of what was in the best interest of Singapore, without representing any particular group or organisation. Still, I felt nervous pressing the nay button. Would this make me *persona non grata* with the ruling party and anything government-related? Would this have an adverse impact on the two organisations (NVPC and CFS) that I was then leading, since both depended on the government for funding? What about the organisations and people that I would want to be associated with and work with in future?

It struck me as I looked at the nay button — if we were truly non-partisan and independent, why would such considerations matter? Why was there behind-the-scenes "lobbying" of specific NMPs, which I assumed was to ensure that the majority of the NMPs would vote for the amended Motion?

For example, I knew that a fellow NMP had a "friendly" call as a reminder that since the NMP's company hired foreign workers, it would be out of line to vote against the Motion. Why was the NMP nudged to give more weight to a personal conflict?

The NMPs' speeches were important because they represented the strong negative public emotions that could erode the moral authority of the ruling PAP Government on this sensitive matter. It would then be political self-harm to carry through the plan in its entirety.

Still, the speeches were taken seriously also because of the ability of NMPs to vote. Ultimately, I find it incongruous in allowing unelected officers, like NMPs, the ability to vote. It would be particularly unacceptable if there comes a time when the NMPs' votes can be the swing vote, when the ruling party and opposition party MP numbers are a lot closer.

The Assessment of NMPs

The substantive evaluation and decision-making in the (re)appointment of NMPs is a black box and lacks transparency.

In the first place, the categories that the NMPs had to fit into are subjective and pre-determined by the government of the day. Thus far, appointments have been mainly represented by the seven functional groups: business and industry, labour, professions, social service organisations, civic and people sector, tertiary education institutions and media, arts and sports organisations.

The Speaker of Parliament appoints Coordinators for each of these functional groups, and he would meet with each Coordinator for its nomination of candidates within their category. Members of the public may be nominated by other proposers, and a Special Select Committee of Parliament, made up of all ruling party MPs bar one, will consider all candidates.

While the appointment process has the appearance of being clearly laid out in terms of procedure, how evaluations and decisions are actually made along the way is opaque. Each Coordinator wields immense power in nominating candidates; but how does each decide?

When I was approached as the nominee for social sector organisations, I did not know how I was deemed to be suitable. I was simply asked if I would consider, and whether I had any intention of wearing white (i.e., joining the PAP as a party member, which would then rule one out). When I agreed to step forward, the entire process was miraculously smooth — all I needed to do was to complete a detailed set of application forms and submissions.

Then, after becoming NMPs, who judges if they have done well? How would they be evaluated especially if they wish to carry on to serve a second term? Nobody tells you. When one looks at the track record of people seeking reappointment for a second term, it is hard to discern any objective criteria that might have been used.

As I considered whether to apply for re-nomination for a second term, I reflected on what I had done during my term. I was not the most hardworking or prolific NMP in my batch — that appeared to be Associate Professor Eugene Tan. I was not the most eloquent — that seemed to be Janice Koh. I was also not the most passionate — that was probably Faizah Jamal. But people, including close friends who have no problems telling me honestly what they thought of my shortcomings, did tell me that I had made a positive difference, raising social issues and painting fresh ways forward.

Towards the end, I felt a little hemmed in. It became clear to me that, in Parliament, PAP MPs started to be designated to rebut me right after my speech. One Minister was particularly harsh in suggesting that I was ignoring the facts, unrealistic and dishonest with the people of Singapore when asking for "a more positive narrative that is grounded in optimism". A Minister joked with former Administrative Service colleagues of mine, at an event, that I had been one of them but had "gone to the dark side". I am pro-Singapore and neither anti- nor pro- towards the PAP Government. Yet, in black-and-white Singapore, where you are either "for us" or "against us", I was increasingly seen as "against us" and hence non-constructive.

In the end, I did not put in a fresh application for a second term, mainly because what I had set out to do had been substantially accomplished and wanted more time for my family. Of course, I must also admit that the negative climate I found myself in, when I thought about what should be constructive differences and disagreements, also did not help.

In any case, who votes against a government motion and expects to be reappointed?

Future of the NMP Scheme

I know the arguments for having the NMP scheme; after all, I have previously publicly defended its relevance. Yes, it can provide an avenue for non-partisan perspectives. Yes, it can give some voice to those under-represented in society. And yes, NMPs can be in a better position to raise issues that are deemed unpopular, inappropriate or too sensitive to be raised by either a ruling party MP or an opposition party MP.

Still, I am of the view that, while making a difference in the short term, the NMP scheme should be abolished in the long term. The scheme was making an impact precisely because of failures in our democratic system — a lack of robust opposition and a lack of alternative platforms for concerned and respected citizens to air perspectives on behalf of fellow countrymen.

Today, the number of Opposition MPs has been on an upward trajectory. Currently, debates with these Opposition MPs in Parliament, even if the ruling party bemoans the quality, are certainly robust. A few sessions even lasted until around midnight, something that never happened during previous terms of Parliament. As the number and quality of Opposition MPs continue to increase in Parliament, there is less justification to have unelected parliamentarians to take away speaking time from elected MPs in parliamentary sessions.

More fundamentally, as highlighted in my personal experience, there are also too many contradictions in the Singapore system and socio-political climate for NMPs to be a truly non-partisan and effective third voice, and to raise uncomfortable issues without fear or favour, whether actual or perceived.

Politics is not simply about the contestation of ideas among elite representatives, solved simply by the persuasion of one's arguments. That might hold true in a different era.

We are currently in a time period when we are facing ill-defined and complex problems and even less certain solutions. And unlike the newly independent Singapore, Singaporeans are much more diverse — not just in ethnicity and culture, but also social wants and normative concerns — the political process must seek to be inclusive. There must be inclusivity in terms of parliamentary representation, but also in terms of the government's direct engagement and partnership with citizens to be part of the hard problem-solving and opportunity-enhancing work that produces societal progress. The dependency on a few elites to solve all problems, big and small, where the wider community has a minimal role, is an unhealthy dynamic.

Hence, instead of having an NMP scheme, we should focus on growing alternative platforms for concerned and respected citizens to air perspectives on behalf of themselves and fellow countrymen. We need to go beyond processes like REACH (which is a government initiative and therefore not perceived as an objective broker) as well as public consultations, which are often perceived as only happening *ex post*. We need genuinely non-government platforms, and these must be allowed to flourish and have real influence.

We need to encourage a wide swathe of citizens to take more ownership of national issues and speak up, even if this comes with dissent. We need non-partisan think-tanks and research centres, filled with diverse teams, exploring the merits and demerits of major public policies, existing and proposed. We need independent non-profits that design, test and scale solutions, harnessing the creative energies of people, even if they have a few sharp edges. Honest third voices who care for Singapore must be encouraged, not extinguished.

Once we address these deficiencies, the NMP scheme should become irrelevant, and be abolished. And when that happens, we should celebrate.

Editor's Cut: A Q&A with Laurence Lien

(This interview has been edited and condensed for length and clarity.)

What is your most memorable moment from your time in Parliament?
My most memorable moment would have to be my maiden speech. It so happened that our first sitting was during the Budget Debate 2012, and during Budget debates, you can make much more substantive speeches. I mentioned that Singapore was in "social recession", where I thought there was a weakening of individual resilience, communities of cohesiveness and so on, as well as a need to review Singapore's social compact.

I used to craft speeches for the frontbenchers while I was in the civil service, and so I was like, who pays attention [to these things], right? I was just doing the same on the other side now, talking to them. But when it came out, the term really resonated, and people started responding to it. Then I realised, wait a minute, this is also about testing ideas — and not just testing, but also mobilisation.

First of all, I wouldn't be saying something that nobody cares about, right? But if I put something out there and people resonate with whatever I'm raising, and I can get support for it, that would influence decision-makers. So I started to realise that the script goes beyond Parliament. And when many of us, by virtue of being NMPs, start to be interviewed by the press for comment on issues or asked to write op-eds as well and so on…all that, I guess, contributes to the difference that you can make.

How did being an NMP change you as a person and/or the work you do?
I guess towards the end, I kind of felt labelled by some in government, and a bit targeted. At an event towards the end of my term, a Minister

joked: "Oh, he used to be one of us". I laughed! But you know, jokes like these are not just jokes.

To me, I'm neither anti- nor pro-government. I am just pro-Singapore. And because NVPC was a sort of quasi-government entity, it did not seem tenable for me to continue in my role there, even though I was going to leave anyway. I was a bit disappointed, like, why can't we all be pro-Singapore? Just because we crossed swords sometimes and I started doing a bit more outside Parliament, all that seemed to be misread and perceived as having a political agenda.

Based on your time in Parliament, what words of advice would you give future NMPs?
I guess change is hard. You need to work in partnership with others both within and outside of Parliament. Again, it's not just about making constructive, logical points to policy makers, but also about testing, mobilising and shaping public opinion, especially if it's bringing attention to underappreciated or underrepresented issues. [For that], you have to work outside of Parliament, like speaking to the press and writing commentaries.

If you're willing to put in this work, it can be useful as well. I'm not saying that it's a must, but it can be valuable to support the work we do as NMPs.

How would you sum up your time as an NMP in one sentence?
It was still a rare privilege to be in a position to raise public social consciousness on matters that are important to Singapore and important to me, be it building a new social compact or tackling poverty.

Endnotes

1. Prime Minister Lee Hsien Loong himself had said in an interview, after he had mooted the idea of NMPs, that having NMPs would give electors a choice of having a voice in the House speak on behalf of them, without driving them to "take a chance and vote against the government just so they would have somebody to articulate the opposition point of view". ("Nothing to lose from having nominated MPs, says BG Lee", *The Straits Times* [Overseas Edition], 9 December 1989, p. 6.)

2. Tan, M. (2014, September 9). 9 notable NMPs who made us sit up and listen. *Mothership*. Retrieved from https://mothership.sg/2014/09/9-notable-nmps-who-made-us-sit-up-and-listen/

Not Just a Youth NMP

Shahira Abdullah
Nominated Member of Parliament (2021–present)

> *Editor's Note: Shahira Abdullah reached out to me when she was appointed as an NMP in January 2021, oddly just like I did with former NMPs Kuik Shiao-Yin and Professor Walter Woon when I was appointed. It is necessary to include, in this section on "Possibilities", the voice of a current NMP to compare and contrast with the experience of the first NMP, Professor Maurice Choo, 32 years before; what has changed and what has not. Touted as the "Youth NMP" and a youth herself (for a couple more years), Shahira reflects the hopes and aspirations of young Singaporeans in embracing multiple and intersectional identities in this essay, ending with a call for the voices of our youth, of possibilities and our future, to be loud and strong in Parliament.*

"Would you have some time today for a chat about potentially applying for NMP?"

It was in the middle of the afternoon. I was still at work, seeing patients — needless to say, the question caught me by surprise. I had to do a quick Google search to get me up to speed on what it was. A lot of questions crossed my mind, but mainly "Why me?".

Even though I was nominated because I have been working on the ground with youths for eight years, I am also a woman, Malay, Muslim and a dentist — in other words, embodying many identities. In a way, I represent a link to many minority groups and communities. It was apparent that my name probably came up as they believed I had the ability to express those communities' points of view, which could always benefit from more representation in the Chamber.

This, I think, is one of the strengths of the NMP scheme. It increases the diversity of voices by ensuring representation of the different sectors and minority groups that may be under-represented in the House. This is important for policy decisions to reflect the experiences of our diverse population — multi-faith, multi-race and of different abilities.

At the same time, how do we ensure that the persons that we choose for this role will and can really give voice to those they are supposed to represent? Just because I am female, Malay, Muslim and a youth, am I therefore automatically able to be the voice of these different identities?

To put it bluntly, I was aware of how big a responsibility it is and was not sure if I was going to be able to do this well with a full-time job without a team to help me on this journey.

Spreading Mercy

I grew up in a family of seven in a Housing and Development Board (HDB) flat. My father was the sole breadwinner and my mother a housewife. Since I was little, they had emphasised to us that the more we give, the more we will receive. We were always reminded to share whatever little we have.

As Muslims, we also strive to embody the spirit of *Rahmatan lil 'alamin*, or being merciful to all of God's creation — fellow human beings, animals and the environment. We believe that nothing actually belongs to us and that when we die, we will be asked what we did to benefit others with the blessings that were bestowed.

On this basis, as much as I was daunted by the prospect of being an NMP, I knew in my heart that I had to step up to this call. After a lot of soul-searching and conversations with past NMPs and family members, I decided to take the plunge and apply.

Once I submitted the application, I wrote an email to my department head informing her of my submission. Before I knew it, I was summoned to the human resources department.

They were very excited and wished me well but had very real concerns, including whether I would receive a salary for my role, whether I would be able to manage my time, how often would I have to go for parliamentary duties and how was I going to manage to be away from work?

"We're assuming you'll be using your annual leave when you have to be in Parliament, right?" was their final question. I answered that if it happens, I hoped that we could discuss it. I came out of the chat feeling a bit perturbed but decided not to think of it too much since my nomination was not yet confirmed.

However, as fate would have it, I did get selected. It has been a whirlwind of an experience so far as I am still in my term as a Nominated Member of the 14th Parliament of Singapore.

Part of the "Yes-Men" Slate

When we were appointed on 14 January 2021, the ground whispers were that the current slate is a group of "Yes-Men" selected so as to agree with the government and not to cause any trouble. I remembered my sister saying, "don't bother reading the comments on Facebook." I did exactly that. Comments such as "so many doctors", "probably born with a silver spoon", "don't know anything on the ground", "they don't even use MRT" were common amongst netizens. I did feel a little indignant when I read them, but also understood what it looked like at face value.

The arts community was also unhappy as there was no representative after having NMPs Audrey Wong, Janice Koh and most recently, Terence

♦ The Nominated Member of Parliament Scheme

Ho in previous Parliaments who were all arts practitioners. As they had done in the past, the community had held a mini-election in a town hall to choose their representatives — Terence Tan, Nabilah Said and Audrey Lim, to represent their diverse needs and specific challenges in Parliament, yet none was selected.

I felt this lack of representation most keenly when we had a special Budget sitting in July 2021 for the extended Covid-19 measures. The arts community was bleeding due to the effects of the Covid-19 restrictions. Although then-MP Raeesah Khan spoke about the slump that the arts sector was facing, someone from the arts community would better understand and make a stronger case for their difficulties. They would also be better placed to recommend solutions in Parliament.

And because of this "Yes-Men" slate, there was that same gripe again that the NMP selection process could be made more transparent. When the nine of us were chosen, I did think that it would have been helpful if some effort were made to explain why certain candidates were picked in the context of the current needs of the country so that Singaporeans can understand the relevance of the scheme as well and lend more credibility to those appointed.

During my interview process, only one member of the Opposition was present. I think the Special Select Committee could have been expanded to include more members of the Opposition as well as past NMPs. This ensures a greater diversity of opinions when selecting the final slate. In addition, this further reinforces the notion that the NMPs are not selected along partisan lines or preferences.

Past NMPs I spoke to assured me that it would be like a chat among friends as I was admittedly anxious. Yet the interview was definitely not a friendly chat. The questions were not meant to find out my opinions regarding sensitive issues and my personal experiences on the ground.

I was asked on a range of topics, and very little about youths. I was sure I would not be appointed given the answers I gave them which I did not think were what they wanted to hear, nor was I diplomatic. Imagine my surprise when I was.

Deeper than Deep End

Although there was an orientation by the Parliament Secretariat to get us acquainted with the system, it was still a steep learning curve for me. To make matters worse, we were thrown into the deep end immediately with the lengthy Budget and Committee of Supply (COS) sessions — and I had to write my maiden speech; it was a lot to learn and do in a short span of time!

After the Budget and COS, we were also introduced to the concept of bills. My fellow NMPs and I realised that, without a legal background, it was actually very difficult for us to read through the legal jargon, understand it, analyse it and let alone debate on it. We found ourselves asking each other and helping each other. We knew that to make full use of our time in Parliament, we had to read those bills but in the end we did not know if we were reading or understanding them correctly.

The Foreign Interference (Countermeasures) Bill, for example, passed in October 2021 was a very large bill at 249 pages that had to be read, understood and analysed in a very short period of time. It was something I really struggled with, confused between sections.

I am extremely lucky to have a close friend who is trained in law to support me to navigate through all the bills to pick out the important points for debate. I think it is important to have this legislative support in order to have quality debate in Parliament.

Currently, elected MPs are entitled to one secretarial assistant and one legislative assistant but not NMPs. To make the NMP's voice effective and useful, I really believe we should be supported with at least a legislative assistant, especially since we have full-time jobs too like the elected MPs.

I am proud of myself for reaching out to previous NMPs in my early days who taught me a lot more than the manual did! I am especially thankful to Anthea for guiding me along so far.

I have also been very fortunate to have a supportive workplace. Recognising it as a form of national service, my hospital agreed to give me 20 extra days of leave per year to attend the parliamentary sessions starting from 2021. I am very grateful for that.

Whither a Youth NMP?

I was Vice President of the Mendaki Club, an organisation focused on the development of Malay/Muslim youths aged 13–35 and beyond, and also part of the SG Youth Action Plan, a platform for youths to share their ideas and vision of Singapore in 2025; we then came up with a plan on how youths can partner with the government to take action. Currently, I am also a board member for the National Youth Council, which explains why I am touted as the "Youth NMP".

But I also wanted to speak for women, minority groups, the dental profession and also other issues I care about. But can I do these groups justice since I was nominated and appointed under the "youth" banner? I decided I did not want to be boxed up in the sector ("youth") that I was from because I am more than that sector; I represent a variety of identities and experiences so that is what I have been doing.

At the time of writing, I have raised concerns of low-income youths being caregivers and supporting the family while trying to upskill so as not to lose out. Youths also feel that more should be done to support vulnerable groups such as low-wage workers, migrant workers and persons with disabilities.

During the debate on the Road Traffic (Amendment) Bill, I took the opportunity to speak about the need for a change in safety standards for migrant workers transported on lorries.

I am determined to highlight the achievements of the Malay/Muslim women community as well as to emphasise their concerns at every opportunity I can. For example, with respect to the online poll ranking of female Muslim religious teachers for sexual attractiveness, I urged for support systems and whistleblowing policies for the victims. In the Empowering Women Motion, I wanted to also highlight the inspirational successes of many Malay/Muslim women to Singaporeans.

When the Dental Registration Bill was tabled, I naturally spoke on it as a dentist to make sure that the changes that were tabled made sense for me as a practitioner.

So essentially, I am trying my best to be "not just a Youth NMP"!

Yes, I will keep pushing for youth voices to be heard in Parliament in my term; they have a lot to say and contribute though many would like to see the government take note of their views and opinions and demonstrate how youth participation has helped/can help to shape future policies. As a consultant for the Youth Action Challenge, a platform for youth to provide solutions that tackle community issues, I have been amazed by the ingenuity of the ideas proposed.

I was inspired to read parts of a Malay song called *Ilham Pujangga (Inspiration of a Poet)* by Singaporeans Ismail Haron and Cikgu Zaharah Salleh in 1972 at the end of my maiden speech to emphasise the value of youth in the wider society.

> *Wahai para belia (To all the young people)*
> *Berikanlah tenaga (Lend a helping hand)*
> *Untuk nusa dan negara (To your motherland)*

◆ The Nominated Member of Parliament Scheme

Ini zaman kemajuan (The new age is here)
Jangan kita ketinggalan (Do not delay any longer)
Kasih sesama manusia (Love humankind)
Seperti anda sayangkan diri anda (As much as you love yourself)
Pandang yang satu kepada yang ramai, sayang (As how each individual beholds the community, my love)
Pandang yang ramai kepada yang satu (And as how the community beholds each individual)

Is a Youth NMP the only way for youths to be represented in Parliament? The National Youth Council and the government are trying their best to engage with youth groups. However, I still feel there are benefits to institutionalise the Youth NMP because what is debated in Parliament affects the kind of future our youths want — they must have a stake in our country.

Editor's Cut: A Q&A with Shahira Abdullah

(This interview has been edited and condensed for length and clarity.)

What is your most memorable moment from your time in Parliament (so far)?

Saying things that people may not agree with. Before you go up to the rostrum, you actually need some courage to say these things.

For example, when I spoke about migrant workers — it actually wasn't even related to the Road Traffic (Amendment) Bill; I just felt that it was something I wanted to speak about, and was going to say it in a speech anyway. I rebutted what Senior Minister of State [Amy] Khor had said before that.

Another time was the RVHS [River Valley High School] incident. I wanted to ask about how we follow up on suicide cases.[1] It was a bit of a prickly question — I could hear [the Minister's] unhappiness when he answered. That was a memorable moment because I remember thinking, oh gosh, he's [the Minister] angry! Yet I'm glad I asked because my question took the government out of its comfort zone. So I think these are memorable moments — when I'm about to say things I think they won't like, feeling scared about it and having that sense of fulfilment after saying it!

How has being an NMP changed you as a person and/or the work you do?

I think it has made me listen to people's problems a lot more and differently. You know sometimes it's just like "Oh, okay, okay," but now I tend to dive a bit deeper and try to understand further, so that I can try to offer solutions or do something more meaningful in Parliament.

When you listen, you do it to try and help. For me now, it's always like: What can I do? What can I ask in Parliament? Overall, I would say that I have matured for sure. At the start of my term, my aim was to do my job as an NMP properly, and if I want to do this, it means I have to step up for certain things. It's not about sitting there in the Chamber and just listening; it's a lot of work.

Based on your time in Parliament so far, what words of advice would you give to future NMPs?
I think you really have to be clear at the start. You need to know why you are doing it, what your term is for and who you are standing up for. At the same time, know that you're going to need help.

There is no way that you're going to be able to do this alone, so reach out to your seniors, like previous NMPs, for help as soon as possible. It's only when you have help that you can make full use of your time in Parliament and not waste this opportunity. So don't be afraid to ask — and yes, I'm still asking for help all the time.

How would you sum up your time as an NMP (so far) in one sentence?
It's been crazy, whirlwind crazy…for now. Yes, I think the most accurate word is crazy!

Endnotes

[1] The 16-year-old boy at the centre of the incident, who was later charged with the murder of a younger schoolmate, had been admitted to the Institute of Mental Health (IMH) for attempted suicide two years before.

Choosing an NMP for the Arts: A Unique Process

Audrey Wong
Nominated Member of Parliament (2009–2011)

Janice Koh
Nominated Member of Parliament (2012–2014)

> *Editor's Note: In curating the chapters for this section on "Possibilities" for the NMP scheme, the first one that came to mind for me is the unique way that the arts community — an impossibly diverse one at that — has organised itself to "elect" their NMP representative(s) at a town hall since 2009. The "elected" representative(s), however, may or may not be successful in the formal process. I reached out first to Janice Koh through a mutual friend of ours; Janice proposed to co-author this essay with Audrey Wong. Their essay discusses advantages and limitations, and takes us behind the scenes of this unique process.*

The atmosphere in the airy warehouse space that was the headquarters of Singapore theatre company, TheatreWorks, was abuzz with anticipation and conversation. Over a hundred actors, visual artists, dancers, theatre designers, production managers, curators, arts managers, stage managers and ardent supporters of the arts chatted with old friends, greeted acquaintances and eagerly discussed what was about to happen. A few veteran arts practitioners sat quietly and intently, aware of the significance of this gathering and perhaps thinking about the pressure on the three people that the crowd had gathered to meet in this specially-convened town hall to select the new Nominated Member of Parliament (NMP) for the Arts.

The three candidates about to enter this room had stepped forward in the bid to represent the arts in Parliament. They had considered their readiness to speak for the diverse groups of arts and creative practitioners conveniently lumped together as the "arts community", and considered the issues they were prepared to champion in the parliamentary arena. They had met a previous Arts NMP to chat about the NMP selection process, the expectations of the role and what it was like to be a member of the august chamber and be counted as a peer to elected MPs who include Ministers and Parliamentary Secretaries. They were now nervously waiting in a separate room, preparing to meet their "constituents", answer questions and clear any doubts that the arts community might have about their suitability as representatives.

Each candidate made a short campaign speech to the room, which was followed by an intense question-and-answer session. Several people in the crowd sought clarification about each candidate's values and preferred causes as well as their stance on controversial issues. A couple of hours later, the community cast their vote for their preferred candidate who would have just a matter of days to prepare and submit the application to the Parliamentary Select Committee.

That year in 2011, the choice of the arts community was Janice Koh, who would be interviewed by the Select Committee and appointed as the second Arts NMP, after Audrey Wong in 2009.

There is of course, no pre-requisite for the NMP nominee from any functional group to come from a voting process. Uniquely, the arts community initiated their own ground-up process of finding a candidate in 2009. It is a process that runs in parallel to the mainstream nomination one often led by sector representative organisations or sector champions.

The Singapore Business Federation, for instance, would typically put forth their candidate to represent the business and industry sector and likewise, the National Trades Union Congress (NTUC) for the Labour Movement. In the case of the arts which is part of the "media, arts and sports organisations" functional group, the search for candidates is usually spearheaded by the Chairperson of the National Arts Council (NAC). As such, after the arts community has made their choice, the candidate would try to seek endorsement from the NAC before submitting their application to Parliament.

However, the arts community's choice is not necessarily the choice of the Parliamentary Select Committee. In 2014, the Select Committee did not choose the arts community's nominee Kok Heng Leun, the Artistic Director of Drama Box, though Kok was eventually appointed an NMP in the next round of selections. In 2018, the two nominees put forward by the arts community, visual artists Dr Woon Tien Wei and Dr Felicia Low, were not selected. Instead, the NMP appointed was Terence Ho, Executive Director of the Singapore Chinese Orchestra, who had not gone through the arts community's town hall nomination process.

Origins of the Arts NMP Town Hall Process

While it is difficult to state exactly what or who the arts community is, one might trace the notion of the existence of a large number of practitioners with shared interests in establishing the value of arts and culture in Singapore, back to a Yahoo e-group initiated in 1999 by Alvin Tan, the Artistic Director of The Necessary Stage.

Alvin is well-known for his ability to bring people together and his involvement in civic causes. The Yahoo e-group, which eventually had 4,000 members, was "a capacity-building tool to share information, discuss issues, and network".[1] Mostly a bulletin board where members posted audition and job opportunity notices or publicised exhibitions and performances, there were occasional lively discussions on issues impacting the arts, such as censorship. Generally though, it was a small number of members who actively and regularly participated in these discussions.[2] It was an online and off-line community as many members were also acquainted with one another through arts work or attending the same performances, exhibitions and seminars.

The idea of a "community" is a powerful mobilising force. In 2009, when a senior theatre practitioner floated the idea via email to friends in the community about proposing somebody for the NMP position,[3] a small group quickly garnered further interest in the idea from their networks and in those early days of social media, quickly organised a town hall to discuss this possibility. Out of this, the first Arts NMP selection town hall was held, also at TheatreWorks.

At that time, there was a sentiment "that there's a need for representation of some of the primary concerns of artists at the highest level in society".[4] As evidenced in the Yahoo group debates, there was more awareness among the arts community on how public policy issues impacted them and were vital to arts practice. These issues include public funding, censorship, education and creativity, spaces for the arts and access to these spaces. With more attention being paid to developing Singapore's cultural and creative economy from the end of the 20th century, the arts sector was ever more tightly enmeshed within the state's orbit.

The government was making huge investments in cultural infrastructure and funding, directed through strategic plans such as the Renaissance City Plan (2000) and the Arts and Cultural Strategic Review (2012). The government's perception of the role and value of the arts in society influences the lives and livelihoods of the arts community. More artists saw the need to have channels to engage with the government, the ministries and the top decision-makers in the nation. The arts — and the view from the ground in the arts — was underrepresented in Parliament.

Mobilising the community to discuss and set up a process to find an Arts NMP was aided by a collaborative spirit among arts practitioners and arts groups, which may be attributed to the fact that in the arts, teamwork and collaboration are necessary to realise projects. Many artists believe that a worthy cause was worth time and effort, even if unpaid. Individuals volunteered their time to reach out to the community and organise the town hall (and eventually assist the NMP too) while TheatreWorks and Emily Hill offered their spaces for the events. TheatreWorks' staff also helped to organise the voting.

This collaborative spirit remains today.

A few arts practitioners committed to the project of a ground-up Arts NMP quickly connect and kickstart the town hall process once Parliament announces a call for nominations. A notice is then circulated through informal arts networks calling for potential nominees to step forward, and the town hall and voting process are swiftly organised. Today, much of it is conducted online through a process of collecting signatures for each candidate. The candidate with the most number of signatories is declared the community's choice. The committee may then approach the NAC to seek its endorsement.

Why the Ground-Up Process?

Other than a few major arts institutions, the arts industry in Singapore is generally made up of a diverse range of freelance practitioners, as well as many independently-run, medium and small-scale arts groups or organisations across various art forms. Unlike other functional groups, there are no formal sector-wide organisations representing the broad spectrum of art forms and arts practitioners. While interest-group associations and societies exist, such as the Federation of Art Societies Singapore, the Association of Artists of Various Resources (APAD), the Singapore Drama Educators Association (SDEA) and so on, they focus on activities catering to the interests of their specific discipline or membership — for instance, organising art exhibitions or capacity-building programmes. They may advocate for more support for the arts but largely steer clear of commenting on and involvement in socio-political issues even when these impact the arts.

There is no umbrella industry association that champions the interests of arts practitioners of different disciplines from visual art to music, dance, theatre, film and design. In addition, it is difficult for a single body to speak for the broad spectrum of disciplines, specialisations and interests in the arts community which includes not only those who "create" but also those in technical and administrative positions, as well as patrons, supporters, audiences and those who participate only peripherally.

This means that, unlike the other sectors such as business, labour movement and social service organisations, there is no formal arts industry body for the government to consult when it comes to matters of policy and changes to the law. Correspondingly, if the arts community wishes to engage the government on national or policy issues, there is no representative body to facilitate this. Artists and arts organisations often only deal with the NAC, which means the NAC ends up playing the role of both mediator and policy maker, which can be contradictory.

When it comes to proposing or surfacing NMP candidates in the other sectors, potential candidates who are already known "on the ground", or who are recognised as having the requisite expertise and credibility are put forward through the industry organisation. In other words, an informal vetting process has already taken place.

This is not the case in the arts. As such, instituting this process of nomination, campaigning and voting serves a useful purpose of surfacing independent candidates who are deemed most suitable to represent the needs of a very diverse arts scene.

Advantages and Limitations of an "Elected" Arts NMP
Advantages
The town hall process is conducted on the principles of openness and transparency, reflecting the values of democratic participation that are important to many in the arts community. Giving voice is an important dimension particularly in contemporary arts practice.

In this section, we cover the positives about the ground-up process.

i. **Legitimacy and accountability.** The voting process and show of support from the community for the candidate by way of signatories gives the candidate legitimacy. It also empowers the candidate to feel they truly represent a constituency of Singaporeans to whom they are accountable.

As the candidate had faced questions from her "constituents" before the selection and given them an opportunity to understand her values and stance on various issues, the candidate feels a sense of responsibility to be accountable to them. She understands that her actions and speeches in Parliament may be scrutinised by the community, while also feeling reassured that there is a community supporting her.

ii. **Unifying diverse stakeholders and allowing the community to rally around an issue.** The town hall process rallies the arts community together in common cause. Having established this, the Arts NMP then provides a platform for the community to debate and discuss issues that impact them, and can convene other town halls for this purpose. Without an industry representative body, these town halls become channels for the Arts NMP to gather responses on policy issues and explore ways that the NMP can help address problems in the sector.

The authors of this article have mobilised the arts community during their time as NMPs on a number of issues. Audrey Wong championed the cause of freelancers in the arts and creative sectors, drawing attention to this issue in Parliament and providing input to the Ministry, which was then beginning to have an interest in measures to support freelancers. She convened town halls and focus group discussions with the community, with the help of non-profit enterprise Six Degrees at Emily Hill. These informed her discussions with policy makers and exploring ways that NTUC could assist the community.

In 2014, the arts community mobilised to express serious concerns to the Proposed Amendments to the Public Entertainments and

Meetings Act. The proposal concerned "Arts Term Licensing", a method of "co-regulating" artistic content by requiring arts companies to have "content assessors" to internally vet plays and artistic content before public presentation. This would effectively formalise self-censorship.

In consultation with the arts community, Janice Koh made an additional submission to the Media Development Authority (MDA) against the scheme.[5] The mobilisation was effective, as MDA removed Arts Term Licensing from the amendments to the Act.

Also during Janice's term, the Singapore Government launched the Our Singapore Conversations movement in 2014, which sought views from the public that would inform the government's planning for the future. Concerned that the arts were excluded from the national process, Janice initiated roundtable conversations with the arts community to contribute an Arts Manifesto to the national programme.

iii. **Capacity-building in the arts.** The informal networks within the arts community provide resources and support to the NMP. Sharing of information about government policies and parliamentary debates also helped build capacity within the community, as practitioners gained insight into matters of political and cultural governance which helped them make strategic decisions pertaining to their areas of work.

The informal nature and ad-hoc organisation of the arts community allows flexibility for individuals to freely enter into active participation and exit if they are unable to commit or have taxing work commitments. This suits the nature of artistic work which is often seasonal and project-based. On the other hand, it can also be considered a disadvantage because there is no permanent support for the NMP's work and when there is no ground-up Arts NMP, the community may disengage from the political engagement process.

Limitations

To the outside eye, the town hall process appears to be a model of democratic participation. It is certainly underpinned by democratic values as observed above, but there are imperfections.

i. **Ad-hoc organisation.** Because of the ad-hoc nature of organising and engagement, and as the work of mobilising is taken on by a small group of volunteers (who also have busy careers in the arts), there are limitations to how far and deep the outreach can be. There is usually a very short runway for outreach to the community and for wide-reaching communications around issues.

   Furthermore, there are no monetary resources to support this work. As a result, there may be a lack of inclusivity in terms of gathering views or votes from across the spectrum of arts practitioners. Considering that there were over 4,000 members in the arts community Yahoo group at its height, a town hall of 200 people and collection of several hundred signatures cannot be said to comprehensively cover the breadth and diversity of the arts community.

   Furthermore, as most outreach is conducted in English, through social media channels or informal networks like WhatsApp, it is possible that some sub-communities in the arts lose the opportunity to participate, for instance those with less interest in political engagement or the older generation who are less tech-savvy.

Participation may be reliant on those who are in the know and arts practitioners who are most vocal.

ii. **Legitimacy of the parallel town hall nomination process.** As the years progress, it is becoming clearer that the parallel process of nomination through a ground-up town hall may lead to a dilemma for the arts community as well as the sector champion (NAC).

The Parliamentary Select Committee cannot endorse the arts community's way because it falls outside the process that it has established with sector champions and industry groups. It is unlikely that Parliament would want to set a precedent of legitimising this method of NMP selection due to the informal and ad-hoc nature of organisation. There are implications to this. There will be instances where the Select Committee does not choose anyone to specifically represent the arts. There will also be instances when the eventual Arts NMP is not the candidate from the town hall but was selected through the mainstream process, which happened in 2018.

The sector champion NAC might also find itself in a difficult position if it is not comfortable with the candidate from the town hall but is approached to endorse the candidate. Or, it might have a preferred candidate of its own. To reject the arts community's request risks accusation that it is not in tune with the very community it claims to champion.

These scenarios also raise the possibility that there are those in the arts community who feel that a candidate not chosen through the town hall cannot truly represent them, and hence, they could challenge the eventual Arts NMP's legitimacy.

Despite these scenarios, the originators of the town hall process (and we) believe that, in the spirit of free choice, anyone who believes they are a good candidate but does not wish to go through the voting process has the right to submit their application directly to the Select Committee and seek endorsement from other parties.

Finally, it is possible that there are unknown candidates from the arts community who quietly submit their applications to Parliament, who are not selected and keep this secret. We have to acknowledge that in Singapore, "face" is still important.

We have no ready answer to the dilemmas presented here; as long as Parliament's selection process remains somewhat shrouded in mystery and as long as there is no independent industry association in the arts with a mission to represent the interests of a diverse arts community, these issues remain.

Conclusion

Speaking for ourselves, we appreciate the process of the town hall where we addressed questions from peers and colleagues. It demanded a level of awareness and sensitivity to multiple concerns, different personalities and perspectives which challenged us personally and professionally. We knew it was impossible to represent everyone in the arts and all perspectives, and we certainly felt the burden of expectation. The legitimacy that this process conferred gave us confidence to take on a role neither of us had attempted before.

The Arts NMP and their selection have always attracted attention from the media and led to a heightened visibility of the arts in public life. The Arts NMP provides a unique opportunity to advocate for the place of the arts in Singapore. There are advantages and limitations to selecting the Arts NMP through the ground-up selection process.

Perhaps what is needed now is the formation of industry groupings and bodies who can raise and champion issues on an ongoing basis and whose elected representatives might be put forward for consideration as Arts NMP.

Ideally, one day, there would no longer be the need for an Arts NMP to represent arts and cultural topics in Parliament because these issues would be widely integrated in parliamentary debates and public pronouncements through elected MPs.

Editor's Cut: A Q&A with Audrey Wong & Janice Koh
(This interview has been edited and condensed for length and clarity.)

What is your most memorable moment from your time in Parliament?
Janice: There are many, but if I had to pick one, I would say it was the long debate over the Population White Paper and being one of three NMPs who voted against the Bill. There was immense pressure to conform simply because there's such a huge majority in Parliament, but I knew I not only had to reflect how I thought about it, but also represent a significant number of people whom I had interacted with and who were strongly against the Bill. As long as the Whip is not lifted, you have two sides of the House that will vote according to party lines, sometimes on rather controversial issues. So suddenly the slate of NMPs become the barometer for how the regular Singaporean thinks about these issues, and all 98 pairs of eyes or whatever are looking at the nine of us. That was a huge moment.

Audrey: We didn't have anything that was so super dramatic in my time, pre-2011. I think mine was probably when my fellow NMP Viswa [Sadasivan] tabled a motion on the National Pledge. *[Editor's note: Viswa shares his reflections on this incident in Section 2, "Merits".]* A lot of people signed up to speak on the Motion because it was something that was so deeply emotional.

I remember I was really very nervous because I think it was one of the first times I actually spoke in the House. Minister Mentor Lee Kuan Yew was also present, and he was kind of sitting opposite me. And I'm like, wow, you know, one of the very first things I'm going to say in this highest law-making body, which is going to be transmitted everywhere, is going to be said right in front of the Minister Mentor. You really do feel that weight of responsibility because you realise this forum is truly massive — it really is national, and you have to be responsible for what you're saying.

How did being an NMP change you as a person and/or the work you do?
Janice: I don't think it changed me so much as it reinforced the idea that you need to walk the talk if you want something to change.

After serving as an NMP, a few things became very clear to me. One, MPs work very hard. Every MP, whether Opposition or the PAP [People's Action Party] — what they do is extremely hard work. Looking at what they do, I don't know whether I even have the capacity to do the same. But basically, stop being a keyboard warrior and be the change. Don't just complain about it.

Audrey: It hasn't changed my personality, but it helped me develop an awareness of the forces in the world that shape us as well as the impact you have on other people — be it intended or unintended — because of things you say or do. You might not think something is that important, but it could actually affect someone, whether positively or negatively. [I guess it's] partly because you're kind of a public figure and you have to watch what you say and do and also because you're aware of being responsible for something. A lot depends on how you present yourself as well as how you present perspectives, particularly perspectives on issues that might not be so mainstream.

Based on your time in Parliament, what words of advice would you give future NMPs?
Janice: Being able to communicate well, clearly and widely with different media, especially now with digital media and so on, is as much a part

of your work in Parliament as being in Parliament itself. If you want something to change, you need to change people's minds and hearts, not just fellow parliamentarians. Also, make friends with your fellow NMPs!

Audrey: I agree with Janice about making friends with your fellow NMPs. Also, one piece of advice I was given by former NMPs before I entered Parliament was to pick your battles. Don't try and fight on all fronts — focus on something that is really important to you, or that you feel is urgent or needs attention, and make that one of your focal areas during your term. You'll probably feel like you achieve more doing that than by, you know, doing a million different things.

How would you sum up your time as an NMP in one sentence?
Janice: Too simplistic! I don't want to answer that question. What is this, Miss Universe?

Audrey: Actually, because people do ask, I did eventually settle on one word over the years. It was educational.

I mean, it was a big learning experience, and I'm sure it was for Janice as well; we had never done something like this before. You also get to interact with people who are making the kinds of decisions that affect your life. Whether they're asking Parliamentary Questions or replying to those questions, you get to see what some of the considerations are when it comes to making decisions for the country. That was really interesting.

Janice: I would say that I learnt a number of things during my time as an NMP. One of them was to choose my battles; you can't please everyone. Second, not to take disagreement personally. Third, to trust my instincts and my gut. And fourth, not to underestimate the power of the media to help get a message across to the wider public. You might be speaking to the House, but your audience isn't just the House. It's national. It's global. You must always tailor your message for the parliamentary hearing, but then you also need to follow up strategically with different platforms and media to let it ripple and reverberate and resonate across the larger sphere, not only now but across time. That was my biggest takeaway.

Endnotes

1. Wong, A. (2012). Artists' Advocacy in Singapore: A Changing Drama. *Asia Pacific Journal of Arts and Cultural Management*, 9(1), 45–52.
2. Tan, A., O'Neil, M., & Davis, L. (2007). The Network Within: Singapore's Arts Community E-group. In *FOCAS: Forum on Contemporary Art and Society* (pp. 278–297). FOCAS.
3. Wong, A. (2012). Artists' Advocacy in Singapore: A Changing Drama. *Asia Pacific Journal of Arts and Cultural Management*, 9(1), 45–52.
4. Sasitharan quoted in Martin, M. (2009, April 22). Wanted: An NMP for the Arts. *Today*.
5. ArtsEngage. *Janice Koh's Additional Submission to MDA*. Retrieved from https://sites.google.com/site/artsengagesg/MDA_Self-Censorship/janice-koh-s-additional-submission-to-mda

The Education Motion: Animus, Process, Potential

Mahdev Mohan[1]
Nominated Member of Parliament (2016–2018)

> *Editor's Note: The "Education for Our Future" Motion moved by NMPs Mahdev Mohan, Kuik Shiao-Yin, Ganesh Rajaram, Kok Heng Leun and Azmoon Ahmad in July 2018 was a significant self-organised effort between NMPs that could set a precedent for future NMPs working together. It sparked a lively and passionate debate amongst eight NMPs and five elected MPs over how best to ensure accessible, inclusive and lifelong education for all with then-Minister for Education Ong Ye Kung supporting the Motion and calling it "a strong chorus in the House". Mahdev gives the backstory and his learnings of this Motion in this essay.*

Hansard indicates that Nominated Members of Parliament (NMPs) have left their *imprimatur* on parliamentary proceedings — rising in the House to ask pointed questions; forward motions; table petitions; vote on whether bills should pass; propose legislative amendments to the government's bills; and even introduce private members' bills of their own. NMPs have not only represented the insights of the functional groups that nominated them, but also spoken to issues of public interest that cut across traditional demographics and that are neglected by political parties.

The question that some ask though is whether these tasks are better left to elected parliamentarians, such as the ruling party's 4th Generation backbenchers to test their mettle; or to elected Opposition MPs to scrutinise and offer counter-points to the government's bills. If the cut and thrust of parliamentary debate has improved and there is unprecedented political participation in the House, they ask if the alternative views are as relevant in Parliament as they might have been in 1990 when the NMP scheme was first introduced.

In a parliamentary debate, aren't two well-articulated opposing views enough? I would submit that it is important for lawmakers (and the electorate) to have the benefit of other diverse views. That is, non-partisan voices that are not accountable to party whips or whims; voices that speak from their lived experiences and expertise to express the sentiments and aspirations of Singaporeans and residents who may not always be heard or even understood; and voices that can attempt to bring together members from either side of the House.

In this chapter, I briefly consider (a) the origins of the *Education for Our Future* Motion; (b) the consultative work that went into gaining support for the Motion in the House and canvassing lived experiences outside it; and (c) my wish-list for structural changes to make NMP motions/proposals more meaningful.

Animus

NMP proposals, in my experience, usually stem from questions that Singaporeans ask and for which there are few readily available or defensible answers.

♦ The Nominated Member of Parliament Scheme

In this case, the question that the Ministry of Education (MOE) was contending with was related to systems design — i.e., in a VUCA (volatile, uncertain, complex and ambiguous) world, how could the education system be tweaked so that students from pre-school to post-tertiary are set up for success?

Yet, there were underlying questions that Singaporeans were asking. Are there equal educational opportunities for social mobility in our schools? Are the curricula and pedagogical processes we have used for decades still relevant today or has standardised testing for children and young persons become outmoded? What can be done to make our schools more inclusive and to prevent popular educational institutions from enabling only high net-worth alumni and their progeny?

Systemic inequality (real or perceived) was at the heart of questions concerning education and had even gained the attention of the front bench of the House.

In May 2018, Prime Minister Lee Hsien Loong singled out popular schools such as Raffles Institution (RI), noting that RI's historically strong tradition of accepting students from diverse backgrounds had eroded in recent years.[2] That more should be done to ensure RI and other schools do not become "self-perpetuating closed circles".

One systems design scholar and architect has termed closed circles as the "boring star system" — one which is uninventive and inherently "problematic given the limited points of view it allows within its reach".[3]

This struck a chord.

First, has the school, i.e., RI, that I had often credited for many of my own values and a space that allowed many of my classmates and I to further our academic and extracurricular pursuits fundamentally changed?

Second, as an MP nominated to represent fellow educators, I wondered if I too was complicit in nurturing self-perpetuating closed circles. How could I do my part to break that loop, and ensure that education was meant to be a *Fibonacci* spiral that grows more diverse, inclusive and expansive?

Together with four other like-minded NMPs, I spoke with the Ministers and officials for education at the time.

Process

At the Members' Room and the Library, places for reflection and discussion between parliamentary sittings, we asked if we could contribute to the review process that the Ministry was involved in. The role we had in mind was not to become auxiliary members of the Ministry's review task force but to meet stakeholders — teachers, students and administrators — in our capacity as independent-minded Singaporeans keenly interested in the future of our education system. Independents who were prepared to highlight aspects of the system that had to be interrogated and to ask how the love for lifelong learning could be inculcated and supported.

While some Ministers and MPs were supportive of our effort, not everyone welcomed the prospect of NMPs having access to MOE's respondents and resources! A few parliamentarians from both sides of the House chuckled and asked whether this was beyond the purview of NMPs who "have the luxury of simply asking questions".

I felt this comment was ironic, as it was because we had questions of the education system designers, educators, parents and students that we had to parse the answers that were being offered firsthand and ask follow-up questions. My fellow NMPs and I believed that it is only when we ask meaningful questions, when we invite lifelong learners to verbalise what they know, that they may be prepared to test the reasoning behind their assumptions (e.g., that continuous assessment in lower primary should persist despite evidence that this was taking a toll on students).

At the minimum, our questions and desire to listen to the answers from stakeholders were not designed to affix blame, but to generate greater interest in the Motion for various stakeholders to look beyond their near-term goals and to become personally involved when their opinions and assumptions are constructively challenged by independent voices. We made the point that if aspects of the education system and the *modus operandi* of educational institutions were to be properly gauged, we needed qualitative data. We intended for the data to ultimately culminate in a parliamentary motion focused on the love of learning as the driving force for education, and that would call for the government and the people to work together to seek to ensure that education is accessible, inclusive and lifelong.

Notably, the Motion gained momentum as the NMPs convened in the next month in less august surroundings (namely, our favourite coffee shops and hawker centres!) to discuss and divide the thematic areas that we intended to cover. We organised small group sessions with the educators and parents to listen to their concerns as well as their aspirations for what the system should prioritise and what methodologies and areas of learning ought to be encouraged, mindful that the markers of resilience for lifelong learners were not simply good grades. There was a genuine concern that the education system had to be significantly re-evaluated so that the insights we were gathering could become, we hoped, the beginning of a more comprehensive review of the education system.

The Education Motion: Animus, Process, Potential ◆

Based on our discussions with educators, parents and students, we noticed that several aspects of the education system had to be refreshed and updated, and that "sacred cows" such as standardised national exams and testing such as the PSLE (Primary School Leaving Examination) had to be reconsidered in order to ensure that students and lifelong learners were future-ready. And as we looked beyond our ranks to interact with and discuss our draft motion with elected MPs who joined the Motion, we noticed greater buy-in from members of the House which even if it was not convincingly bipartisan, ultimately culminated in a framework proposed for an action plan to implement the Motion beyond the session that we introduced it.

As we met to iron out the details of the Motion and the aspects that various members would speak to, we realised that the Motion stirred different emotions which went to our own experiences with the education system and the MOE respondents and stakeholders whom we had met. We also realised that we had different views amongst ourselves as to which aspects of the Motion we should emphasise more and what needed to be changed as a priority and what could be tackled at a different time. As we wrote our speeches, we decided that we would not only speak to our researched positions and expertise, but also from our personal experience with the education system. Personalising the Motion to make it true to our lived experiences and the schools, educators and students who left a mark on us.

NMP Ganesh Rajaram and I questioned the ethics of an over-reliance on tuition for academic and sports education which appear to privilege certain segments of society over others. In addition to highlighting the changes that RI was making to ensure a level playing field for its students, I shared the challenges that some neighbourhood primary school students face which can be addressed by "tough love" from firm yet supportive teachers who make house visits to convince parents to send their children to school.

NMP Kuik Shiao-Yin highlighted the importance of recognising the talents of every student and suggested ways to refine how assessments are conducted in primary and secondary schools so as to progressively encourage students to become independent and confident in their thinking.

MP Louis Ng asked that performance-based rankings of teachers be reviewed. He suggested that pre-school and lower primary students should be encouraged to play and explore; and that we should not be overly focused on academic content in early childhood education.

NMP Kok Heng Leun suggested how humanities education should be promoted as a means to encourage critical thinking and asked if it is finally time to do away with the PSLE given that more than 70% of respondents to a survey had found the PSLE out of step with the times and wanted to see alternatives this "sacred cow" being discussed by MOE.

NMP Chia Yong Yong and MP Rahayu Mahzam asked that special education schools and mainstream schools work together to ensure that students with special needs are integrated in settings that appropriately meet their needs and allow for different education pathways.

NMP Associate Professor Randolph Tan asked that we build on the strengths of the current system and anticipate the challenges of technological disruption with effective and future-ready policies deployed in comparable economies; while NMP K. Thanaletchimi wondered if old barometers for success were outmoded in view of new opportunities for innovation.

In the lead up to the Motion and during the parliamentary session, we noticed that the Motion had garnered a great deal of interest from members of the public. In addition to what we were proposing, they were also keenly interested in the fact that the Motion was meant to prompt MOE to act, that it was not, as is often the case, a polemically opposed position between the government and certain NMPs. In this case five NMPs were proposing a motion based on an ongoing review by a Ministry and that other NMP colleagues and certain government MPs were joining in to echo and add to.

In our preparatory discussions, we noticed that our speeches resonated with many Singaporeans who, regardless of whether they agreed or disagreed with us, appeared to celebrate the fact that different members of the House were attempting to work together to suggest improvements to the education system. After all, education is a defining aspect of our shared experience as Singaporeans and one that many of us agree should be periodically reviewed to ensure that our students are set up for success and all of us are encouraged to be lifelong learners.

One might suggest that the process leading up to the Motion, the speeches and the coordination amongst proposers and ruling party MPs who were suggesting an action plan to enable the Motion's tangible implementation; and the reassurance by the education Ministers to consider this in the changes they wished to implement could be seen as an example of how proposals on matters of public interest should be prepared, canvassed and ultimately presented in the House.

Potential

Looking back on the Motion, I am indeed pleased to say that some of our suggestions and calls for further review have been taken on board by the MOE. While the "sacred cow" was not killed, some aspects that cause stress to students and parents were put to pasture.

For example, to ease off the pressure of standardised exams, the PSLE did away with aggregate scores in 2021, so children would no longer be graded relative to one another. This reduces fine differentiation at a young age and recognises a student's achievement regardless of how their peers have done. This will help them focus on their own learning instead of competing with others. Results for the PSLE are also now released without the top scorers and without the highest and lowest scores.

Throughout their secondary school education, students will have tailored opportunities to transfer across courses based on their aptitude and readiness at that time to study the curriculum offered in each of these courses.

Notwithstanding this result, the experience proposing the Motion (and petitions and legislative amendments in the past) makes me question if more can be done to allow for a more constructive role for NMPs who are willing and able to gather qualitative data and surveys to support their views and strengthen their recommendations.

I would suggest three points for revitalising the design underlying NMP-led motions.

Engagement

NMPs should as a rule be given access to resources and research assistance in order to make data-driven and substantive proposals to a legislative or policy review process, and make their recommendations to both the relevant Government Parliamentary Committee (GPC) and a caucus of the Opposition prior to a parliamentary motion being proposed and moved in the House.

Such assistance is vital to ensuring that contributions from NMPs, whether in the form of motions, petitions or proposed amendments to legislation (as driven by NMPs from 2016–2018 in relation to the Administration of Justice (Protection) Bill and the Protection from Falsehoods and Manipulation Bill in 2019), are well researched and structured. This will also encourage NMPs to step outside their comfort zone more often and speak on topics that may be less crucial to the functional groups they represent, but which impact Singaporeans in general, or certain communities, in particular. Increasing the length of time NMPs are given to conduct research that is well documented and allowing for a longer incubation period ahead of motions from NMPs being submitted to the House enables NMPs to engage with the intricacies of the parliamentary system more deeply, and to test their ideas in less formal settings and with focus group respondents prior to parliamentary debates.

Impact

At the sitting of the main motion or at the next sitting, a Subsidiary Motion of consideration should be filed to lay the motion on the table and arrive at an actionable decision (e.g., a call for division of the House and a vote on the main motion) that makes clear the position of the political parties and a clear accounting of why members may choose to vote for, against or abstain from voting for a motion that is ostensibly filed by independents and is in the public interest. Where a Minister, the head of a GPC or the Leader of the Opposition has indicated interest in studying proposals that stem from the motion, a parliamentary record of the outcome of this study should be made and be transparently shared with all members of the House and a summary of the same should be made publicly available. This will help to build accountability and institutional memory regardless of the final outcome.

Iterative Review

To implement the recommendations decided upon in the context of a motion, there should be accountability for the action plan that follows. There should be a role that independent NMPs play in keeping the legislative agenda from previous main motion/petition sessions alive and finding opportunities to present the conclusion of the action plan, which should include both legislative and non-legislative options. This should be presented to the relevant Minister(s), leader of the relevant GPC, Leader of the Opposition and Leader of the House before it is presented in a parliamentary sitting for broader discussion and debate.

Conclusion

In my term as an NMP, I had the opportunity to leverage my experience as an academic and lawyer. This ranged from criminal justice-related bills which contemplated deferred prosecution agreements and renewing the Criminal Law (Temporary Provisions) Act ahead of schedule; to commercial ones relating to changes to the mediation and arbitration legislation in view of Singapore's prominence as a dispute resolution hub and the passage of the Singapore Convention on mediated settlement agreements in 2018.

Beyond this, I cherished the opportunity to inquire into matters of general concern to Singaporeans, such as the housing options for older Singaporeans who may not be able to finance their Housing and Development Board (HDB) loans, what a lease buyback scheme represents to them and how the application process could be simplified and made more accessible. Oral and written Parliamentary Questions I asked also provided greater clarity on the Lasting Power of Attorney (LPA) scheme. Despite its benefits in allowing a person to specify a representative to look after his/her interests in the event of mental incapacity, I underscored the need for updates to the law to guard against fraud.

I fully support the NMP scheme and the diversity of perspectives that it allows in the House in addition to two opposite views from the government and the Opposition. Nonetheless, to remain relevant and be impactful, the NMP scheme should be fine-tuned as this chapter has outlined.

Editor's Cut: A Q&A with Mahdev Mohan

(This interview has been edited and condensed for length and clarity.)

What are some memorable moments from your time in Parliament?
One major thing was the amendments to the Administration of Justice (Protection) Bill, which were tabled by [fellow NMPs] Shiao-Yin, Heng Leun and myself around August 2016. As a lawyer, I was keen to ensure that it accurately codified the common law crime of contempt of court, Shiao-Yin had done a lot of work with students and underserved communities who expressed views on matters of public interest, and Heng Leun is a noted theatre practitioner, so we brought different resources and perspectives on the issues that the Bill appeared to raise.

When we proposed the amendments, though the Ministry of Law took the time to engage with us, there was less of an appetite to consider the possibility of amendment. When we spoke with the Opposition, we realised that they were not keen to consider our amendments because they were minded to vote against the Bill, whereas our position was that we didn't really believe in the Bill altogether, regardless that several aspects represented the law as it stood at that time. The three of us went to the Ministry of Law to make our case for clarifications and modifications, engaged in scenario-planning exercises where we gave examples of how different groups might be affected by the Bill and had discussions with other MPs in the Members' Room. Basically, it was an opportunity for us to ask questions and discuss policy outcomes, and I think it informed the contributions we made in Parliament, the clarificatory questions that we asked, and in my view, made the basis of the eventual Bill clearer.

Although some may feel that all of our amendments should have remained, there are limits in ensuring this is the case without a larger number of MPs who are willing to vote for them. Ultimately, I was pleased that this has generated interest in issues that should be discussed, and that important clarifications on the nature and scope of the offences and defences were made in Parliament and recorded in Hansard, to make sure that the legislative debates are a point of reference for jurists and the court.

I still have a piece of paper with the handwritten words of the proposed amendments from all three of us on it.

How did your time as an NMP change you as a person and/or the work you do?
I guess the most tangible change is that it inspired me to pursue my current passion for online trust and safety. I learnt that some of the greatest risks that Singapore faces are not just from traditional sources as a low-lying island nation, but in maintaining our cyber-security and guarding our citizens against online misinformation. The reality/real possibility of cyber-attacks and online mis/disinformation campaigns was something I noted and had to discuss during my term (e.g., the health data of more than 160,000 SingHealth patients, including PM Lee Hsien Loong, was targeted and stolen). This came to the fore in the context of the Cybersecurity Bill and the Green Paper on Deliberate Online Falsehoods (which in the next parliamentary term culminated in a Select Committee and eventually the passage of the Protection from Online Falsehoods and Manipulation Act). These were significant legislative initiatives, and during my term I witnessed the importance of getting the private and people/civic sector involved in fine-tuning legislative and non-legal options that policy makers were considering. In both instances, I saw policy makers and parliamentarians having at times to rethink and revise their original formal positions on matters

that may not have been, strictly speaking, within their core professional/domain expertise or lived experience.

I would also say my time in Parliament made me a bit more sceptical, and perhaps more practical, than I used to be. What are the steps a policy maker needs to take to make a course of action practicable, even if it is not the preferred course for some? Who are the people who need to join you in this conversation and advocate for a similar position? These are points I think I ask now in part because of my experience as an NMP. It isn't always a fun debate, because as many of us learnt, just as you can ask pointed questions, an NMP — and any MP for that matter — has to be prepared to carefully account for and defend a policy position you take in the House.

What advice would you give future NMPs, based on your time in Parliament?
The first is to "work the room". The nine of us were encouraged to cultivate relationships with each other, but I'd say to just go out there and make friends with both the ruling party and the Opposition. Talk to them as a fellow Singaporean, not like you're someone who's trying to outshine them. I think the Opposition might have worried, at times, about whether some of us were trying to do their job for them; and the ruling party might have wondered whether we had an "agenda" or whether we were aligned too closely with the Opposition. If our job is to do our best for Singaporeans, then go and make those friends and strategic alliances in the House. There should not be unhealthy competition or one-upmanship among MPs if the end goal is to do right by Singaporeans.

The second is to make sure you've done your research. In the past, the way we'd get shown up was to be told we didn't have empirical evidence. You can't do things broad-brush, so even if it's just anecdotal evidence, you've got to find some way of canvassing the ground, like we did with the *Education for Our Future* Motion. NMPs will never be on the same footing for making changes legislatively because we don't have constituents, but you have to find a way to gather some reliable data. If you can show that NMPs are involved in speaking to ordinary Singaporeans, that's a game-changer.

Finally, I would say that it's important to be open-minded, but always decide for yourself. Organisations and people will approach you — and they might be entirely well-meaning — and want you to present their view on certain bills or issues that society is going through. I'd say hear them out, but ultimately apply your own mind and make sure you're not parroting what they say. Maybe they haven't done their homework in forming their views, like checking the veracity of their sources. Check everything, including the footnotes!

How would you sum up your time as an NMP in one sentence?

It was inspiring to see legislators committed to improving the lives of Singaporeans, but there's also a need for systemic refinements to the NMP scheme to ensure it remains capable of making socially impactful contributions to our laws and parliamentary process.

Lessons and action plans from past NMPs should stand as a guide for future batches. Former NMPs should be invited by future batches to discuss their views for the benefit of the latter's consideration. Such institutional memory is imperative and should be built upon and preserved to empower the NMP scheme. Otherwise it becomes a rinse and repeat exercise of near-term strategic planning every two-and-a-half years. If the NMP scheme is to live on, NMP-led proposals should be more actionable; and with appropriate support, be representative of the actual views and concerns of Singaporeans.

Endnotes

1. The author thanks Siraj Shaik Aziz for his valuable support as his legislative research assistant during his tenure as a Nominated Member of Parliament (NMP).
2. *Yahoo News*. (2018, May 16). MOE to work with popular schools to ensure they do not become closed circles: PM Lee.
3. Levinson, N. (2010), Critical Beats, Places Journal, March 2010. Retrieved from https://placesjournal.org/article/critical-beats/?cn-reloaded=1

Constitutionally Engineering Non-Partisanship

Eugene K B Tan
Nominated Member of Parliament (2012–2014)

> *Editor's Note: It is safe to say that Associate Professor Eugene Tan could be the most quoted NMP and political observer in local and international media, though this was not the reason I reached out to him for this book. He was the first MP to call out the need for a quorum on the passage of bills for constitutionality; in fact, he raised this more than a few times during his term and one bill was even delayed to the following day for third reading so as to fulfill the quorum. I found myself counting the number of MPs whenever the Chamber seemed decidedly bare, thanks to his precedents. In this essay, Eugene offers suggestions on strengthening the selection process for further legitimacy of the NMP scheme as he justifies the relevance of this parliamentary innovation.*

On 8 December 1965 when Parliament sat for the first time after Singapore's independence, not a single Opposition Member of Parliament (MP) attended. Barisan Sosialis (BS) MPs, a breakaway faction of the People's Action Party (PAP), had boycotted the sitting in protest of Singapore's "phoney" independence and the "undemocratic laws" of the PAP Government. In the following year, all the BS MPs vacated their parliamentary seats. BS also boycotted the 1968 General Election, opting to take their political struggle outside of Parliament. This boycott was a massive strategic blunder as it left the PAP unchallenged in the political arena. No Opposition MP was elected into Parliament until J. B. Jeyaretnam of the Workers' Party (WP) won the Anson seat in a by-election in 1981.

Placid politics from independence have evolved to become relatively more contested, somewhat divisive and increasingly partisan. The political contexts are very different when the Nominated Member of Parliament (NMP) scheme was first introduced in 1990 and today, 32 years later. The first two NMPs in 1990, together with Opposition MP Chiam See Tong and Non-Constituency MP Lee Siew Choh, were the only non-government MPs then. Various cohorts of NMPs witnessed the ruling PAP remain politically dominant despite a general downward trend of popular electoral support. In 2020, the WP won a bumper crop of 10 seats.

In that sense, the creators of the NMP scheme were prescient that there was a constitutionally significant role for NMPs, specifically to articulate non-partisan, independent views in Parliament. For a legislature to perform its constitutional roles well, the combination of partisan (government and opposition) and non-partisan views not only speaks to the legislature being more representative but also reduces the perception that Parliament is but a mere rubber stamp institution in a one-party dominant political system.

In other jurisdictions that have modelled their legislative systems on the Westminster parliamentary system, unelected legislators are not unusual but they are often political creatures as card-carrying members of political parties. The Singapore NMP is perhaps unique.[1] She cannot claim to represent her functional group as the latter has neither the legal power to appoint an NMP nor to censure an NMP ostensibly from the functional group. In reality, the NMP is only accountable to herself and to Parliament for her actions or acts of omission. Put simply, an NMP represents herself and speaks only for herself. Moreover, although a lawmaker, an NMP is not a politician. She is, at best, a political actor in Parliament's process of law-making.

Non-Partisanship amid One-Party Dominance

In a one-party dominant system co-existing with a growing number of Opposition MPs, parliamentary debates can and have taken on an increasingly partisan complexion. It is not that elected MPs cannot or do not voice non-partisan views. Rather, elected MPs are bound by a certain party line and the party whip. This leaning towards partisanship is more likely than not in a more politically competitive landscape. Without the burden of toeing a party line, NMPs have full autonomy to speak freely in Parliament. This is of course a broad generalisation. All MPs must endeavour to speak without fear or favour as Singaporeans expect them to.

I had the privilege of serving as NMP (2012–2014) after the so-called "watershed" 2011 General Election. As a constitutional law scholar keenly observing the dynamics of Parliament, I would say that the NMP scheme still has an important role to play.

The NMP innovation also flags the clear institutional preference for "alternative" or non-partisan voices, rather than opposing or partisan ones. This perspective of what Parliament should be, one characterised by consensus instead of contention even in the realm of politics, is in keeping with the harmony philosophy and discourse encouraged by the PAP Government.

NMPs have made legislative debates more representative by providing a wider range of opinions and not inflected by partisan concerns. Partisan politics influences the workings of Parliament such that certain issues and viewpoints are not given adequate airing. During my term of service, I witnessed the strident, seemingly irreconcilable views during the Population White Paper debates and the debates on the Little India riot. I believe NMPs' inputs have promoted the legislative process through broadening political participation and representation. NMPs have enhanced consensus building by the airing of a wider range of concerns and of speaking up for stakeholders who are sometimes inadequately represented such as civil society, migrant workers and small and medium enterprises.

One thought experiment that could be attempted is to hypothetically expunge all Parliamentary Questions (PQs) and speeches by NMPs from Hansard and assess whether parliamentary proceedings would be the poorer for it in terms of the diversity and quality of views expressed and ideas put forth as well as holding the Executive accountable.

As one-party dominance persists amid a more competitive political landscape, non-partisan views take on greater importance. Without the non-partisan input, parliamentary debates could generate more heat than light; it might leave the larger population none the wiser on major issues of the day. Ultimately, it is in Singaporeans' best interest to have laws and policies thoroughly examined, and for Parliament to better function as a check and balance to the Executive.

My Experience in Parliament

NMPs can be a bellwether, a barometer of public sentiments, especially on controversial matters. Take for example, the contentious Population White Paper debates of February 2013. How did the nine NMPs vote when a division was called after days of strident debates? Four for, four against and one abstention. This, I thought, reflected quite well the sentiments on the ground over the White Paper proposals.

I provided the sole abstention. I had abstained from supporting or rejecting the Motion because I had concluded both positions were untenable. I was initially going to vote against the Motion but re-evaluated my position after the Prime Minister took pains in his speech to specifically address and provide assurance on the concerns I had.[2] Although Singapore would require immigration for some time to come, I was also not persuaded by the government's approach in the White Paper.

A key objection I made in my speech was,

> *"The White Paper's emphasising the need for immigration — or the alternative scenario of a lower quality of life — remains quintessentially material and pragmatic. There is limited appeal to and a lack of definitive assurance of the affective dimension that a contested major policy like immigration is so badly in need of. A consequence of close to half-century of nation building, Singaporeans are beginning to imbibe an aspirational approach towards citizenship. This precipitation of a Singapore national identity and belonging means that a hyper-rationalistic justification of immigration is not likely to nurture an affective acceptance of the immigration policy and regime."*

I reasoned that an abstention was my way of indicating that Singaporeans must keep an open mind about immigration, and that the government must always address the genuine concerns of Singaporeans over immigration and demonstrate that immigration unequivocally benefits Singapore and Singaporeans in meaningful ways.

Another related observation from my NMP stint was that the front bench was, more often than not, keen to engage and persuade NMPs ostensibly to win them over, especially those with critical views of the matter under debate. The fact that NMPs are not hewed to a party or ideological position and were not perceived to be engaging in posturing or rhetoric or political point-scoring perhaps necessitated a differentiated treatment of NMPs and Opposition MPs.

Further, where an NMP had expertise in the matter under debate, I would say the engagement was even more pronounced. During my term, other controversial bills included the Criminal Law (Temporary Provisions) (Amendment) Bill 2013 and the Public Order (Additional Temporary Measures) Bill 2014, both of which I spoke out strongly against.

In contrast, and perhaps understandably so, the Opposition MPs did not see it as a priority to engage with the NMPs, even where an NMP's position was not disposed towards the government. This was a wasted opportunity but I recognise that it is the reality of partisan politics.

I participated in parliamentary debates as often as possible, filing numerous PQs and speaking on a wide array of bills.[3] Unlike our elected colleagues, NMPs' sole function is to participate in parliamentary debates. My expertise in the government and politics of Singapore and my vocation as a public law academic meant that a broad swathe of interests and issues before Parliament appealed to me. I enjoyed the labour of preparing well for parliamentary sittings.

Of particular interest to me was the broad theme of governance, especially the advocacy of the social dimensions of governance. Having attained phenomenal economic success through a focus on material well-being, the time had come for Singapore to shift the focus to the seldom-asked "how" questions of governance. These included concerns such as how do we build a fair and just society? How do we live up to the founding ideals of our improbable nation? How do we progress on our National Pledge for a better Singapore? These considerations must form the bedrock of governance and policy making in Singapore if we are to remain cohesive and resilient and a society defined by its values.

In nation-building, process must matter as much, if not more, than the outcome. I believe that we will reach our societal objectives in good shape and as one people, if we journey well together and are true to our founding aspirations and ideals, well-captured in our National Pledge. However, we will be impoverished if wealth and asset enhancement are the be-all-and-end-all of the Singapore Dream and they are derived without due regard to the shared values that Singaporeans hold dear.

Indeed, such post-material aspirations and concerns have grown in importance in Singaporeans' hierarchy of needs and increasingly define what it means to be Singaporean, what Singapore stands for and what we expect of good governance. Too much focus on value in policy making, at the expense of values, can set back the sense of belonging and identity so crucial in nation-building.

In this regard, as an educationist, I had spoken on the particular concerns about our education system and meritocracy as it is practised and their impact on income inequality, social mobility, national identity and inclusiveness.[4] These issues were raised by NMPs in Parliament even before the government and the Opposition took particular interest in them.

This should not surprise us. The government will not dwell on such issues until it has decided on policy shifts. It would not want to draw unnecessary attention to its policies that have not fared so well or are not popular with the people. The Opposition is perhaps wary of wading in until it has clear policy proposals and is more interested in critiquing extant policies. Taken in totality, they reflect the different concerns of NMPs and elected MPs — the former trending towards aspirational concerns and the latter on operational/policy matters with political considerations as the subtext.

It should therefore not surprise us that NMPs have raised issues over the last three decades that seemed ahead of their time but are now mainstream concerns such as gender equality, immigration, disability, mental health, environmental protection, the role of the arts and sports in our maturing society.

Perhaps, one concern of mine which irked some parliamentary colleagues was my insistence that there must be a quorum whenever Parliament is sitting whether as a House or as a Committee.[5] Some MPs take the view that a sitting can proceed despite there being no quorum, so long as no MP raises an objection.

As a constitutional law scholar, I am conscious that any bill passed by Parliament without the requisite quorum runs the risk of it being challenged in a court of law for unconstitutionality. During my term, I had flagged on no fewer than seven occasions that there was no quorum, including when bills were about to be passed. For example, there was no quorum when the debate for the Land Transport Authority of Singapore (Amendment) Bill 2012 concluded on 9 July 2012; the Bill could only be passed when sitting resumed the following day.

But it was always with trepidation when I rose to raise the point of order of whether there was a quorum. From my seat in the Chamber, I did not have a clear sight of every MP on my side of the aisle, which might mean that my own headcount of MPs in the Chamber could be wrong.

Looking Ahead

Although Parliament had institutionalised the NMP scheme by making it a permanent feature of Singapore's legislature in 2010, the persistent question of the scheme's relevance and legitimacy is something that NMPs have to live with.[6] How can the NMP scheme be revitalised?

That challenge falls primarily on each new cohort of NMPs. While it is expected that NMPs bring their expertise and experience to bear on matters affecting the functional groups they come from, they must not be seen as speaking almost exclusively for those functional groups. NMPs should endeavour to speak on a broad range of issues rather than on selected issues and to speak without fear or favour.

Equally important is for Parliament's Special Select Committee to nominate individuals who can contribute on a variety of issues for appointment as NMPs rather than being "one issue" NMPs.

Another area for improvement would be to clothe the selection process of NMPs with more transparency and robustness. I had raised in Parliament that the selection process can be more transparent, including making public the names of all applicants.[7] My premise for more transparency in the selection process is that anyone wanting to serve in our highest law-making body should be made public. Why should NMPs be treated differently from people running for elected office such as the MPs and the Elected Presidency?

If one is afraid of the embarrassment of not being selected as NMP, as then-Leader of the House Ng Eng Hen alluded to in reply to my PQ, it raises the question of whether such a person should be serving as an NMP in the first place.[8] Although NMPs have limited voting rights, they enjoy the same parliamentary privileges as elected MPs. NMPs can speak on matters even where they have no constitutional right to vote on them subsequently. More transparency in the selection process would add to the credibility of the scheme and can help avoid the perception in some quarters that the NMP scheme is a "back-door" mode to having more pro-establishment voices in Parliament.

I appreciate that "merit" is a polycentric consideration when the Special Select Committee determines the suitability of the applicants for appointment as NMPs. It has to fulfil the constitutional requirement for each slate of NMPs "to reflect as wide a range of independent and non-partisan views as possible". But that should not stop Parliament from publishing a list of individuals who applied to be NMPs. I must emphasise that this is not a criticism of the selection process by the Special Select Committee but rather that there are clear benefits of more transparency which outweigh the disadvantages. Opportunists, resume builders and timorous souls will then be discouraged from applying if they find it embarrassing to be identified publicly and not appointed as an NMP. So be it. They can contribute in other fora.

It is also crucial that within each functional group, the process of selection be transparent and robust. Former PAP stalwart and now leader of the Progress Singapore Party Dr Tan Cheng Bock, a long-time critic of the NMP scheme, had articulated his concern that NMPs represent narrow sectoral interests.[9]

For instance, the sole nominee of National Trades Union Congress (NTUC) is always appointed as NMP.[10] This raises questions as to why certain sectoral interests should be privileged over others. Presently, NMPs are mostly nominated under one of seven functional groups, including business and industry, social service organisations and media, arts and sports organisations. NMPs can be appointed even if they are not nominated by any functional group but this is rare. In the selection process, the functional groups operate to varying degrees as administrative mechanisms by which potential nominees are surfaced to the Special Select Committee for its consideration.

NMPs should also be included in and commit themselves to the activities of Parliament as much as possible. During my term, I readily agreed to be a part of Parliament's delegation meeting visiting parliamentarians from other countries. I am also grateful to then-Speaker Halimah Yacob for the opportunity to be part of the four-MP delegation she led to Thailand in August 2013 at the invitation of the Thai National Assembly and the Thai Senate. Due to an urgent major surgery to fix a broken shoulder, I had to withdraw as a member of Parliament's delegation to the 33rd ASEAN Inter-Parliamentary Assembly (AIPA) in Lombok, Indonesia, in September 2012.

Closing Thoughts

The NMP scheme is a product of careful constitutional engineering and adaptation for one-party dominance. It has come of age and it has added to the quality of debates in Parliament with non-partisan ideas and perspectives not bootstrapped by party loyalties or the quest for popularity.

The NMP will eventually become irrelevant — it is not a question of whether but when. It will become irrelevant when Singapore becomes a two-party parliamentary democracy or a multiparty parliamentary democracy. Political parties seeking election to Parliament then will have no choice but to be as catholic in their representation, to raise and advocate a broad swathe of issues and concerns in the legislature. It is probable then that in such a political-partisan environment, the value of non-partisan views may become less appreciated and the value of unelected MPs increasingly questioned despite their small number and very limited legislative powers.

But until that comes to pass, NMPs still have a key role to play so long as they ensure their relevance to the legislative process and as an additional, if inchoate and limited, check-and-balance mechanism in our system of government. They will also have to keep an eye on reinforcing the legitimacy of the scheme. The watchwords of relevance and legitimacy remain pertinent as they were when the first two NMPs took their oath of office in 1990.

All said and done, it was an honour and a privilege to have served as an NMP!

Editor's Cut: A Q&A with Eugene K B Tan
(This interview has been edited and condensed for length and clarity.)

What were some memorable moments from your time in Parliament?
There was not really a single moment, but something which does stand out was founding Prime Minister Lee Kuan Yew's dedication to attending parliamentary sittings. I was in Parliament from 2012 to 2014 and he passed away in 2015, and he was quite frail by then. What really struck me was how he made it a point to be there, and even when he was in a wheelchair, he would refuse any assistance as he walked into the Chamber and made his way to his seat. I think it was only in one of his last sittings that he was helped to his seat by his security officer.

The MPs had a gathering in the Members' Room to mark Mr Lee's 90th birthday in September 2013. We sang the birthday song and had a birthday cake. He made brief remarks. His simple message was that it was important that Parliament continued to command the trust and confidence of the people. Here I was, kind of naive and bright-eyed, and there he was, a founding father having been in Parliament since 1955. Mr Lee was someone who was dedicated to the cause right to the very end. That, to me, was both humbling and inspiring.

How did your time in Parliament change you as a person or influence the work you do?
The experience gave me a better understanding of the practical workings and the realities of parliamentary government: why it is important that the government of the day prevails in its legislative agenda, the role of the Whip and so on. It also certainly reinforced in me the importance of speaking one's mind and being very mindful of the need to back up what you say. It could be an opinion — that doesn't matter — but the

question is, how did you arrive at it? I do think this is the sort of discourse that we must nurture in Singapore. You're entitled to your views, but be mindful to say how you arrived at them and to substantiate it and to speak from the heart.

It was very easy for me to transition from being an NMP to an ordinary citizen. I mean, NMPs *are* ordinary citizens! Singapore Management University, where I teach, is very close to Parliament, and I would walk to and from Parliament. I think I was one of the few MPs who used Parliament's public entrance, which I think the auxiliary police officers on duty were a little surprised by at first. Using the public entrance was a very good reminder that, ultimately, NMPs are all still private citizens, albeit with a public role.

The NMP stint has given impetus to my serving the community in various capacities. I have continued to be active in the public square after my NMP term. Parliament provided an elevated platform to raise issues, and I felt it was important to find other ways to contribute to the community and nation. For instance, I have continued to write newspaper op-eds and commentaries and made submissions to the Constitutional Commission in 2016 and the Select Committee on Deliberate Online Falsehoods in 2018. I also continued with my active community involvement volunteering at various charities and community organisations. Since 2019, I have also served as Singapore's Alternative Representative to the ASEAN Intergovernmental Commission on Human Rights (AICHR).

What advice would you give future NMPs?

Immerse yourselves in the life of Parliament. When I was appointed, I was very clear that I wasn't going to be a one-issue MP; that I would speak on a variety of issues, not just those specific to my functional group or area of expertise. I was also very conscious that NMPs have a very limited, if any, role beyond parliamentary sittings. We don't have constituents and don't sit on any parliamentary committees — so our legitimacy, our standing, very much hinges on what we do within Parliament rather than outside it. So take an active part in parliamentary sittings. File questions. Take part in the debates. But prepare well for them — whether it's research or discussing the topics with people who know the topics well. It is foolhardy to be ill-prepared for a sitting especially when one is taking part in the debates. Being a pedestrian is not any better.

I am convinced that as an NMP I represented no one other than myself, not even my functional group. I would try to articulate their concerns in Parliament where appropriate. While a functional group might surface names to the Special Select Committee, the functional groups have no power to determine what NMPs say or to censure them for it, even if they are unhappy with their functional group NMP's views. That's why it's such an immense responsibility: You have to speak responsibly, not so much as to make your stakeholders unhappy, but so that you can represent their concerns as accurately as possible and propose ideas or even solutions.

The two-and-a-half-year NMP term goes by so quickly. In the first year, you're getting used to the procedures and getting into the swing of things. The second year is probably when you get more comfortable and familiar, but before you know it, the last six months will just come and go. If you look at NMPs' appointments in the last decade or so, it's increasingly rare for NMPs to serve more than one term. In a more competitive parliamentary landscape and a more contentious atmosphere in Parliament, NMPs will have to try a lot harder to have their voices heard and demonstrate that they are relevant — that the scheme as a whole is relevant.

How would you summarise your time in Parliament in one sentence?
I'd say my term was enlightening because I got to better understand the nuances and limitations of Parliament, and it reaffirmed my commitment and desire to continue being active in the public square.

It was also productive. It can get quite stressful the weekend before a sitting as I finalise my preparation for the sittings that week. Looking back, I would say there were many highlights, but something my parents and Brother Emmanuel [the late religious brother from the Gabrielite order and long-time director of Boys' Town] always impressed upon me was not to get used to the trappings of any office. All that disappears — often sooner rather than later. In the end, it's really about what you did that matters, not the office you had.

Endnotes

[1] The inspiration for the NMP scheme can perhaps be traced to the 1966 Constitutional Commission, chaired by Chief Justice Wee Chong Jin. The Commission had recommended the creation of a "Council of State", a non-elected advisory body of "able, mature citizens irrespective of race, colour or creed who have attained eminence or responsible positions in their respective walks of life but who are not members of any political party" with particular emphasis on "ensuring against legislation discriminatory of racial, linguistic or religious minorities...". This Council of State is the present-day Presidential Council for Minority Rights (PCMR), which is chaired by the Chief Justice and comprises elected politicians, former politicians, religious leaders, jurists and distinguished citizens. The NMP scheme tracks closer (than the PCMR) to the original conception of the attributes of the Council of State: an unelected body with no political affiliations that is part of the legislative process. For a robust examination and critique of the NMP scheme, see Garry Rodan, *Participation without democracy: Containing conflict in Southeast Asia* (Ithaca, NY: Cornell University Press, 2018), chapter 4.

[2] See Hansard of 8 February 2013 at https://sprs.parl.gov.sg/search/sprs3topic?reportid=motion-102 for my speech. For Prime Minister Lee Hsien Loong's speech on 8 February 2013, see https://sprs.parl.gov.sg/search/sprs3topic?reportid=motion-106

[3] A review of Hansard would show more than 190 distinct mentions of my participation in debates during my stint, comprising 40 speeches on bills and motions and 141 PQs. *The Straits Times* cheekily gave me the "Range Far And Wide Award" "for having something to

say on almost everything — even the attendance of MPs": see "At the end of the day, NMPs make the House better," *The Straits Times*, 6 August 2014.

4 This is best captured in my speech during the debate on the President's Address on 28 May 2014, available online at https://sprs.parl.gov.sg/search/sprs3topic?reportid=president-address-234

5 Article 56 of the Singapore Constitution provides that, excluding the Speaker or MP presiding, one-quarter of the total number of MPs constitute a quorum. See also my interview in "Of manic Monday and MPs' no-show," *The Straits Times*, 9 August 2014.

6 Prior to it being institutionalised, the Constitution provided a "sunset" clause for the NMP scheme. Parliament, when it sat for the first time after a general election, had to decide by resolution whether there would be NMPs for that new term of Parliament. This proviso was to assuage the concerns from the ruling party's backbenchers who felt that unelected MPs had no place in Singapore's unicameral legislature. The sunset clause was repealed in 2010 vide the Constitution of the Republic of Singapore (Amendment) Act 2010.

7 See my PQ, "Disclosing Identities of Applicants for Appointment of Nominated Members of Parliament," 16 September 2013: https://sprs.parl.gov.sg/search/sprs3topic?reportid=oral-answer-550

8 Then-Leader of the House replying to my supplementary question stated: "The reasons why the process should not be made public, as recommended by the then-Special Select Committee [in 1990 to examine in detail the merits and demerits of various modes of selecting NMPs], are still valid. The Member says that those who want to put themselves up for public service should not feel embarrassed or discomfort. I would presume he is speaking for himself and for others who wish to reveal. But the truth is there may be others who do. It is a balance and I think we would keep to this system because it has worked well. Certainly, I think the Members who have been selected into this House as NMPs have done credit to the House".

9 As a PAP MP, Dr Tan Cheng Bock had described NMPs as "armchair MPs" and the scheme as "a dilution of the democratic process, a dilution of the one-man-one-vote parliamentary system". See also Lim, J. (2021, January 23). 30 years of NMP scheme — are non-partisan, unelected voices still needed in Parliament? *TODAY*. Retrieved from: https://www.todayonline.com/big-read/big-read-30-years-nmp-scheme-are-non-partisan-unelected-voices-still-needed-parliament

10 For a recent affirmation of the PAP–NTUC symbiotic ties, see PAP's Secretary-General Lee Hsien Loong's 36th Ordinary Party Conference Speech on 8 November 2020 at https://www.pap.org.sg/news/secretary-general-lee-hsien-loong-36th-ordinary-party-conference-speech/

Are Elected MPs Enough?

Anthea Ong
Nominated Member of Parliament (2018–2020)

Editor's Note: This final essay of the book and the section on "Possibilities" inverts the question of whether unelected MPs are still necessary: Are elected MPs enough in a supermajority Parliament and a majoritarian democracy? I ask many questions in looking at the possibilities for the NMP scheme and propose a possible reframe of NMP as Non-Majority Members of Parliament (NMMPs) to proportionally represent minority groups and alternative views even in a balanced Parliament. Mostly, I do not think we can examine the NMP scheme in isolation from a discussion on what a future-ready Parliament looks like. I also spill some beans and share some stories from behind the scenes!

"The Nominated Member of Parliament or NMP scheme is a parliamentary innovation in a unicameral system that is uniquely Singapore...,"[1] was how I began my earnest sharing on a wintry morning in London at the UK Commonwealth Parliamentary Association's 68th Westminster Seminar on Effective Parliaments on 25 November 2019. Representing Singapore with MP Murali Pillai, I found myself as an NMP (and my choice of that Prussian blue cheongsam) the subject of much curiosity for my fellow parliamentarians from all over the Commonwealth. Through the week of many questions and conversations, I was shamelessly self-justifying and zealously defending the merits of this feat of electoral engineering, peculiar to the political context of my country with its supermajority Parliament and single-party dominance since independence.

Yet it was only eight years before, following the 2011 "watershed" General Election,[2] that I had promptly turned down a nomination invitation from a civic sector luminary. I was not suitably convinced then of the usefulness of the NMP scheme in an electoral democracy. Nor was I persuaded that being an NMP could be more impactful for the communities that I care about than being a social entrepreneur solving problems directly with people on the ground.

Notably, in those eight years, nothing about the NMP scheme changed, nor did the parliamentary supermajority held by the People's Action Party (PAP). Unfortunately, neither did the mounting challenges facing mental health, marginalised communities (including migrant workers) and Mother Earth (I call these the "3Ms" of my heart) that we were and are still grappling with as a society.

So my mind changed when the second invitation came from the National Volunteer & Philanthropy Centre (NVPC) in early 2018. I stepped forward, no longer asking whether unelected voices should be in Parliament but determined to serve the "3Ms" and curious to find out if elected MPs are indeed enough in a supermajority Parliament amidst rising inequality.

Of "Hobby Horses" and "Unvotables" in a Majoritarian Democracy

I sometimes forget that this supermajority Parliament we have had since independence came as a result of the "extra parliamentary struggle" boycott of elections by the Barisan Sosialis in 1968.[3] It prompted a slew of parliamentary innovations, including the Group Representation

◆ The Nominated Member of Parliament Scheme

Constituency (GRC), Non-Constituency MP (NCMP) and NMP schemes.

During the heated 1989 debate on the NMP scheme,[4] amongst other reasons, then-PAP MP Dr Tan Cheng Bock argued against the scheme on grounds of NMPs "peddling self-interest",[5] quoting then-Prime Minister Lee Kuan Yew by his use of "hobby horse". Dr Tan also added that "…we must beware of the eager-beavers who are supporting this scheme because they want to get into this House to serve their own ends and not the interest of Singaporeans".

I must say I am happy to have proved him right 29 years later — about the "horse" part, not the "beaver" ("eager" would have seen me say yes the first time round)!

"How are you able to speak about mental health in just about every bill?", asked a fellow NMP earnestly midway through our term. Indeed, I was relentless in surfacing my "hobby horse" of mental health during the two years to underscore the widespread impact that policies have on the mental health of the population.[6]

My volition in championing mental health began in 2006 following my own brush with depression.[7] For too long (and in some quarters even today), mental health was merely deemed a "medical" issue but where and how we learn, live, play, work and age clearly impacts our mental well-being. Social inequalities are also associated with increased risk of mental disorders.[8]

Therefore, everything we do — or do not do in Parliament — affects the mental health and well-being of our people.[9] The absence of a robust mental health discourse in Parliament when I joined was thus deafening and disturbing, so was the lack of public engagement on mental health policies. My team and I conducted a public consultation on mental health that informed and substantiated my Budget 2020 debates.[10]

"Hobby horses" are necessary if elected MPs are not talking about them because they are not seen as majority issues. Flagging mental health as a national priority and the urgent need for a national coordinating body in 2019[11] was unintentionally prescient given the devastating impact of the Covid-19 crisis on mental health since 2020.

The first-past-the-post electoral system means our Parliament is based on majoritarian representation, not proportional. We may have built-in constitutional safeguards for racial and religious minorities with the Presidential Council for Minority Rights,[12] but not for all other minority groups, e.g., persons with disabilities, single mothers, migrant workers, the LGBTQ+ community, sex workers and so on, to ensure that bills passed do not discriminate against them. These minorities — some more than other — are what I call "unvotables", as speaking up for them may put elected MPs, including Opposition MPs, in political peril with the majority of voters.

For instance, the government has defended its stance on not repealing Section 377A of the Penal Code, an inherited colonial law that criminalises consensual sex between men, on grounds of majoritarianism, despite the "antiquated law"[13] being challenged repeatedly by eminent legal experts like former NMP Professor Walter Woon, Professor Tommy Koh and former Chief Justice Chan Sek Keong. In October 2007, former NMP Siew Kum Hong bravely tabled the parliamentary petition to repeal Section 377A in response to the Penal Code (Amendment) Bill; although a heated debate expectedly ensued, the law was retained.[14]

Similarly, in order to placate the burgeoning NIMBY ("not-in-my-backyard") sentiments of residents and voters, swathes of migrant workers were moved to the periphery of the island, following calls by MPs in the 1990s. The inadequate enforcement regarding their living conditions[15] and emergency preparedness provisions under the Foreign

Employee Dormitories Act (2015) prior to the Covid-19 pandemic, coupled with seeing the harrowing ground situation unfolding first-hand,[16] compelled me to ask the government if it would consider issuing an apology to our migrant workers during the Ministerial Statements debate in May 2020. This was particularly in light of the stringent confinement of workers to their rooms/dormitories in order to contain the spread of the disease, which has continued even at the time of writing in January 2022.

That question and the response that followed took on a life of its own. I was subjected to an unsolicited crash course on hate memes, trolls and internet brigades. Suffice to say, I came to understand clearly the ills of majoritarian democracy and why elected MPs from both sides of the House — save for activist MP Louis Ng — treaded carefully and stayed away from migrant worker issues, even if these residents are a significant part of our society serving our needs and living in our midst.

Being purposeful with my "hobby horses" and "unvotables" gave me clarity in strategy and courage to show up in the Chamber without fear or favour (most of the time anyway) during my term. NMPs like Dr Kanwaljit Soin ("women and ageing issues"), Braema Mathiaparanam ("human rights"), Faizah Jamal ("environment"), Laurence Lien ("social recession"), Associate Professor Eugene Tan ("constitutionality") and Janice Koh ("arts and censorship"), to name just a few, were similarly resolute and perspicuous over why and what they were in Parliament for.

I am not saying that elected MPs cannot or did not raise these important issues; a good number have. However, I am not convinced they would/could do it with the same focus, consistency and fervour, given that (a) their foremost priority as town council chairs would understandably be the wide-ranging municipal needs of their residents;

(b) they may not have the lived experience or proximity to such issues to appreciate their wider implications across the population; and (c) they may not believe representing these invisible issues and "unvotables" would endear them to the majority of their constituents for the votes they need.

Scrutinising a Supermajority Government: Are Elected MPs Enough?

In the 1989 debate on the NMP scheme, then-MP and now Minister for Law and Home Affairs, K. Shanmugam, argued that the scheme will "make the Government more responsive" because "trenchant criticism" or votes against the government by NMPs who are "honourable and decent" cannot be "explained away easily", unlike that from the Opposition which can be explained away on partisan grounds. The government is also secure in the knowledge that its MPs are subjected to the Whip, no matter the scrutiny. He further argued that trenchant views from NMPs could signal to the people that the government "has not been able to carry the day".[17]

This might be why the good Minister penned a commentary for CNA headlined "NMPs agree with major points of the Falsehoods Bill" on 3 May 2019, in response to the Amendment Motion for the controversial Protection from Online Falsehoods and Manipulation Bill (POFMA) filed by myself, Associate Professor Walter Theseira and Irene Quay (see chapter by Associate Professor Theseira titled "POFMA: Duty, Conscience or Both?"). I would argue that the headline should have more accurately stated that "NMPs *did not* agree with the Falsehoods Bill on *three* major points", but I understand the optics of having NMPs on the side of the proposed Bill. There was widespread public outcry on the Bill; our Amendment Motion received much media attention.[18]

◆ The Nominated Member of Parliament Scheme

"It must be remembered that the function of Parliament is not only to pass good laws but to stop bad laws", said Winston Churchill. As a first-term parliamentarian, I was naively hopeful that the government would concede to some, even if not all, of the amendments proposed, especially given the good faith meetings and negotiations we had with the Minister and the Ministry staff prior to the debate on 7 May 2019. This, to my mind, would demonstrate a well-functioning parliamentary democracy at work — that the government is open to alternative views expressed in a civil manner through existing parliamentary mechanisms — but it was not to be. Instead, I was soon pugnaciously updating my speech in real time as it hit me that some Ministers and PAP MPs were taking turns to gun down our Amendment Motion, perhaps to demonstrate that the government was "able to carry the day".

Choosing to abstain was my way of agreeing with the intent of the Bill but disagreeing over the exclusion of the three major points we raised for the law to be fair and just. Truth be told, I almost pressed the "no" button on my seat at the call for division, as I was rather indignant from the seemingly co-ordinated offensive. Thankfully, I refrained in that split second because doing so would perpetuate a parliamentary culture that is partisan, binary and blunt — that context, reasoning and nuances have no place in debates and law-making, despite the complexities that we are dealing with as a society.

The POFMA experience solidified for me that the government takes scrutiny by NMPs rather seriously; the absence of a partisan agenda apparently makes any disagreements or alternative views by NMPs more weighty in the public's eyes. A senior political office-holder even remarked that our objections to the POFMA Bill could make Singaporeans think that "there must be something wrong with the law".

I also became braver in speaking up after that baptism of fire.

Unnerving as it was to come between the crossfires, I participated in the Motion on Aljunied-Hougang Town Council. In the wake of the Yale-NUS saga involving Alfian Sa'at, I spoke on youth activism and questioned the government's uncompromising stance on activism and dissent, in support of Associate Professor Walter Theseira's Adjournment Motion on liberal education.[19]

Several senior political officeholders tried to "persuade" me in the tea room not to go ahead with the speech that evening.[20] I understood their concerns, given the spate of youth-led protests in Hong Kong at the time, but I would rather have our youths raise their views and concerns — through me in this case — to the right forum for debate in Parliament than via other insidious channels. The "unsayable" *has* to be said in Parliament, which is, in my view, the most important forum for citizen participation, rather than left to lurk and have their flames fanned in echo chambers created by the algorithmic manoeuvres of social media that can only polarise and cause division.

I also strongly believe that *how* parliamentarians debate on controversial and sensitive issues in the Chamber, beyond merely what is said, is role-modelling to the people, especially youths, how we must engage with each other as fellow citizens on the same.

"Inconvenient" I may have been in the Chamber with my "hobby horses", "unvotables" and "unsayables", but several ministries have been sincere in taking up engagements with me beyond the Chamber and turning talk into action; a few have continued till today. The fear of what might happen is usually greater than reality, or it might be that I am still oblivious to the "cost" of speaking up!

Notwithstanding that we must continue to strive towards a balanced Parliament, the truth remains that we do not have one now. As long as the Whip system remains, I would argue that there would not be enough scrutiny of the government by a majority of government MPs.[21] Neither could the growing number of Opposition MPs in a supermajority Parliament practically give voice to all "unvotables" if they need the majority on their side. For example, will the Opposition raise the repeal of Section 377A?

Elected MPs are therefore not enough in a parliamentary supermajority, but are they enough for a balanced Parliament when in a majoritarian democracy, majority interests and dominant narratives are (understandably) always foremost in the minds of elected politicians?[22]

Ask Not if NMPs Are Still Relevant but Whether Our Parliamentary System Is

The NMP scheme today, save for being made a permanent feature and the introduction of the seven functional groups, has stayed much the same in mechanics as recommended by the Select Committee back in 1990 despite the changing contexts of our society.[23]

Notwithstanding the opacity of the selection process and performance measurements, the arguments against the NMP scheme on the grounds of it being undemocratic are a tad too convenient and binary — as are the arguments for the scheme based on the merits of NMPs.

Now that I have been one, I would submit that the question to ask is not whether the scheme is still relevant more than three decades on, or if NMPs will be necessary with more Opposition MPs in the House. Instead, we should be curious about the possibilities for this electoral engineering "experiment" in the context of Singaporean society today.

In much the same way that we have three branches of government under the Constitution, could Parliament also be an equally weighted three-branch structure where the NMP scheme is sufficiently strengthened to be a non-partisan check against the divisiveness of a two-party system from mature democracies we are seeing in the US and the UK? If NMPs are expected to participate in parliamentary debates with the same rigour in research and substance, why aren't they provided the minimal level of secretarial and legislative support as other MPs?[24]

Beyond democratic ideals, we must urgently consider the intergenerational impact of social stratification in an almost perfect meritocracy over 57 years, especially the equity and availability of opportunities for the minorities in our midst. What kind of Parliament will truly represent all Singaporeans and residents, not just the majority? How can the NMP scheme evolve to mitigate rising inequality and widening divides amidst growing political polarisation? Can the NMP scheme be reframed into a "proportional" system as Non-Majority Members of Parliament (NMMPs) that ensures our minority groups, invisible issues, "unvotables" and "unsayables" are represented?

Truth be told, I am still baffled that the functional groups of business, labour and professions were introduced to the NMP scheme in 1997. Aren't business owners and professionals already aptly represented, given their active participation as grassroots leaders and volunteers within the political party system? Aren't Labour MPs more than entrenched in representation through the ruling party? With the economy, jobs and cost of living high on all partisan agendas, these three sectors would hardly ever be at risk of becoming "minority interests"; in fact, they might be "over-represented" by both ruling and Opposition MPs alike. I would argue that these sectors need not be represented by NMPs or NMMPs.

Albert Camus famously said that "democracy is not the law of the majority but the protection of the minority". Issues that fall outside majority support such as arts, sports, migrant workers, the LGBTQ+ community, civic and people sectors should be given voice by design, but who should decide which groups and sectors "NMMPs" should be nominated from? Could we exercise participatory democracy and let the public decide what minority and/or national issues are important to them?

Some open mandate is better than no mandate. If the public is asked to vote for Singaporean of the Year — which is positioned not as a popularity exercise but in recognition of the human ideals we aspire towards — can we ask for votes to shortlist NMP candidates for the eventual slate? Or maybe we could institutionalise the same town hall process of representation and accountability that the arts community has employed over the years to mandate their representative?[25]

Or perhaps, going even further, should we have district elections for non-partisan candidates to be Mayors who will also be in Parliament as NMPs?

I have more questions than answers but that curiosity, I humbly think, is exactly what we need for the system we are in to see itself. We need a national conversation on what a future-ready Parliament looks like and how the NMP scheme needs to evolve accordingly.

We may have a supermajority Parliament but we also have, by all measures, a strong and effective government that is more than benign in intention for Singapore. It, however, could no longer hold *all* the answers for *all* Singaporeans as we mature and evolve as a society. The government is accountable to Parliament, and Parliament represents the people who must necessarily be part of this ongoing effort to strengthen our system of government with a robust, responsive and inclusive Parliament.

We cannot become what we want if we remain what we were 32 years ago.

Ending a Chapter with Love and Gratitude

I love Singapore. There is no greater honour than to serve my country and humanity, and no greater privilege than to serve this way as a member of the 13th Parliament, especially as part of a pandemic Parliament tackling the crisis of a generation.

I would not have imagined that the deep dark place of despair back in 2006 would lead me on a trajectory that saw me speaking up in Parliament for those who cannot speak for themselves as an NMP. I was also speaking for myself as a Singaporean.

This "uniquely Singapore" electoral innovation may not have truly belonged since its birth but I felt deeply the significance of my seat in the hallowed Chamber and also strangely at home. The quote, "Work is love made visible" by poet Khalil Gibran could not describe my experience more accurately, I was wholeheartedly assiduous.

Perhaps, no matter what the NMP scheme becomes, it will always be up to the NMP to choose what this privilege means personally.

On that same trip to London at the end of 2019, I was introduced by a mutual friend to Lord Andrew Stone, a peer with the House of Lords, with whom I share a strong aspiration for the world to have more mindful parliaments to transform politics. Together with a group of House of Commons MPs, he filed a motion for mindfulness training to be part of Parliament business for all MPs in 2014; the Motion passed. I had planned to do the same in Singapore, but it was not to be as Covid-19 hit and then Parliament dissolved shortly after. This remains my only unfulfilled wish.

I completed my 21-month term on 23 June 2020 when Parliament dissolved for the 2020 General Election. I did not intend to seek a second

◆ The Nominated Member of Parliament Scheme

term as I was completely certain that I would not be re-selected, but finally relented the week before the closing date when a group of young changemakers earnestly asked me to. How could I not show them that it is okay to throw yourself in the arena, even if the odds are stacked against you? Or that there is no shame in not being selected after publicly sharing that you are applying for a second term, knowing that either result says something about the NMP scheme and its selection process?

I turned down the NMP invitation the first time round; perhaps it was befitting that I would be turned down for a second term. I am thankful that I gave my all when I could.

Editor's Cut: A Q&A with Anthea Ong
(This interview has been edited and condensed for length and clarity.)

What is your most memorable moment from your time in Parliament?
Too many! The first one would be getting the House to take three mindful breaths with me before I made my maiden speech. I do this centering practice at each meeting and/or talk, whether with CEOs or 15-year-old students. What we do in Parliament is an immense responsibility which affects everyone in this country, so how can we not be totally present and engaged for each sitting? I went in with that thought, but was a real ball of nerves — wondering if there was something in the Standing Order that could mean breaking the rules since this hasn't been done before, or if I was going to be seen as un-parliamentary…but I did it, and everyone went along with it. I was delighted that the Prime Minister, who also meditates himself, gave me an encouraging smile and started thumping the armrest! As a rookie NMP and a dedicated meditation practitioner, with all the nerves I was carrying, that was a very very special moment.

POFMA, obviously, is another. Being so deeply involved in the law-making process of such a significant piece of legislation was incredibly hard work but also strangely energising and empowering…When I look back, I'm like: Was that really me doing and saying all that in Parliament? There was indignation too, like when Minister Shanmugam stood up and said that we NMPs weren't legally trained in a way that seemed to be slighting our effort, and the seemingly coordinated offensive against our amendments by the PAP MPs. Where did that courage and clarity come from in standing up and responding to all that in real time? I'm still clueless.

There are many little things too, like PM Lee coming up to me in the tea room after reading my book, *50 Shades of Love*. His jaw dropped a bit when he asked me how long I meditate and I said sometimes two hours! Such encounters are very special, because they're such human moments in an otherwise very officious setting.

How did being an NMP change you as a person and/or the work you do?
Before being an NMP, I was already very invested within civil society, inhabiting these diverse spaces and communities — sometimes being an ideator, sometimes playing an advisory or mentorship role — so being an NMP was an extension, albeit a significant one, of my role as a changemaker.

Having said all that, the experience was still very transformative for me. It's very strange, because it's not like I'd never been in a position of power or influence from my C-suite experience, but I felt quite strongly throughout that this was a very different, a higher kind of authority and responsibility. The responses I got towards some of my speeches, and the sheer number of strangers who reached out to me — this sense that people really believed in me or had high hopes for what I would do, was all very new and humbling.

I'm human, and I would be lying if I say it didn't feel good to be received so positively — it also really helped when the hate memes came! — but at the same time, I knew that if I wasn't mindful, it would be easy to get carried away with all the attention and forget my purpose and the people I was there for. This privilege wasn't given to me, for me. I wanted to come to it as the Singaporean I am, who loves my country and my people, and was therefore very intentional about the need to ground myself so I bring the voices of the people into Parliament, not just mine. Every morning when I meditated and journaled, I would bring myself back to my true nature without all the labels. It was strange but I don't think my spiritual practice was deeper than it was during those two years as a parliamentarian! The higher I went on the outside, the deeper I had to go inside.

Based on your time in Parliament, what advice would you give future NMPs?
There are practical aspects to this, and then there are more introspective ones.

In terms of the practical, I would say organise yourself. I don't just mean getting legislative help, but actually doing some strategic planning as to the support systems you will need for the next two-and-a-half years, and having a clear vision in mind as to what you want to achieve.

It takes a while to get into the swing of things — there's a very brief onboarding process, and suddenly there are all these bills to read and it can be so, so daunting when you're not trained in reading legalese or know about the drafting process. I was thankful that I had years of C-suite experience in strategic planning and was already active in civil society. So, like a professional beggar, I went out and asked who would like to join me as my support team. By the end of my term, I had a vibrant collective of almost 40 outstanding volunteers that I called Legislative Angels to discuss strategies with, do research and offer moral support. But in mobilising these volunteers, it's also really important to know your vision during your term — how else are you going to convince them to give you their time?

I think it's also important to try and align with your fellow NMPs. For example, I supported Associate Professor Walter Theseira in his Adjournment Motion on liberal education, and Professor Lim Sun Sun supported my Adjournment Motion on closing the digital divide. My cohort had discussed tabling a motion together on mental health but the spate of Covid-19 Budget debates and then Parliament dissolving shortly after made that moot. Associate Professor Walter Theseira and I also discussed a possible motion on repealing Section 377A.

Becoming a public figure overnight is not always comfortable for everyone, nor is the great responsibility that comes with such privilege.

It's not helpful too that the narrative of NMPs is not always flattering or empowering. In my early days as an NMP, during a coffee with Professor Tommy Koh, he wisely said, "Whether the NMP scheme is tokenistic or not is up to you." I think it's important to set your intention as an NMP. Who am I, what are my values? Who am I giving voice to, how will I do that? What do I want to bring to this role?

There are no right or wrong answers, but I do think that if you don't ask yourself these questions, it might not be a very fulfilling journey even if you're well-organised because you may not be able to act without fear or favour. Nor do you want to get caught out when your term ends and find yourself asking, what have I done and who have I been in my time here?

How would you sum up your time as an NMP in one sentence?
It was a gift in the most monumental way, because it wasn't just about getting to bring all the people who trusted in me along on this journey, but also allowed me to see my own gifts and vulnerabilities in the most humbling manner.

I'm still only just beginning to accept that I deserve this as my place to be — that of a leader, advocate, activist working for change from the ground all the way to the highest law-making body of the country. Yes, there were uncomfortable parts like losing my anonymity and stretching myself beyond exhaustion given the lack of institutional support, but those were small inconveniences. It was such an expansive and empowering process for me and ultimately a deep, deep privilege to get to serve in this way. In showing up wholeheartedly, I finally got to understand what it means to be part of something larger.

Endnotes

1. In many bicameral parliaments of the Westminster system, nominated members for the Upper House are common for e.g., House of Lords in the UK, House of Senators in Canada, Dewan Negara in Malaysia and Rajya Sabha in India. However, in the 1990 debate on introducing the NMP scheme in Parliament, then-First Deputy Prime Minister Goh Chok Tong also mentioned that 20 countries including Botswana, Pakistan and Bangladesh also had nominated members in their parliaments which were incidentally met with some slight disdain by some MPs for that comparison made (Hansard vol. 54, 1989). See more on appointed MP systems in Appendix E.

2. The ruling party faced challengers in every electoral division for the first time since 1963. GE 2011 was the first elections in which the Workers' Party managed to secure a Group Representation Constituency (GRC), which had previously seemed impenetrable. The Opposition secured nearly 40% of the popular vote and observers characterised it as a "watershed" moment in Singaporean politics. Tan, K. Y. L., and Lee, T. (eds.) (2011) *Voting in change: Politics of Singapore's 2011 General Election*. Ethos; Chong, T. (2012). A Return to Normal Politics: Singapore General Elections 2011. *Southeast Asian Affairs*, 283–298. http://www.jstor.org/stable/41714000

3. Lee, T. H. (1996). *The open united front: The communist struggle in Singapore, 1954–1966*. South Seas Society.

4. Hansard, 29 November 1989, vol. 54, col. 695. Second Reading Speech by Goh Chok Tong, Constitutional (Amendment) Bill (No. 2).

5. Hansard, 29 November 1989, vol. 54, col. 723. Dr Tan Cheng Bock, Constitutional (Amendment) Bill (No. 2).

6. Excluding Parliamentary Questions and Committee of Supply (COS) speeches, I made 36 parliamentary speeches during my two-year term — half of which were either completely on mental health or have parts mentioned.

7. I have shared the story of this colossal collapse of my life openly and widely as part of my mental health advocacy.

8. More literature on "Social Determinants of Mental Health" can be found on the World Health Organization (WHO) website.

9. It was also with this in mind that I invited the House to take three deep breaths with me at the start of my maiden speech because it is important that we as parliamentarians bring our full presence to the Chamber. Hansard, 20 November 2018, vol. 94. Anthea Ong, Employment (Amendment) Bill.

10. This was the first public consultation on mental health in Singapore conducted by my volunteers and I that attracted 500 respondents and numerous mental health groups. This effort became SG Mental Health Matters, a citizen-led initiative comprising mental health practitioners, researchers and advocates to engage the public on mental health policies. We conducted another in 2021 and put forth a policy recommendation for a permanent mental health office under the Prime Minister's Office to the Prime Minister and relevant Ministers.

11. In Budget and COS 2021, the government announced three new priorities in mental health to be established: (1) a national mental wellbeing strategy; (2) a national mental health resource platform; and (3) a national mental health competency framework.

◆ The Nominated Member of Parliament Scheme

12 I filed a Parliamentary Question asking if we should consider establishing a similar body that ensures that all bills passed in Parliament are scrutinised to ensure that they do not discriminate against key minority communities, outside of race and religion. Anthea Ong, Singapore Parliamentary Debates, Employment Rate for Differently-abled Persons in Last Three Years (19 November 2018), vol. 94, sitting 85. Retrieved from https://sprs.parl.gov.sg/search/sprs3topic?reportid=written-answer-na-4342

13 Tembusu College Article by Professor Tommy Koh, 25 September 2018.

14 Hansard, 22 October 2007, vol. 83. Penal Code (Amendment) Bill.

15 The government announced in June 2020 that a major programme will be put in place to build additional dormitories with higher standards for migrant workers.

16 I initiated a WhatsApp group of migrant worker non-governmental organisations (NGOs) as founder of A Good Space (a community of changemakers) at the onset of the pandemic in February 2020 which quickly grew to a pseudo-humanitarian effort when the Covid-19 outbreak spread quickly across the dormitories.

17 Hansard, 30 November 1989, vol. 54, col. 820. K. Shanmugam, Constitutional (Amendment) Bill (No. 2).

18 Please read Associate Professor Walter Theseira's chapter on "POFMA: Duty, Conscience or Both?" where he dedicated his essay to the process of the POFMA Amendment Motion that we undertook and his views on the role of NMPs as a check on the parliamentary processes.

19 Hansard, 7 October 2019, vol. 94. Adjournment Motion on A Liberal Education and Corruption of the Youth.

20 Whether it is a smart thing to do, I always give my speeches beforehand — in good faith and also in response to request by the relevant Ministry.

21 In the debate on the NMP scheme, two quotes by MPs S. Chandra Das and Dr Aline Wong stood out as validation for this claim I make. Both did not support the NMP scheme and spoke passionately against it but they concluded their speeches with these statements. Chandra Das: "Sir, much as I am not in favour of the Bill, party discipline does not allow me to do anything else but to say 'Aye' when the Bill is put to a vote." (Hansard, 29 September 1989, vol. 54, col. 720); Dr Aline Wong: "Under the circumstances where the Party Whip is not lifted, voting is compulsory but speaking is not, I beg the First Deputy Prime Minister to interpret the silence of some Members judiciously." (Hansard, 29 September 1989, vol. 54, col. 746).

22 It is noteworthy that even balanced parliaments in liberal democracies like the UK, Canada and the US have appointed members or political appointees systems. See Appendix E.

23 Report of the Select Committee on the Constitution of the Republic of Singapore (Amendment No. 2) Bill (no 41/89) (Presented to Parliament on 18 December 1990).

24 I raised this issue of lack of legislative and secretarial support directly to Speaker Tan Chuan-Jin twice. My fellow NMP Associate Professor Walter Theseira also raised this in Budget/COS 2019.

25 Please read the chapter by former NMPs Audrey Wong and Janice Koh on the arts community town hall process. In 2020, the green sector attempted to do the same and put forth all three nominees as their representatives.

Appendix A: Constitutional Provisions

Excerpted from the Fourth Schedule (Appointment of Nominated Members of Parliament) of the Constitution of the Republic of Singapore

Timeline for Appointment

Section 1(2): Subject to the provisions of this Constitution, the President shall, within 6 months after Parliament first sits after any General Election, appoint as nominated Members of Parliament the persons nominated by a Special Select Committee of Parliament.

Length of Term

Section 1(4): Subject to Article 46, every person appointed as a nominated Member of Parliament shall serve for a term of 2 1/2 years commencing on the date of his appointment.

Call for Names and Nomination Process

Section 2(1): In preparing the list of persons to be appointed as nominated Members of Parliament by the President, the Special Select Committee shall invite the general public to submit names of persons who may be considered for nomination by the Committee.

Section 2(2): Every name submitted under subsection (1) shall be made in such form as the Special Select Committee may determine, and shall be signed by 2 persons as proposer and seconder, respectively, and by not less than 4 other persons, all of whose names shall appear in any current register of electors.

Section 2(3): Before making any nomination for the appointment of nominated Members of Parliament, the Special Select Committee shall, wherever possible, consult other Members of Parliament in such manner as it thinks fit.

Number of NMPs and Selection Criteria

Section 3(1): The Special Select Committee shall, from the names of persons submitted to the Committee under section 2, nominate not more than 9 persons for appointment by the President as nominated Members of Parliament.

Section 3(2): The persons to be nominated shall be persons who have rendered distinguished public service, or who have brought honour to the Republic, or who have distinguished themselves in the field of arts and letters, culture, the sciences, business, industry, the professions, social or community service or the labour movement; and in making any nomination, the Special Select Committee shall have regard to the need for nominated Members to reflect as wide a range of independent and non-partisan views as possible.

Composition of Selection Committee

Section 1(3): The Special Select Committee of Parliament shall consist of the Speaker as Chairman and 7 Members of Parliament to be nominated by the Committee of Selection of Parliament.

Appendix B: Timeline of Key Developments

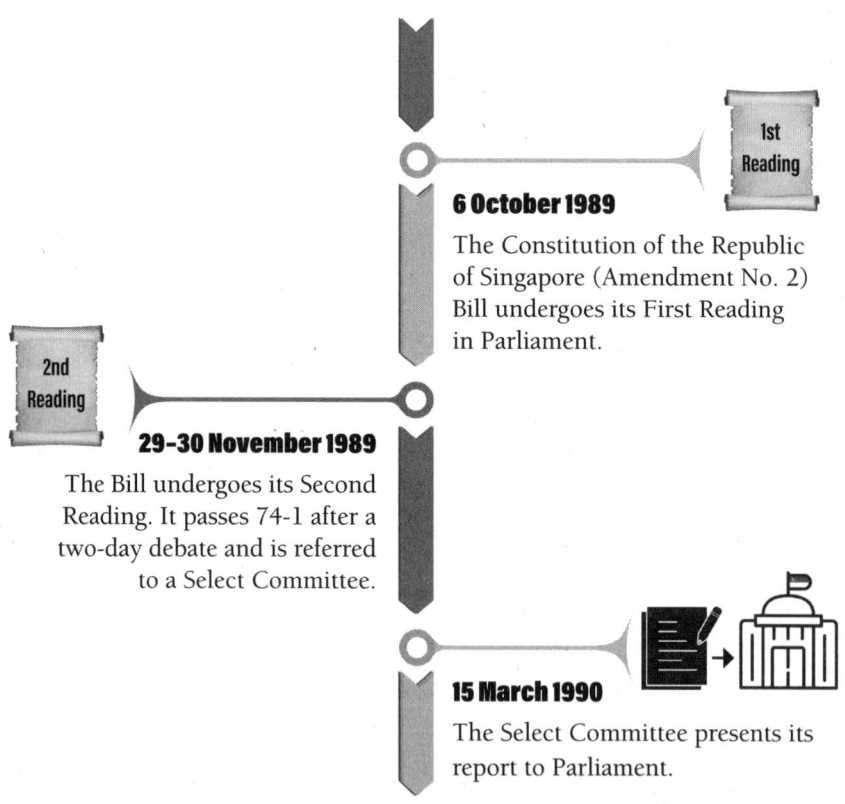

6 October 1989 — 1st Reading
The Constitution of the Republic of Singapore (Amendment No. 2) Bill undergoes its First Reading in Parliament.

29–30 November 1989 — 2nd Reading
The Bill undergoes its Second Reading. It passes 74-1 after a two-day debate and is referred to a Select Committee.

15 March 1990
The Select Committee presents its report to Parliament.

Appendix B: Timeline of Key Developments ◆

29 March 1990

The Bill undergoes its Third Reading and is enacted as the Constitution of the Republic of Singapore (Amendment) Act 1990.

It allows for a maximum of six NMPs to be appointed for a two-year term, with Parliament given the discretion to decide whether to appoint NMPs by passing a resolution.

10 September 1990

The NMP scheme is introduced in Parliament, with the Constitution of the Republic of Singapore (Amendment) Act 1990 going into effect.

22 November 1990

The first two NMPs, Professor Maurice Choo and Leong Chee Whye, are appointed from a slate of 10 candidates.

◆ The Nominated Member of Parliament Scheme

31 July 1997

The Constitution of the Republic of Singapore (Amendment) Act 1997 is passed, raising the maximum number of NMPs from six to nine.

> Three Proposal Panels, representing business and industry, the professions and the labour movement, are also set up to recommend candidates for consideration.

27 August 2002
The Constitution of the Republic of Singapore (Amendment) Act 2002 is passed, extending NMPs' term of service from two to two-and-a-half years.

27 May 2009

Prime Minister Lee Hsien Loong proposes that the people sector be added to the list of interest groups from which NMP nominations are sought (business and industry, the professions, the labour movement, social and community organisations, media, arts and sports and higher education institutions).

26 April 2010

The Constitution of the Republic of Singapore (Amendment) Act 2010 is passed, effectively entrenching the NMP scheme.

The amendments abolish the requirement for a parliamentary resolution to appoint NMPs for that term, replacing it with the requirement to appoint NMPs within six months after Parliament first sits following a general election.

Appendix C: Comparison of NMPs and NCMPs

	Nominated Members of Parliament (NMPs)	Non-Constituency Members of Parliament (NCMPs)
Year scheme introduced	1990	1984
Political affiliation	None. Candidates may be considered as official nominees from one of the functional groups or as independent applicants	Opposition political party which has lost in a general election. NCMP seats will be offered to the losing candidates with the highest percentage of votes in their electoral division, subject to several conditions (see below)
Number	Capped at nine	Twelve less the number of Opposition MPs elected to Parliament

Appendix C: Comparison of NMPs and NCMPs ♦

(Continued)

	Nominated Members of Parliament (NMPs)	Non-Constituency Members of Parliament (NCMPs)
Length of term	Two-and-a-half years from date of appointment or until Parliament is dissolved	Five years, non-renewable or until Parliament is dissolved
	NMPs may reapply to serve further terms	
Salary/ remuneration	Currently pegged at 15% of an MP's annual allowance	
Qualifying criteria	Same as elected MPs, i.e.: • Singapore citizen aged 21 or above • Name must appear in a current register of electors • Must have been a resident of Singapore for at least 10 years • Must be able to speak, read and write in at least one of the four official languages • Must not be disqualified under Article 45 of the Constitution (e.g., bankruptcy, a criminal conviction resulting in a sentence of at least one year's imprisonment or a fine of S$2,000, or renunciation of Singapore citizenship) **and**	

(Continued)

♦ The Nominated Member of Parliament Scheme

(Continued)

	Nominated Members of Parliament (NMPs)	Non-Constituency Members of Parliament (NCMPs)
Additional requirements	The final list of appointees is drawn up following interviews by the Special Select Committee Candidates must have a record of public service, brought honour to Singapore, or distinguished themselves in one of eight fields (arts and letters, culture, the sciences, business, industry, the professions, social or community service or the labour movement)	For NCMP seats to be offered: i) fewer than 12 Opposition candidates must have won elected seats; ii) candidates for the NCMP seats must receive at least 15% of the votes for their constituency; iii) there can be no more than two NCMPs from one GRC, and no more than one NCMP from one SMC
Timeline for appointment	Within six months from when Parliament first sits following a general election	If NCMP seats are offered following a general election, the returning officer must be notified of acceptance of the seats within seven days

Appendix C: Comparison of NMPs and NCMPs

(Continued)

	Nominated Members of Parliament (NMPs)	Non-Constituency Members of Parliament (NCMPs)
Powers	Can speak and vote on any bill or motion, except for: - Amendments to the Constitution - Any motion pertaining to a bill to amend a supply bill, supplementary supply bill or final supply bill (bills authorising the government to expend public money) - Any motion pertaining to a bill to amend a money bill - A motion of no confidence in the government - Removal of the President from office	Same as elected MPs since 2017

Appendix D: Fun Facts and Figures

What started out as merely highlighting some fun facts and figures about Nominated Members of Parliament (NMPs) became an opportunity to assess the NMP scheme in a more meaningful and "scientific" manner.

The research became a rather onerous endeavour, partly due to complete reliance on the way Hansard is organised and the limitations of its search function.

Dr Rayner Tan, a post-doctoral researcher, led the research and analysis effort, with support from Sophie Chew and Teo Ye Heng. He employed research methods such as imputation and box plots to highlight pertinent comparative data.

We believe this is the first time such an effort has been undertaken, and that the data and charts presented here have never been published in this way.

Appendix D: Fun Facts and Figures ◆

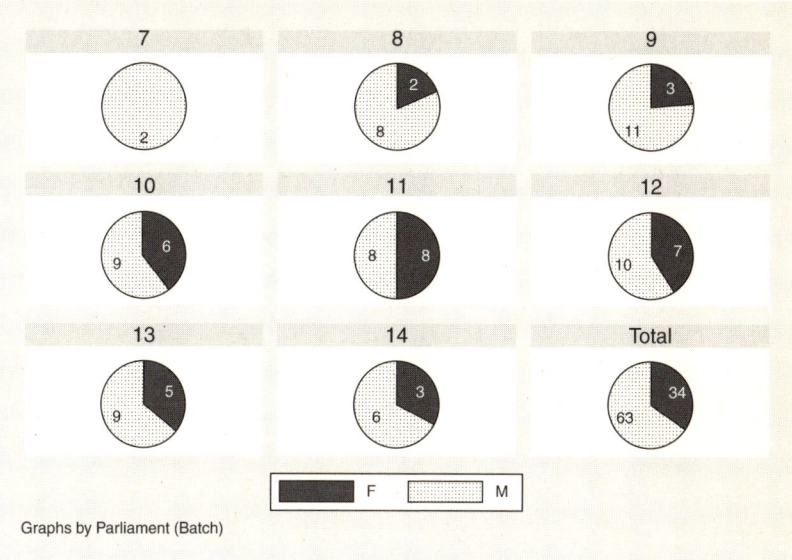

Figure D1. Gender distribution of NMPs by Parliament session

Of all NMPs from the 7th to 14th parliamentary batches, about 64.9% (63/97) were Male NMPs, while 35.1% (34/97) were Female NMPs.

◆ The Nominated Member of Parliament Scheme

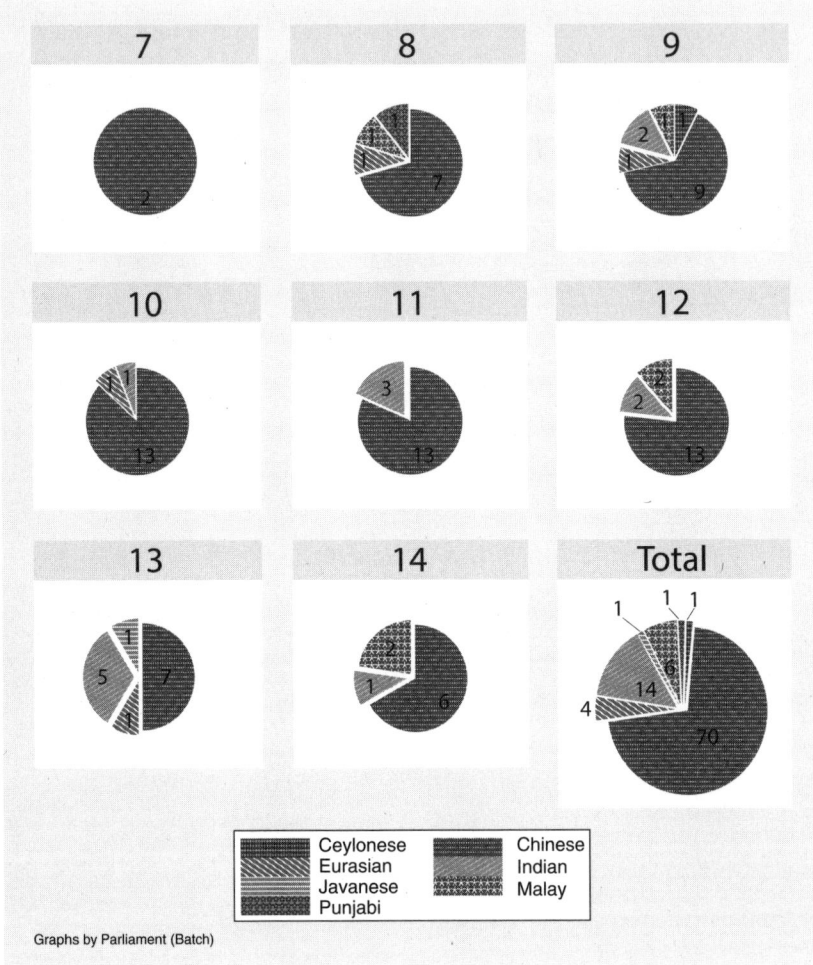

Figure D2. Race distribution of NMPs by Parliament session
Data were verified with the Singapore Parliament Human Resources unit.

Of all NMPs from the 7th to 14th parliamentary batches, about 72.2% (70/97) were Chinese NMPs, 14.4% (14/97) were Indian, 6.2% (6/97) were Malay and 7.2% (7/97) were of other races.

Appendix D: Fun Facts and Figures ♦

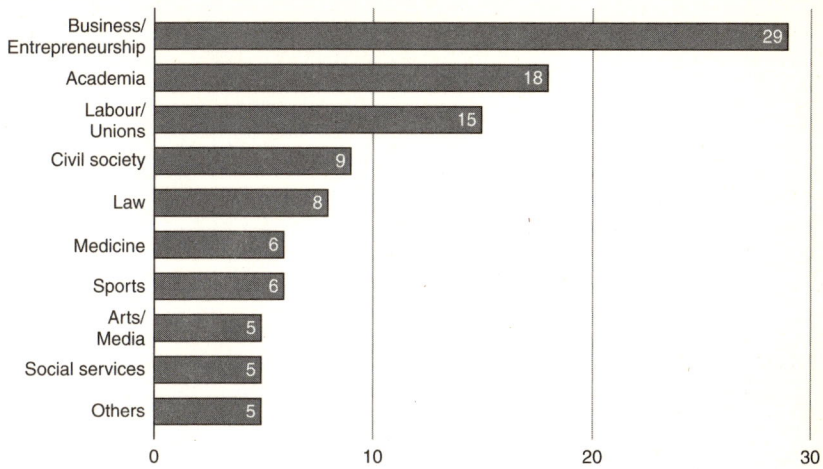

Figure D3.   NMPs by professional background and expertise

Professional background and expertise categories were derived through a process of inductive coding by two analysts. Any discrepancies were discussed and resolved, with any unresolved categorisations being referred to the book editor for a final decision.

The professional backgrounds or expertise that were reflected most commonly among NMPs were business/entrepreneurship, academia and labour/unions. It should also be noted that these numbers are a function of when the different functional groups were introduced, and professions or expertise with smaller numbers tend to reflect functional groups that were introduced at a later time (e.g., civic and people sector being introduced last).

◆ The Nominated Member of Parliament Scheme

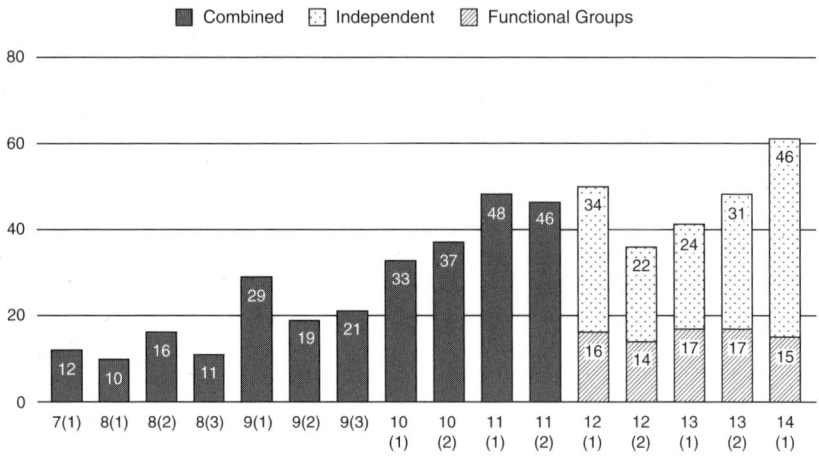

Figure D4. Number of NMP applications per NMP batch

Numbers in parentheses indicate separate NMP application batches within a given Parliament session. Data for applications made through functional groups were derived from Select Committee reports and were only available from batch 12(1) onwards.

Overall, the number of applicants for the NMP scheme has been on the rise, spanning from a low of 10 applications in the first batch of the 8th Parliament, to a peak of 61 applications (46 independent applications and 15 from the functional groups) in the first batch of the 14th Parliament.

Appendix D: Fun Facts and Figures ◆

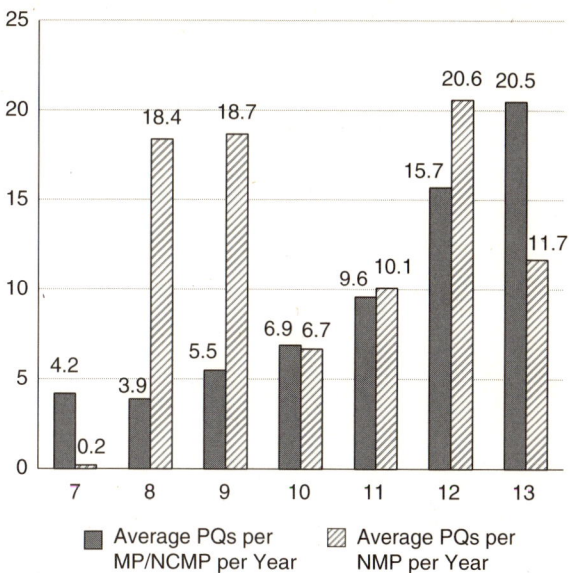

Figure D5. Comparison of Parliamentary Questions asked per year (with Political Office Holders removed)

On average, NMPs have asked more PQs than MPs and NCMPs, except for the 7th, 10th and 13th parliamentary sessions. The average number of PQs by MPs and NCMPs has been steadily increasing, whereas average number of PQs by NMPs fluctuates depending on the NMPs in the respective parliamentary sessions. More details can be found in "Explanatory Notes (Methodology)".

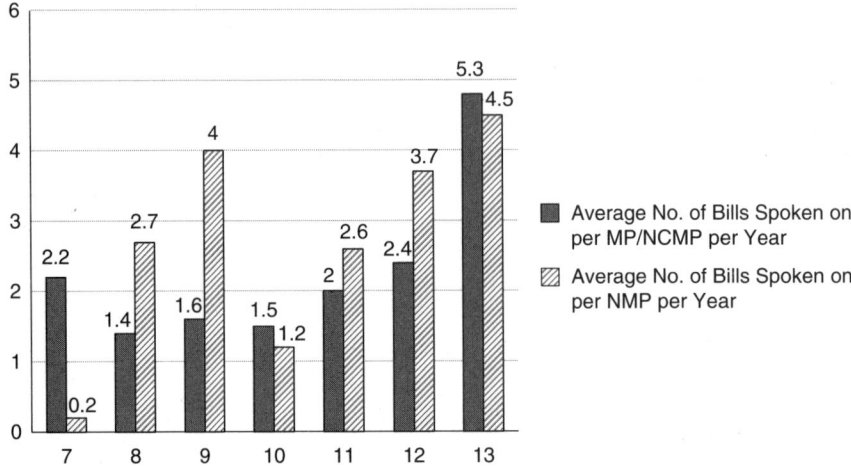

Figure D6. Comparison of bills spoken on per year (with Political Office Holders removed)

On average, NMPs have spoken on more bills than MPs and NCMPs, except for the 7th, 10th and 13th parliamentary sessions. The average number of bills spoken on by MPs and NCMPs has been steadily increasing, whereas the average number of bills spoken on by NMPs fluctuates depending on the NMPs in the respective parliamentary sessions. More details can be found in "Explanatory Notes (Methodology)".

Appendix D: Fun Facts and Figures ◆

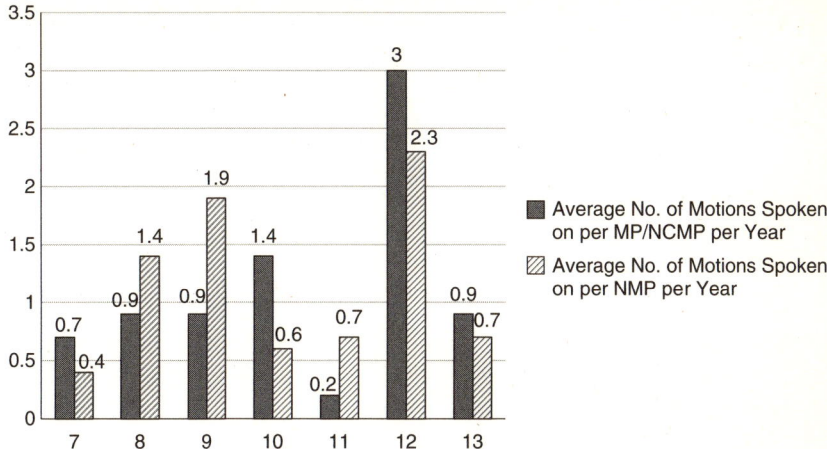

Figure D7. Comparison of motions spoken on per year (with imputation of scores for Political Office Holders)

On average, MPs and NCMPs have spoken on more motions than NMPs, except for the 8th, 9th and 11th parliamentary sessions. Motions are more often tabled by MPs rather than NMPs due to the amount of preparation needed (NMPs do not have legislative support). A motion would involve giving a substantive speech and being prepared to engage in a robust debate on it. More details can be found in "Explanatory Notes (Methodology)".

◆ The Nominated Member of Parliament Scheme

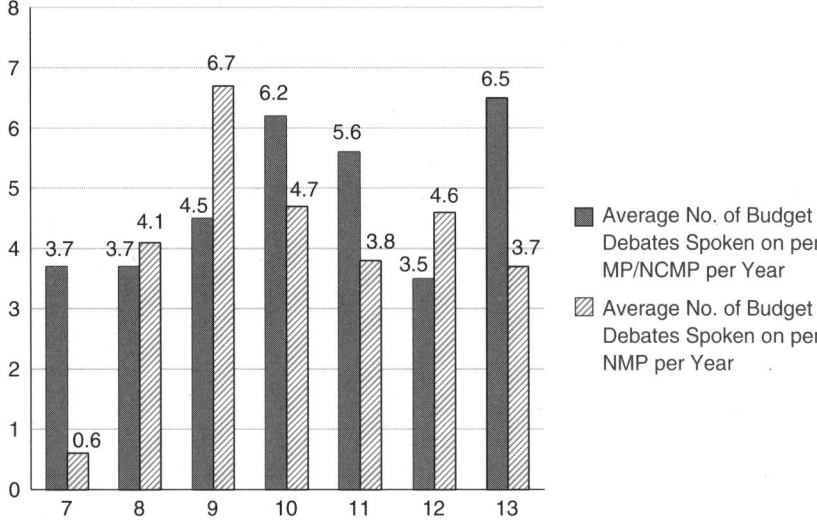

Figure D8. Comparison of Budget debates spoken on per year (with imputation of scores for Political Office Holders)

On average, MPs and NCMPs have spoken on more Budget debates than NMPs, except for the 8th, 9th and 12th parliamentary sessions. More details can be found in "Explanatory Notes (Methodology)".

Table D1: List of Adjournment Motions

#	Title of Adjournment Motion	Spoken on by	Sitting Date
1	Compulsory Teaching of Home Economics and Technical Studies for All Students in Lower Secondary Classes	Kanwaljit Soin	30-8-1993
2	Quota on Female Medical Students	Kanwaljit Soin	25-8-1994
3	Revised Allocation System for New HDB Flats in Non-Mature Estates	Chia Shi Teck Toh Keng Kiat Kanwaljit Soin	26-8-1994
4	Beyond Economic Fundamentals	Claire Chiang See Ngoh	19-11-1997
5	Support for and Concerns Over Economic and Business Development with China	Claire Chiang See Ngoh	25-9-2001
6	Social Service Professionals	Braema Mathiaparanam	27-8-2002
7	Public Information Processes	Braema Mathiaparanam	14-8-2003
8	Charity Practices	Braema Mathiaparanam	19-4-2004
9	Supporting Sports Excellence in Singapore	Ng Ser Miang	1-9-2004
10	Singapore's National Research and Development Strategic Thrusts	Ong Soh Khim	19-9-2005

(Continued)

◆ The Nominated Member of Parliament Scheme

Table D1: (*Continued*)

#	Title of Adjournment Motion	Spoken on by	Sitting Date
11	Policies and Services for an Ageing Population	Kalyani Kirtikar Mehta	17-11-2008
12	Voice of Small and Medium Enterprises	Teo Siong Seng	12-11-2012
13	Sustainability of Small and Medium Enterprises	Teo Siong Seng	21-10-2013
14	Building World-Class Singapore Enterprises	Thomas Chua Kee Seng	4-11-2014
15	Emerging Gaps in Singapore's Sports Participation	Benedict Tan	19-1-2015
16	Preserving Our Heritage, Culture and History — Conserving Dakota Crescent	Kok Heng Leun	10-10-2016
17	Addressing Issues that Limit Artistic Expression in Everyday Places	Kok Heng Leun	10-9-2018
18	The Arts as an Integral Part of Our People and a Strategic National Resource	Terence Ho Wee San	14-1-2019
19	Achieving Arts Excellence in Singapore	Terence Ho Wee San	8-7-2019
20	A Liberal Education and Corruption of the Youth of Singapore	Walter Theseira Anthea Ong	7-10-2019
21	Building a Sustainable and Vibrant Community Arts Eco-system	Terence Ho Wee San	6-1-2020

Table D1: (*Continued*)

#	Title of Adjournment Motion	Spoken on by	Sitting Date
22	Why Fear the Fear of Failure — Imperatives for Refining Our Education System	Lim Sun Sun	3-2-2020
23	Working Together Towards a Zero Suicide Singapore	Anthea Ong	25-3-2020
24	Rational Immigration Policy in an Irrational Age	Walter Theseira	26-3-2020
25	Closing the Digital Divide for SGUnited: Learnings from COVID-19	Anthea Ong Lim Sun Sun	26-5-2020
26	Unending Project of Building Racial Harmony in Singapore	Joshua Thomas Raj	5-7-2021

◆ The Nominated Member of Parliament Scheme

Table D2: List of Private Members' Bills

Name of Bill	Year Introduced	Description of Bill	NMP who Introduced Bill	Bill Passed?
Maintenance of Parents Bill	1994	An Act to make provision for the maintenance of parents by their children and for matters connected therewith.	Professor Walter Woon	Yes. Came into force on 24 November 1995 as the Maintenance of Parents Act 1995.
Family Violence Bill	1995	An Act to protect spouses, children and other family members in situations of family violence or threatened family violence and to make provisions for purposes connected therewith.	Dr Kanwaljit Soin	No, but some of its provisions included in amendments to the Women's Charter.

Table D3: List of parliamentary petitions

Name of Petition	Year Presented	NMP who Presented Petition
That Section 377A of the Penal Code (Cap. 224) be repealed	2007	Siew Kum Hong

Appendix D: Fun Facts and Figures ◆

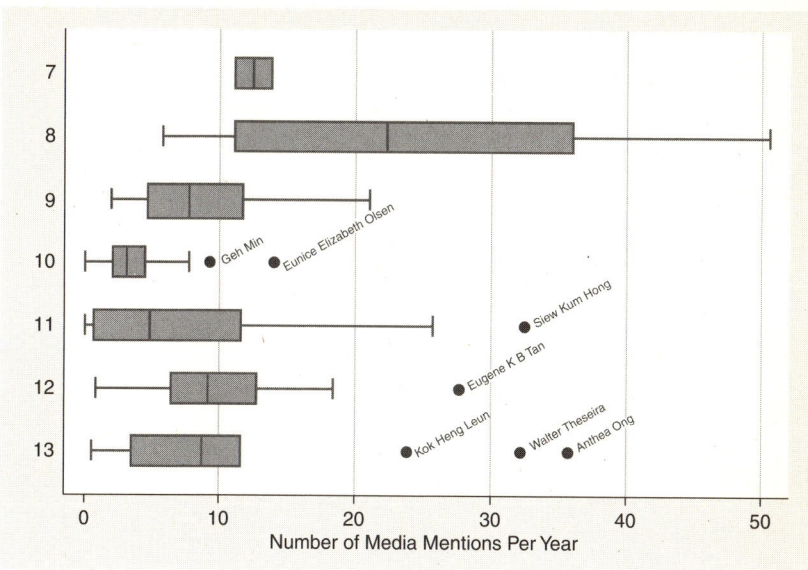

Figure D9. Box plots for media mentions of NMPs per year by Parliament session

Box plots indicate the minimum, lower quartile, median, upper quartile and the maximum per parliamentary session. Outliers on the right side of the boxes indicate that an NMP has had a lot more media mentions than the average NMP in that given parliamentary session. These include Geh Min and Eunice Elizabeth Olsen in the 10th Parliament, Siew Kum Hong in the 11th Parliament, Eugene K B Tan in the 12th Parliament as well as Kok Heng Leun, Walter Theseira and Anthea Ong in the 13th Parliament. More details can be found in "Explanatory Notes (Methodology)".

◆ The Nominated Member of Parliament Scheme

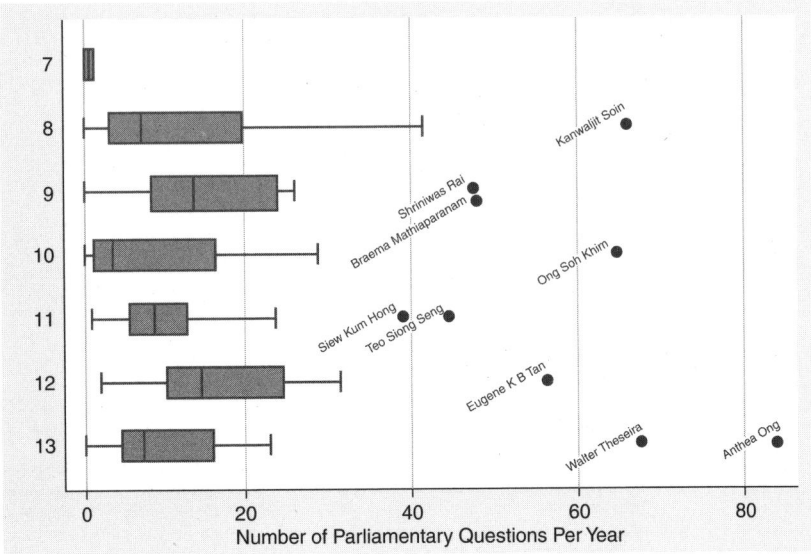

Figure D10. Box plots for Parliamentary Questions asked per year by NMPs in each Parliament session

Box plots indicate the minimum, lower quartile, median, upper quartile and the maximum per parliamentary session. Outliers on the right side of the boxes indicate that an NMP had asked a lot more PQs than the average NMP in that given parliamentary session. These include Kanwaljit Soin in the 8th Parliament, Shriniwas Rai and Braema Mathiaparanam in the 9th Parliament, Ong Soh Khim in the 10th Parliament, Siew Kum Hong and Teo Siong Seng in the 11th Parliament, Eugene K B Tan in the 12th Parliament as well as Walter Theseira and Anthea Ong in the 13th Parliament. More details can be found in "Explanatory Notes (Methodology)".

Appendix D: Fun Facts and Figures ◆

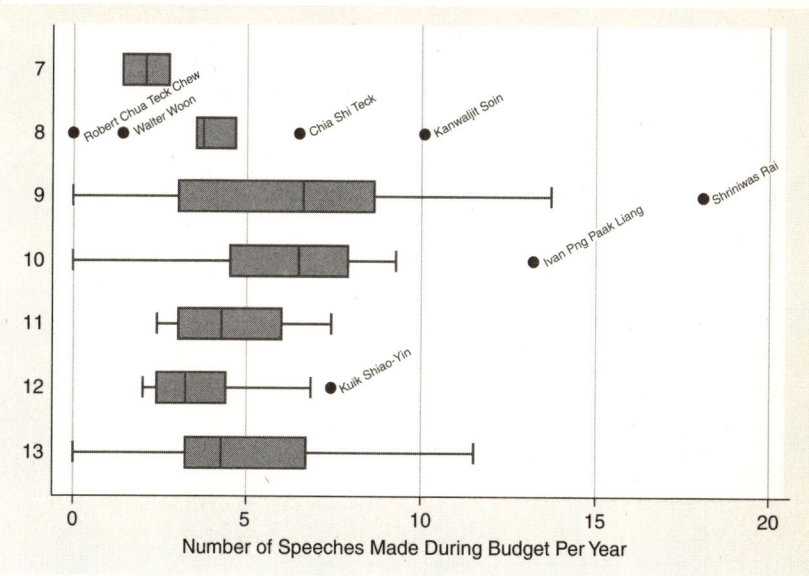

Figure D11. Box plots for Budget debates spoken on per year by NMPs in each Parliament session

Box plots indicate the minimum, lower quartile, median, upper quartile and the maximum per parliamentary session. Outliers on the right side of the boxes indicate that an NMP had spoken on a lot more Budget debates than the average NMP in that given parliamentary session. These include Chia Shi Teck and Kanwaljit Soin in the 8th Parliament, Shriniwas Rai in the 9th Parliament, Ivan Png Paak Liang in the 10th Parliament and Kuik Shiao-Yin in the 12th Parliament. More details can be found in "Explanatory Notes (Methodology)".

◆ The Nominated Member of Parliament Scheme

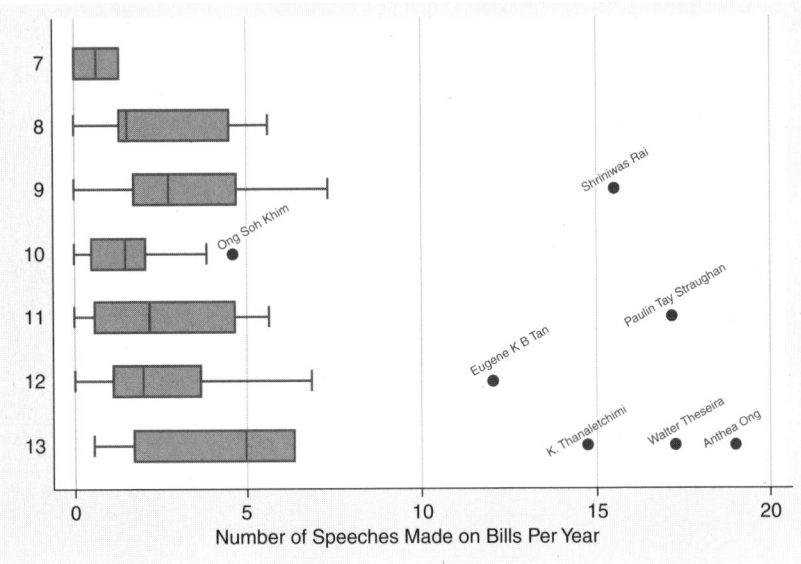

Figure D12. Box plots for bills spoken on per year by NMPs in each Parliament session

Box plots indicate the minimum, lower quartile, median, upper quartile and the maximum per parliamentary session. Outliers on the right side of the boxes indicate that an NMP had spoken on a lot more bills than the average NMP in that given parliamentary session. These include Shriniwas Rai in the 9th Parliament, Ong Soh Khim in the 10th Parliament, Paulin Tay Straughan in the 11th Parliament, Eugene K B Tan in the 12th Parliament as well as K. Thanaletchimi, Walter Theseira and Anthea Ong in the 13th Parliament. More details can be found in "Explanatory Notes (Methodology)".

Appendix D: Fun Facts and Figures ◆

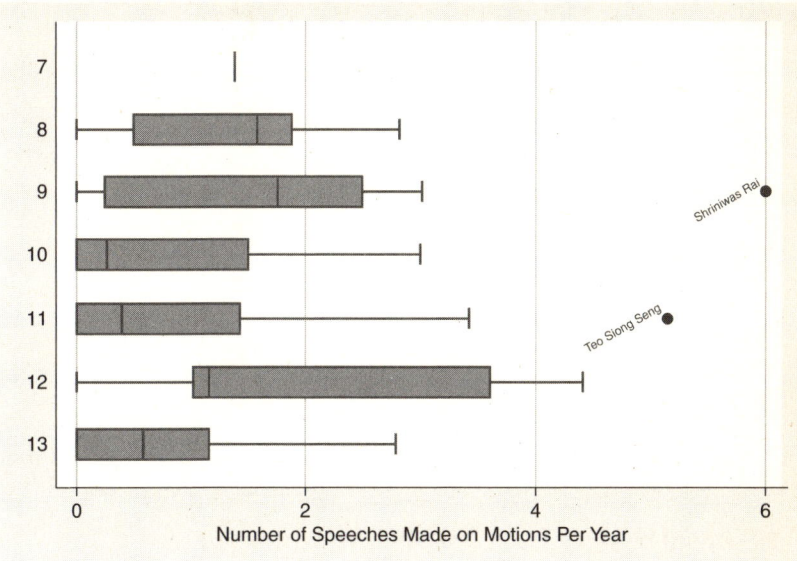

Figure D13. Box plots for motions spoken on per year by NMPs in each Parliament session

Box plots indicate the minimum, lower quartile, median, upper quartile and the maximum per parliamentary session. Outliers on the right side of the boxes indicate that an NMP had spoken on a lot more motions than the average NMP in that given parliamentary session. These include Shriniwas Rai in the 9th Parliament and Teo Siong Seng in the 11th Parliament. More details can be found in "Explanatory Notes (Methodology)".

◆ The Nominated Member of Parliament Scheme

Explanatory Notes (Methodology)
Figures D5–D8

Data were derived from the Parliament of Singapore Hansard. Using the search function, we generated a list of all Members of Parliament (MPs) from the 7th Parliament onwards, when Nominated MPs (NMPs) were introduced. The search function allowed us to select MPs and the categories of documents that they had spoken or been mentioned on. We used the absolute number of Parliamentary Questions (both written and oral), bills spoken on, motions spoken on and Budget speeches made for each MP to generate this dataset.

To calculate the contribution by NMPs, we used the total number of NMP seats for that Parliament session, not the total number of NMPs which would be greater, since NMPs do not serve for the full length of a parliamentary term.

We assumed that Political Office Holders (POHs) would have inflated numbers in the Hansard search due to their responsibility to respond. Since POHs typically do not ask PQs or speak on bills, they are not included in the calculation for average PQs and bills spoken on for elected MPs. For the ones on Budget debates and motions where POHs do participate, we used an imputation method for their data. To do so, we calculated the mean scores for the entire parliamentary session for all other elected MPs (i.e., non-POHs) and imputed these means (rounded to one decimal place) for the POHs, making the assumption that these estimates would be a proxy for the average participation of elected MPs in that given parliamentary session.

We detected glitches with the Hansard search function and attempted to alleviate inaccuracy by doing a second round of the same search.

Appendix D: Fun Facts and Figures ◆

Figures D9–D13

Data were derived from the Parliament of Singapore Hansard. Using the search function, we generated a list of all MPs from the 7th to 13th sessions of Parliament. The search function allowed us to select MPs and the categories of documents that they had spoken or been mentioned on. We used the absolute number of Parliamentary Questions (both written and oral), bills spoken on, motions spoken on and Budget speeches made for each MP to generate this dataset.

Box plots indicate five important summary figures for a given dataset. These include the minimum, lower quartile (25th percentile; start of box), median (50th percentile; line within box), upper quartile (75th percentile; end of box) and the maximum. Outliers are data points that are located outside the whiskers of the box plot and are calculated as being outside 1.5 times the interquartile range (IQR) (the difference between 25th and 75th percentile) above the upper quartile and below the lower quartile (Q1 − 1.5 * IQR or Q3 + 1.5 * IQR).

Appendix E: Examples of Other Appointed Member Systems

Unicameral Parliaments

Botswana

The majority of members of the National Assembly are directly elected under the simple majority system. They appoint another six members from a list provided by the President, who also serves as an *ex officio* Member of Parliament (by virtue of their post) with the Attorney-General.

Dominica

Representatives of the House of Assembly are directly elected under the simple majority system. They then decide whether a further group of Senators are to be appointed or elected by their vote. If Senators are appointed, five of these are on the advice of the Prime Minister, while four are on the advice of the Opposition leader.

Kuwait

The majority of members of the National Assembly are directly elected. The remaining seats are filled by appointed Cabinet Ministers (capped at one-third the number of directly elected members) who are *ex officio* members, with some limits on their powers vis-a-vis their elected colleagues.

Zambia

The majority of members in the National Assembly are elected under the simple majority system. A further eight are appointed by the President, and three others (the President, Speaker and Deputy Speaker) are *ex officio* members.

Bicameral Parliaments with Appointed Members in Upper Houses

Canada

Members of the Senate of Canada are appointed by the Governor-General on the advice of the Prime Minister, with seats assigned on a regional basis.

India

The majority of members of the Rajya Sabha are directly elected under the single transferable vote system. The President can appoint another 12 members for their contributions to or expertise in areas like art, literature, science and social services.

Malaysia

The Dewan Negara consists of a mix of elected and appointed members. Each of the 13 state assemblies elects two members. Of the appointed members, four are appointed by the Yang di-Pertuan Agong (the constitutional monarch and head of state) to represent the three federal territories, while another 40 are appointed by the Yang di-Pertuan Agong on the advice of the Prime Minister.

United Kingdom

Membership of the House of Lords can be by appointment, hereditary peership or *ex officio* roles. Members who sit by virtue of their ecclesiastical offices are known as the Lords Spiritual. The Lords Temporal, their secular counterparts, include hereditary peers and life peers, who form the largest group in the House of Lords overall. Life peers are appointed by the Monarch on the advice of the Prime Minister, with an independent House of Lords Appointment Commission also making recommendations and vetting nominations.

Bicameral Parliaments with Appointed Members in Both Houses

Egypt

Up to 5% of members of the House of Representatives (the Lower House) can be appointed by the President, while the rest are directly elected. Similarly, one-third of the Senate's seats (the Upper House) are appointed by the President, while the remainder are directly elected. Ten per cent of all Senate seats are also reserved for women.

Kenya

The majority of members in the National Assembly (the Lower House) are directly elected, while 12 are nominated by parliamentary political parties to represent groups like youth, persons with disabilities and workers. The Senate (the Upper House) consists of 47 directly elected members, 16 women members who are nominated by parliamentary political parties according to their Senate vote share, two appointed members each to represent youth and people with disabilities and the Speaker (an *ex officio* member).

Appendix F: Further Readings

Book Chapters

Ho, K. L. (2003). Legitimation, Legislature and Legislators in Policy-Making. In *Shared responsibilities, unshared power: The politics of policy-making in Singapore*. Eastern Universities Press.

Rodan, G. (2018). Nominated Members of Parliament in Singapore. In *Participation without democracy: Containing conflict in Southeast Asia*. Cornell University Press.

Tan, K. P. (2013). The Singapore Parliament: Representation, Effectiveness, and Control. In Zheng Y. N., Lye L. F., & Hofmeister W. (Eds.), *Parliaments in Asia: Institutional building and political development*. Routledge.

Journal Articles

Abdullah, W. J. (2016). Electoral Innovation in Competitive Authoritarian States: A Case for the Nominated Member of Parliament (NMP) in Singapore. *Japanese Journal of Political Science*, 17(2), 190–207.

Hansard

Parliament. *Parliamentary debates: Official Report.* (29–30 November 1989). Constitution of the Republic of Singapore (Amendment No. 2) Bill. (vol. 54, sitting 8).

Parliament. *Parliamentary debates: Official Report.* (31 July 1997). Constitution of the Republic of Singapore (Amendment) Bill. (vol. 67, sitting 15).

Parliament. *Parliamentary debates: Official Report.* (26 April 2010). Constitution of the Republic of Singapore (Amendment) Bill. (vol. 87, sitting 1).

Author Bios

Audrey Wong served as an NMP from 2009–2011. She is a cultural policy expert, civil society advocate and arts and cultural scholar. She is the programme leader for the MA in Arts & Cultural Leadership programme at LASALLE College of the Arts. From 2000–2010, Audrey was the artistic co-director of The Substation, where she was the first woman to be appointed to this role. She has served on boards and advisory committees in the arts and is currently on the board of non-profit theatre company, Nine Years Theatre.

Braema Mathi served as an NMP from 2001–2004. She has worked as a teacher, a journalist, a researcher, a trainer and in programme development, corporate communications and strategic visioning. She led MARUAH, a human rights group, and is a founder of Transient Workers Count Too (TWC2), a former president of the Association of Women for Action and Research (AWARE), former Board

Advisors at ONE (SINGAPORE) and was the Regional President (Southeast Asia and Pacific) of the International Council of Social Welfare. Braema was also an award-winning journalist with *The Straits Times*, where she initiated the Straits Times School Pocket Money Fund.

Chandra Mohan Nair served as an NMP from 2001–2004. He is a partner at the law firm Tan Rajah & Cheah, a Commissioner for Oaths, a Notary Public and a Justice of The Peace. He has been active in the Law Society of Singapore since the late 1970s, and served as its President as well as Vice-President of the Singapore Academy of Law from 1995 till 1997. He has also served as a member of the National University of Singapore Board of Trustees from 2000 till 2021 and was on the Board of Governors for Duke-NUS Graduate Medical School and NUS High School of Maths and Science. He served in the National University of Singapore Society (NUSS) from the 1980s to the 2010s and was its President from 2005 to 2007. He was and continues to serve in various committees in several ministries, including the Ministry of Home Affairs, Prisons, Infocomm Media Development Authority (IMDA), as a Marriage Solemniser and charitable and sports bodies.

 **Eugene Tan** served as an NMP from 2012–2014. He is an Associate Professor at the Singapore Management University's Yong Pung How School of Law, where he specialises in constitutional and administrative law and the government and politics of Singapore. He obtained his JSM from Stanford University on a Fulbright scholarship. Outside of academia, he is active in serving on several public bodies and comments frequently on local politics and policy issues in the media.

 **Faizah Jamal** served as an NMP from 2012–2014. Currently a facilitator of Breathwork, a mindfulness modality, she is passionate about healing and wholeness through environment and cultural consciousness. Formerly an Intellectual Property lawyer with Drew and Napier, she was awarded a European Commission scholarship to study Environment Law at King's College London. After returning to Singapore, she transitioned into a second career teaching environment education. She has been a member of the Nature Society since the 1980s. Faizah is devoted to sharing the untold stories of Kampong Gelam, where she was born, grew up and still resides.

◆ The Nominated Member of Parliament Scheme

Janice Koh served as an NMP from 2012–2014. She is a well-respected stage and screen actress and has received multiple awards for her performances. She obtained a Masters with Distinction in Theatre Administration from Goldsmith's, University of London under a Public Service Commission Scholarship and has previously worked at the National Arts Council. In June 2022, Janice was awarded Chevalier dans l'Ordre des Arts et des Lettres (or Knight of the Order of Arts and Letters) by the French government. She also serves on various boards in the non-profit arts and education sector, including Wild Rice Ltd.

Lim Sun Sun served as an NMP from 2018–2020. She is Head of Humanities, Arts and Social Sciences at the Singapore University of Technology and Design. She has written extensively on the social impact of technology, her most recent book being *Transcendent Parenting: Raising Children in the Digital Age* (Oxford University Press, 2020). She was named to the inaugural Singapore 100 Women in Tech list in 2020 and frequently offers her expert commentary in diverse media outlets. Outside of academia, she contributes actively to public bodies, including the Media Literacy Council and the Singapore Environment Council.

K. Thanaletchimi served as an NMP from 2016–2018. She is currently the elected Vice-President of the National Trades Union Congress (NTUC) Central Committee and President of the Healthcare Services Employees' Union. She also served on the Executive Board of the Singapore Council of Women's Organisations (SCWO) between 2018–2020. She has chaired the Labour Movement's Healthcare Cluster, NTUC Women's Committee and NTUC Training Committee (Essential Domestic Services) and served on the Families for Life Council and People's Association Board. She received the National Day Award (Public Service Medal) in 2019.

Kuik Shiao-Yin served as an NMP from 2014–2018. She is a cultural change strategist, facilitator, coach, trainer and speaker who helps organisations shape their approaches to cultural transformation and human development. She was a founding director of The Thought Collective from 2002–2021 and is currently the Executive Director at Common Ground, a civic centre that builds whole communities. Her 2018 parliamentary speech, "The Power of a People", was published by Epigram Books as part of their Rational Conversations collection of writings by prominent Singaporeans.

Laurence Lien served as an NMP from 2012–2014. He is the Chairman and founding CEO of the Asia Philanthropy Circle and the Chairman of the Lien Foundation as well as the Chairman of Lien AID, the Foundation's humanitarian arm. He was the CEO of the National Volunteer & Philanthropy Centre (NVPC) from 2008–2014 and served as the Chairman of the Community Foundation of Singapore from 2013–2019. Laurence is also a Board Member of the Lien Centre for Social Innovation at Singapore Management University. Prior to joining the non-profit sector, he worked in the Administrative Service in the Singapore Government.

Mahdev Mohan served as an NMP from 2016–2018. He is currently a senior policy adviser in a multinational technology company and was formerly an academic and practising lawyer in the field of international law, which he taught as an Assistant Professor at the Singapore Management University's Yong Pung How School of Law. Mahdev is also the co-founder of Access to Justice Asia LLP, a non-governmental organisation comprising scholars and lawyers dedicated to *pro bono* legal representation, social justice and capacity-building for victims of mass crime in Asia.

Maurice Choo served as an NMP from 1990–1991. He is a senior physician at Farrer Park Hospital, where he practises cardiology and internal medicine, and Chairman of The Farrer Park Company. He has held various titles at the National University of Singapore, including Professor of Medicine, Vice Dean (Research) and Director of the National University Medical Institute. He is also currently an Adjunct Professor at the Nanyang Technological University (Lee Kong Chian School of Medicine) and has served on the boards of various public and private organisations and committees.

Nicholas Fang served as an NMP from 2012–2014. He is currently a Senior Advisor to The Asia Group and is the founder and managing director of Black Dot, a leading strategic communications consultancy. He was previously a journalist for almost a decade at *The Straits Times* and CNA and was also Deputy Chief Editor of Singapore news at national broadcaster, Mediacorp. Nicholas has represented Singapore in fencing and triathlon as a national athlete and was chef de mission for Team Singapore at the 2015 Southeast Asian Games. He received the Public Service Medal at the 2015 National Day Awards.

Dr Shahira Abdullah began serving as an NMP in 2021 and is currently in the middle of her term. She is an associate consultant and orthodontist with the dental surgery team at Khoo Teck Puat Hospital. Outside of her medical practice, she is a dedicated youth leader and a current member of the National Youth Council (NYC) as well as an immediate past vice president of the Mendaki Club. In 2019, she was appointed by the Ministry of Culture, Community and Youth (MCCY) as an SG Youth Action Plan member.

Simon Tay served as an NMP from 1997–2001. He is a lawyer, academic and public intellectual. He is currently a Senior Consultant at the law firm WongPartnership, an Associate Professor at the National University of Singapore's Faculty of Law and the Editor of the *Asian Journal of International Law*. Professor Tay is concurrently the Chairman of the Singapore Institute of International Affairs (SIIA), a leading think-tank, and regularly comments on regional and public affairs for the media. He is also a prize-winning fiction author and received the Singapore Literature Prize in 2010.

Author Bios

Thomas Thomas served as an NMP from 1999–2001. He was then the General Secretary of the Singapore Shell Employees' Union, a Central Committee Member of the National Trades Union Congress (NTUC) and active with global unions. He has worked at the intersections of corporate social responsibility (CSR), industrial relations and business and human rights for many years. He is currently the CEO of the ASEAN CSR Network and was previously the executive director of the Singapore Compact for Corporate Social Responsibility (CSR) (now Global Compact Network Singapore). He was awarded the Public Service Medal in 2002 and the Comrade of Labour Star in 2008 for his contributions to the labour movement.

Viswa Sadasivan served as an NMP from 2009–2011. He has worked in media and public policy for over three decades and is the founder and CEO of Strategic Moves, a corporate strategy consulting practice. A former broadcaster, he has spoken at numerous public policy events and served on the boards of several government agencies and as a member of various national groups and committees, including the Singapore Feedback Unit, the Economic Review Committee and the Singapore Indian Development Association (SINDA). He served in the Singapore Armed Forces as a national serviceman for 41 years, holding the rank of Colonel in the last decade. He holds a Masters in Public Administration from Harvard University's Kennedy School of Government.

Walter Edgar Theseira served as an NMP from 2018–2020. Walter is Associate Professor of Economics, School of Business, Singapore University of Social Sciences; and Adjunct Senior Research Fellow, Asia Competitiveness Institute, Lee Kuan Yew School of Public Policy. His Ph.D. is in Applied Economics and Managerial Science from the Wharton School, University of Pennsylvania. His areas are applied microeconomics, behavioural and experimental economics. His research has been published in the *Proceedings of the National Academy of Sciences* and the *Journal of Economic Behavior and Organisation*. His policy research covers housing integration with the Ministry of National Development, vehicle quota auctions with the Land Transport Authority, and the Singapore Retirement and Health Survey. He has advised the Economist Service of the Ministry of Trade and Industry, the Ministry of National Development, the Ministry of Social and Family Development and with the Civil Service College.

Photo courtesy of Parliament Secretariat.

Walter Woon, SC served as NMP from 1992–1996. He is Lee Kong Chian Visiting Professor at the Yong Pung How School of Law, Singapore Management University, having formerly been David Marshall Professor at the National University of Singapore Faculty of Law and founding Dean of the Singapore Institute of Legal Education. He is also currently Chairman of regional law firm

RHTLaw Asia LLP and Patron of the Gunong Sayang Association, founded in 1910 to promote Baba culture. He was Attorney-General from 2008–2010 and Solicitor-General from 2006–2008, as well as Singapore's ambassador to Germany, Greece, the European Communities, the European Union, Belgium, The Netherlands, Luxembourg and the Holy See from 1998–2006.

Editor's Profile

Anthea Ong served as an NMP from 2018–2020 in the 13th Parliament. As a self-described "full-time human being, part-time everything else", she is a mental health advocate, social entrepreneur and impact investor, life and leadership coach, strategy consultant, yoga and wellness instructor and author, amongst many other roles. She is never seen without headgear to match her multiple hats.

She enjoys bringing disparate groups of people together, especially where this highlights our common humanity amidst our differences. As such, she divides her time, energy and love across many different communities and has founded or co-founded several initiatives in her main focus areas of migrant rights, mental health, environmentalism and social impact, including SG Mental Health Matters, WorkWell Leaders, A Good Space Co-operative, Hush TeaBar and Welcome In My Backyard. She also served and serves on several boards and committees in these fields, including Unifem (now UN Women), Society for WINGS, Daughters of Tomorrow, Social Service Institute, National

Volunteer & Philanthropy Centre and the Tripartite Oversight Committee for Workplace Safety & Health. Prior to devoting herself to civil society and social impact work full-time, she spent over 25 years in the corporate world as a C-suite leader. Her new mantra, as a former banker and reformed business leader, is "why start a business when you can start a movement, or two?"

A sought-after speaker on human-centred leadership, mental health and social entrepreneurship, Anthea has also published numerous commentaries and contributed to anthologies such as *My Life, My Story* by the National Library Board and the recently-published *Social Context, Policies, and Changes in Singapore* edited by Dr Intan Azura Mokhtar and Dr Yaacob Ibrahim. Her wood-cover memoir, *50 Shades of Love*, was shortlisted for the Best Illustrated Non-Fiction Title in the 2019 Singapore Book Awards. A podcast series, *Shades of Love*, followed in 2021.

Anthea finds wisdom through her intrepid travels that have taken her to all seven continents and over 80 countries including Antarctica, Mt Everest Base Camp, The Amazon, Machu Picchu, Sinai desert, Iran, Tibet, Siberia and more. A passionate scholar of self and student of life, she believes that the farther out she explores, the deeper in she travels as she continues to be amazed by each new chapter in her journey of becoming.

www.antheaong.com

Acknowledgements

The acknowledgement of a single possibility can change everything. With gratitude and humility, I would like to start by acknowledging that better part of me which chose to listen to, and act on, that loud and clear vision of this book in my meditation that morning in June 2021. I thank my parents wholeheartedly for this better part of me.

Clearly, this book would not even exist or be possible without the 19 NMP colleagues who gamely agreed on my first invitation to co-create this vision as contributors. I am immensely grateful for their trust and confidence as well as enthusiasm and co-operation during the strategy development and writing phases of the project. What an indescribable joy for me that this book also served as launchpad for an NMP Alumni WhatsApp group with past NMPs which is planting the seed for an alumni group to be formed. Whether this continues to be informal or be formalised in some manner in the foreseeable future remains to be seen.

I want to thank Max Phua and Chua Hong Koon of World Scientific Publishing who offered me a publishing contract without seeing a single word except believing in my audacious idea that we can bring 20 NMPs to create this collection of essays as the first book on NMPs by NMPs

◆ The Nominated Member of Parliament Scheme

in Singapore. And their Editor, Jiang Yulin, who has been such a breeze to work with.

It was a long shot then but I am grateful to Prime Minister Lee Hsien Loong for so generously agreeing in-principle to provide a foreword when I asked before we even started writing and then stayed true to his word when the book was done. His agreeing to endorse this book from the start emboldened my conviction to stay the course.

I wish to acknowledge Speaker Tan Chuan-Jin for kindly agreeing to Lim Puay Ling, the Parliament Librarian's help to my research team as well as giving them access to the library for the onerous work needed to produce Appendix D on Fun Facts and Figures.

For good measure, I should also mention the National Volunteer & Philanthropy Centre for nominating me for NMP in 2018 which put me on this unexpected trajectory that led to this book.

Last but certainly not least, I owe the most gratitude to Sophie Chew and Dr Rayner Tan. The only reason we kept to schedule and quality is because of these two dedicated and generous friends who supported me as my research and project management team despite their packed professional obligations. Sophie's journalist-trained eye for details as well as Rayner's curiosity and analytical insights as a post-doctoral researcher made them perfect partners to have for the monumental task, giving me the space to focus on the editing of each essay with care. I felt immensely supported by them. I thank them too for the arduous work needed for the Section Prefaces, Q&As and Appendices. I'm sure this will not be our only project together, especially as I have also openly encouraged Rayner to consider being an NMP himself!

The mistakes in this book are all mine; whatever is good in it is due in enormous measure to the contributors and my team.

Index

4G leadership, 45
1984 Committee on the Problems of the Aged, 30
1988 Advisory Council of the Aged, 30
1997-98 haze, 41
2011 General Election, 105, 214

Abdullah Tarmugi, 166
absolute power, 52
abstain, 294
accountability, 166
ActiveSG, 107
adjournment motions, 93
Administration of Justice (Protection) Bill, 191, 263, 266
ageing, 15
ageing population, 214
Albert Camus, 297
Aline Wong, 66
Alvin Tan, The Necessary Stage, 240
Anglophone, 33

Anson by-election, 22
Anthea Ong, 96, 133, 136–138, 140
anti-colonial struggle, 150
Arasu Duraisamy, 94
Arts and Cultural Strategic Review, 241
arts community, 238–248
Arts Manifesto, 245
Arts NMP, 238–241, 243, 244, 246–249
Arts NMP town hall, 230
ASEAN passport, 56
ASEAN university, 56
Association of Artists of Various Resources, 242
Association of Southeast Asian Nations, 42, 45, 54, 56
Athenian democracy, 31
atypical employment, 155
Audrey Wong, 229, 237, 238, 244, 250
AWARE, 66

backbenchers, 143, 255
Barisan Sosialis, 21, 271, 289
barometer of public sentiments, 274
behind the curve, 48
bicameral parliament, 72
big data, 89, 91
boring star system, 256
Braema Mathiaparanam, 292
breastfeeding, 126
British Labour Party, 149, 151
Budget Debate, 15, 27, 120, 156, 157, 180, 215, 224, 230, 231, 290
Bukit Brown debate, 114
burden of proof, 141, 142

call for a division, 117, 118
career suicide, 27
censorship, 240
Central Catchment Nature Reserve, 122
Central Provident Fund, 156
Chan Chun Sing, 180
Chan Sek Keong, 291
Charles Chong, 180
chef de mission, 105
Chiam See Tong, 12, 26, 51, 158, 196, 272
Chia Yong Yong, 260
chilling effect, 141
Christopher de Souza, 125
Civic and People Sector, 118, 125
civil society, 36–38, 40, 42, 45–48, 67, 68, 71, 302, 303
climate of fear, 166
Committee of Privileges, 173

Committee of Supply debate, 108, 231
common cause, 244
Community Foundation of Singapore, 214, 218
community ownership, 214
Companies Act, 156
Companies (Amendment) Bill, 26
conservation, 41, 43, 44
constituents, 238, 244
Constitutional Amendment Bill, 182
constitutional engineering, 281
constitutionality, 271, 292
Constitution of the Republic of Singapore, 49
Constitution Review Body, 58
Consumers Association of Singapore, 152, 157
continuing dominance, 36
convenient inconvenience, 69
co-operatives, 152
Corrupt Practices Investigation Bureau, 53
Covid-19, 92, 96, 101, 141, 230, 291, 292, 299, 303
credible Opposition, 48
Criminal Law (Temporary Provisions) Act, 154, 264
Criminal Law (Temporary Provisions) (Amendment) Bill, 276
Cross Island Line, 122
cultural infrastructure, 241
cyber-security, 267

David Marshall, 57
Defence Science and Technology Agency (DSTA) Bill, 153
democracy, 62, 69–72, 75, 170, 173
Dental Registration Bill, 233
Desmond Lee, 127, 129
digital literacy, 91, 96
Director of Public Prosecutions, 58
dissent, 24, 25
diverse and inclusive representation, 72
diversity of voices, 228
Dover and Clementi forests, 125
dual citizenship, 53

eco-services, 126, 127, 129
Education for Our Future Motion, 255, 269
education reforms, 94, 95, 256, 259, 261
Edwin Tong, 135
Elected Presidency, 184
Elected President, 23–25, 49, 52, 58, 182, 184, 279
electoral college, 24
electoral democracy, 289
electoral engineering, 289, 296
elite sports, 108
Emily Hill, 241, 244
emotional resistance, 33
Employment of Foreign Manpower Act, 68
Empowering Women Motion, 233
en bloc redevelopment laws, 43
environment, 40, 42, 44

environmental consciousness, 120
Environment Impact Assessment, 119
Environment NMP, 125, 126
ethics, 259
Eugene Tan, 124, 220, 292
exceptionalism, 162, 163
excessive discretion, 133
extra parliamentary struggle, 289

Fair Trading Act, 157
Faizah Jamal, 220, 292
fake news, 133
family-friendly employer, 177
faux experts, 92, 98
Federation of Art Societies Singapore, 242
Feedback Unit, 161
female workforce, 177
Fire Safety (Amendment) Bill, 143
first IT Plan, 89
first nominated members, 10, 25
first-past-the-post system, 63
flexible work arrangements, 182
food, water and energy security, 123
Foreign Employees Dormitories Act, 292
Foreign Interference (Countermeasures) Bill, 126, 231
foreign workers, 156
functional groups, 64, 219, 242, 279, 280, 285, 296, 297

Galileo Galilei, 134
Ganesh Rajaram, 259

gender, 40
gender diversity, 66
gig workers, 155
Gini coefficient, 164
Goh Chok Tong, 11, 23, 24, 26, 37, 56
Goods and Services Tax, 27, 28, 157
Goury Govin, 51, 52
Government Parliamentary Committee, 63, 262–264
Grace Fu, 180
gross domestic product, 169
Group Representation Constituency, 63, 214, 289
guillotine time, 161

Halimah Yacob, 66, 122, 129, 180, 281
Hansard, 14, 34, 53, 101, 139, 254, 267
Hawazi Daipi, 155
haze pollution, 41, 42, 46
healthcare costs, 15
Healthcare Services Employees' Union, 175
heliocentrism, 134
Heritage Society, 43
higher education subsidies, 16, 17
hobby horse, 290
Housing and Development Board, 38, 264

idealism, 52, 59
identity stories, 188
Ilham Pujangga (Inspiration of a Poet), 233

ILO Declaration on Fundamental Principles and Rights at Work, 153
income divide, 214
inconvenient convenience, 69
independent task force, 71
Inderjit Singh, 124
industrial action, 154
industrial relations, 149, 152, 154–156
Industrial Relations Act, 154, 156
information discordance, 15
institutional objectivity, 190
Intermediate and Long-Term Care Sector, 178
international environmental law, 41
International Labour Organization, 153
Internet, 13, 16, 56
interracial, 54
Irene Ng, 96
Irene Quay, 133, 136, 138
Istana, 54

Janice Koh, 124, 127, 190, 220, 229, 237, 238, 245, 250, 292
Janil Puthucheary, 135
Jayakumar, S., 52
Jeyaretnam, J. B., 22, 23, 39, 57, 158, 272
Junior Parliament, 53

Kallang Roar, 104
Kanwaljit Soin, 292
Khalil Gibran, 299
knowledge-based economy, 89

Kok Heng Leun, 191, 239, 260, 266
Kranji forest, 125
Kuik Shiao-Yin, 260, 266

Labour Movement, 148, 149, 151
Labour NMP, 148, 151
lacuna, 141
Land Transport Authority of Singapore (Amendment) Bill, 278
Lasting Power of Attorney, 265
Laurence Lien, 124, 127, 190, 292
Law Society, 51, 53
Leader of the Opposition, 69, 126, 263, 264
Lee Bee Wah, 191
Lee Hsien Loong, 26, 52, 256, 267
Lee Kuan Yew, 10, 40, 46, 57, 160, 166–170, 283, 290
Lee Siew Choh, 19, 57, 272
Legal Profession Act, 53
legislative support, 157, 231, 297
legitimacy, 279, 282
Leong Chee Whye, 10, 25
LGBTQ, 40
libel and defamation, 39
liberal education, 295, 303
Lim Biow Chuan, 180
Lim Sun Sun, 303
Lim Swee Say, 40, 46, 166
Lim Yew Hock, 150
Little India Riot Bill, 127, 274
lobbying, 218
Louis Ng, 101, 191, 260, 292
loving critic, 52, 57
loving-kindness, 196

Lower Peirce Reservoir, 128
Low Thia Khiang, 26, 51, 117, 126, 129, 158, 191, 217

Mah Bow Tan, 121, 166
Maintenance of Parents Bill, 27, 30
majoritarian representation, 291
majority issues, 291
Malayan Communist Party, 149
Malay-Muslim women community, 233
Margaret Thatcher, 137
marginalised communities, 289
Matthias Yao, 167
Maurice Choo, 25
Mayor, 58
Media Literacy Council, 90
mediation, 60
mediocrity, 32
MediShield Life, 181
Members' Room, 19, 67, 124, 129, 157, 158, 166, 167, 172, 257, 266, 295, 301
Mendaki Club, 232
mental health, 289–291, 303
microaggressions in classrooms, 94
migrant worker issues, 67
    employment of foreign domestic workers, 67
    migrant workers and lorries, 233
    social security for foreign domestic workers, 74
migrant workers, 67, 289, 291, 292, 297

mindfulness in Parliament, 299
Ministry of Peace, 53
minority interests, 297
moral duty, 28
moral legitimacy, 216
Mother Earth, 289
motion, 161, 164–167, 169
motion on Aljunied-Hougang Town Council, 295
multiparty parliamentary democracy, 281
municipal needs, 292
Murali Pillai, 288

Nathan, S. R., 52
National Arts Council, 239, 242, 243, 247
National Council for Youth Guidance and Rehabilitation, 91
National Environment Agency, 44
National Pledge, 161–163, 165, 167, 168, 277
national reserves, 23
National Service, 104, 110, 111, 232
National Trades Union Congress, 148, 150–152, 155, 157, 158, 174, 175, 179, 239, 244, 280
National Volunteer & Philanthropy Centre, 214, 218, 225
National Youth Council, 90, 232, 234
natural capital, 120, 127, 129
nature and heritage, 120
nature-as-healer, 120

nature reserves, 43
Nature Society, 43, 118, 119, 127, 128
Ng Eng Hen, 279
NIMBY ("not-in-my-backyard"), 291
Non-Constituency Member of Parliament, 39, 49, 63, 64, 67, 107, 124, 290
non-elected parliamentarians, 174
Non-Majority Member of Parliament, 297
non-partisan, 174, 178, 182, 183
non-partisan check, 296
non-partisan Mayors, 298
non-partisanship, 271, 273
non-partisan voices, 25

old National Library, 43, 44
omakase, 21
one-party dominant system, 273
one-party power, 23
one-party system, 57
Ong Teng Cheong, 19
online falsehood, 133, 135, 137, 139, 141
Orang Asli, 121
Our Singapore Conversations, 121, 245
over-reliance on tuition, 259
overseas electronic voting, 54

pandemic Parliament, 299
parenting, 94, 95
parliamentary democracy, 27

parliamentary innovation, 288
parliamentary mechanisms, 294
parliamentary privileges, 279
Parliamentary Questions, 182
parliamentary representation, 222
Parliamentary Select Committee, 238, 239, 247
Parliament revamp, 54
participatory democracy, 298
partisan politics, 274, 276
Penguingate, 126
pentathlon, 105
People's Action Party, 10, 19, 23, 24, 33, 36–39, 43, 44, 46, 47, 51, 52, 57, 59, 137, 143, 150–152, 155, 158, 185, 214, 217, 218, 220, 251, 271–273, 280, 289, 294, 301
    PAP monopoly, 45
People's Association, 56
performance-based ranking, 260
personhood, 190
Pioneer Generation Package, 181
poppycock, 32
Population White Paper, 107, 114, 119, 121, 217, 218, 274
    call for a division, 117, 118
pre-school education review, 169
Presidential Council for Minority Rights, 291
Primary School Leaving Examination, 259, 260, 262
Prime Minister, 49, 52, 54, 56, 57
principles of openness and transparency, 243

Pritam Singh, 69, 126
Progress Singapore Party, 280
proportional representation, 18
Proposed Amendments to the Public Entertainments and Meetings Act, 244
pro-Singapore, 220, 225
Protection from Online Falsehoods and Manipulation Act, 126, 132, 133, 139, 141, 142, 267, 293, 294, 301
    Amendment Motion, 135
    call for a division, 140, 141
    Committee Stage, 140
    First Reading, 135
    Second Reading, 135, 137, 139, 140, 143
protection of workers, 156
public funding, 240
public law academic, 276
Public Order (Additional Temporary Measures) Bill, 276
public sense-making, 194

quorum, 271, 278

race-focused politics, 64
Raeesah Khan, 230
Raffles Institution, 256, 259
rage of poverty, 175
Rahayu Mahzam, 260
Rahmatan lil'alamin, 228
Rajaratnam, S., 162, 163, 167
Randolph Tan, 260
REACH, 222

referendum, 58
relevance, 279, 282
Renaissance City Plan, 241
retirement adequacy, 181
Richard Hu, 27, 30, 31
rising inequality, 289, 297
River Valley High School incident, 235
Road Traffic (Amendment) Bill, 99, 233, 235
rubber stamp institution, 272

sacred cows, 259
secretarial support, 55, 60
Section 377A, 291, 296, 303
sectoral representation, 65
security of small states, 14
selection process, 271, 279, 280
self-government, 11
self-perpetuating closed circles, 256, 257
sentient common citizen, 13
Serjeant-at-Arms, 117, 141
SG Youth Action Plan, 232
Shanmugam, K., 293, 301
showboating, 190, 193
Sidek Saniff, 19
Siew Kum Hong, 291
Silver Support Scheme, 181
Singapore 21, 39, 40, 41, 43, 44, 46
Singaporean Singapore, 162
Singapore Business Federation, 239
Singapore Concept Plan 2000, 43
Singapore Convention, 264

Singapore Democratic Party, 26, 51
Singapore Drama Educators Association, 242
Singapore Dream, 277
Singapore Environment Council, 42
Singapore Improvement Trust, 50
Singapore Institute of International Affairs, 42, 45, 47
Singapore National Olympic Committee, 105
Singapore Sports Hub, 104
Singapore Sports School, 113
Singapore Trades Union Congress, 150
single mothers, 177
single women, 74
SkillsFuture, 177
Smart Nation blueprint, 89
social democratic parties, 149, 151
social leveller, 169
social media, 17, 37, 39, 45, 47, 56, 69, 71, 76, 92, 95, 295
social recession, 215, 224
social renaissance, 215
social reset, 215
Speakers' Corner, 38
Special Select Committee, 179, 279, 280, 285
speech-actions, 194
sporting ecosystem, 107
sporting nation, 104, 112
sports-focused NMP, 112
Sports NMP, 103, 106, 112
sports university, 110

strike, 154
Sungei Road Thieves Market, 126
Sun Xueling, 143
supermajority Parliament, 52, 57, 289, 296, 298
Super Seven team, 67
sustainability, 127
sustainable and affordable healthcare, 178
Sylvia Lim, 122
symbiotic relationship, 151, 152
systemic inequality, 256

Tan Cheng Bock, 280, 290
Tan Soo Khoon, 52
technological utopianism, 88, 91
technology domestication, 89, 96
technology explosions, 15
Teo Chee Hean, 40, 46
Terence Ho, 229, 239
Thanaletchimi, K., 260
TheatreWorks, 237, 240, 241
The Next Lap, 37
the Roundtable, 38
The Working Committee 2, 67
Tommy Koh, 291, 304
Tony Tan, 179
Town Hall, 238–241, 243, 244, 246–248
Trade Disputes Act, 154
trade unions, 149, 151, 154–156
Trade Unions Act, 154, 155
Transboundary Haze Pollution Act, 42

Transient Workers Count Too (TWC2), 67
transparency, 279, 280
trust, 191, 193, 197
two-party parliamentary democracy, 281

union leaders, 149–151
universal digital access, 96, 97
unsayables, 295, 297
unvotables, 289, 291–293, 295–297
useful idiots, 138

VUCA world, 256
vulnerable groups, 232
vulnerable workforce, 181

wage parity, 175
Walter Theseira, 293, 295, 303
Walter Woon, 291
weaponisation of information, 16
WhatsApp, 100, 180, 246
Whip, 30, 55, 138, 151, 273, 283, 293, 295
wholeness, 189
Wong Kan Seng, 166
words-deeds, 194
workers-in-transition, 181
Workers' Party, 26, 51, 69, 106, 117, 122, 124, 137, 139–141, 143, 217, 272

Yahoo e-group, 240, 246
Yale-NUS saga, 295

Yeo Cheow Tong, 42
"Yes-Men" slate, 229, 230
Youth Action Challenge, 233
youth activism, 295
Youth NMP, 227, 232–234

Youth@SGNature, 127
Yu-Foo Yee Shoon, 66

Zainudin Nordin, 166, 167
Zulkifli Baharudin, 42, 46